T0272414

FORTRESS AI

ULTIMATE CYBERSECURITY STRATEGIES

KEN WATSON

PrimeTrust Publishing

Book Cover by Usama Zaheen

Illustrations by Usama Zaheen

This book is devoted to the pillars of my life: my mother Ruby Watson, my father Kenneth Watson, and my son Lovell Watson. Their unwavering love and support have shaped me into the person I stand as today. In life's rollercoaster of highs and lows, the steadfast presence of a nurturing family is as crucial as the most sophisticated security in safeguarding a system from breach. My family is my fortress, offering the resilience needed to face life's myriad challenges. To them, my deepest love and heartfelt gratitude.

.

CONTENTS

1. Chapter 1: Introduction to AI and Cybersecurity   1

    Section 1.1: The Intersection of AI and Cybersecurity

    Section 1.2: The Benefits of AI for Cybersecurity

    Section 1.3: The Challenges of AI in Cybersecurity

    Section 1.4: The Ethical Implications of AI in Cybersecurity

    Chapter 1 Conclusion

2. Chapter 2: AI Fundamentals for Cybersecurity   8

    Section 2.1: Understanding AI and Machine Learning

    Section 2.2: Key AI Techniques for Cybersecurity

    Section 2.3: Applications of AI in Cybersecurity

    Section 2.4: Challenges and Considerations for AI in Cybersecurity

    Chapter 2 Conclusion

3. Chapter 3: AI for Network Security   16

    Section 3.1: Introduction to Network Security

    Section 3.2: AI for Network Threat Detection

    Section 3.3: AI for Network Incident Response

    Section 3.4: AI for Network Behavior Analytics

    Section 3.5: AI for Network Forensics and Analysis

    Chapter 3 Conclusion

4. Chapter 4: AI for Endpoint Protection   27

    Section 4.1: Understanding Endpoint Security

    Section 4.2: AI-Powered Malware Detection

    Section 4.3: AI for Endpoint Behavioral Analysis

    Section 4.4: AI for Autonomous Threat Hunting

    Section 4.5: AI-Powered Endpoint Response and Remediation

    Chapter 4 Conclusion

5. Chapter 5: AI for Application Security   42

    Section 5.1: Introduction to Application Security

    Section 5.2: AI for Secure Software Development

    Section 5.3: AI for Application Vulnerability Detection

    Section 5.4: AI for Application Runtime Protection

    Section 5.5: AI for Application Security Testing and Validation

    Chapter 5 Conclusion

6. Chapter 6: AI for Cloud Security   58

    Section 6.1: Introduction to Cloud Security

    Section 6.2: AI for Cloud Threat Detection and Response

    Section 6.3: AI for Cloud Access Control and Identity Management

    Section 6.4: AI for Cloud Security Posture Management

    Section 6.5: AI for Cloud Compliance and Governance

    Chapter 6 Conclusion

7. Chapter 7: AI for IoT Security   81

    Section 7.1: Introduction to IoT Security

    Section 7.2: AI for IoT Device Security and Vulnerability Management

    Section 7.3: AI for IoT Network Security and Anomaly Detection

    Section 7.4: AI for IoT Data Security and Privacy

    Section 7.5: AI for IoT Security Operations and Incident Response

    Chapter 7 Conclusion

8. Chapter 8: Quantum Computing and AI Security   105

    Section 8.1: Introduction to Quantum Computing and its Implications for Cybersecurity

    Section 8.2: Quantum Computing Basics and Key Concepts

    Section 8.3: Post-Quantum Cryptography and Quantum-Safe Security

    Section 8.4: Quantum Machine Learning and its Applications in Cybersecurity

    Section 8.5: Quantum Cybersecurity Challenges and Future Directions

    Chapter 8 Conclusion

9. Chapter 9: AI for Cybersecurity Policies and Governance   125

    Section 9.1: Introduction to AI Governance and Policy Considerations

    Section 9.2: AI Ethics and Principles for Cybersecurity

Section 9.3: AI Security and Robustness for Cybersecurity Systems

Section 9.4: AI Governance Frameworks and Standards for Cybersecurity

Section 9.5: The Future of AI Governance in Cybersecurity

Chapter 9 Conclusion

10. Chapter 10: Cybersecurity Landscaping and AI   143

Section 10.1: Introduction to Cybersecurity Landscaping

Section 10.2: Cybersecurity Threat Landscaping with AI

Section 10.3: Cybersecurity Risk Landscaping with AI

Section 10.4: AI for Cybersecurity Compliance Landscaping

Section 10.5: The Future of AI in Cybersecurity Landscaping

Chapter 10 Conclusion

11. Chapter 11: AI and Cybersecurity Awareness and Education   160

Section 11.1: The Importance of Cybersecurity Awareness and Education in the Age of AI

Section 11.2: Strategies for Developing Effective Cybersecurity Awareness and Education Programs

Section 11.3: The Role of AI in Enhancing Cybersecurity Awareness and Education

Section 11.4: Measuring the Effectiveness of Cybersecurity Awareness and Education Programs

Section 11.5: Emerging Trends and Best Practices in Cybersecurity Awareness and Education

Chapter 11 Conclusion

12. Chapter 12: AI and Cybersecurity Ethics and Social Responsibility   177

Section 12.1: The Importance of Ethical AI and Cybersecurity Practices

Section 12.2: Designing and Implementing Ethical AI and Cybersecurity Frameworks

Section 12.3: Promoting Transparency, Accountability, and Fairness in AI and Cybersecurity

Section 12.4: Addressing Bias and Discrimination in AI and Cybersecurity Systems

Section 12.5: Promoting Diversity, Equity, and Inclusion in AI and Cybersecurity

Chapter 12 Conclusion

13. Chapter 13: The Future of AI in Cybersecurity   192

    Section 13.1: Emerging Trends and Technologies in AI and Cybersecurity
    Section 13.2: Preparing for the AI-Driven Cybersecurity Landscape: Strategies and Best Practices
    Section 13.3: Overcoming Challenges and Barriers to AI Adoption in Cybersecurity
    Section 13.4: The Role of Policy and Regulation in Shaping the Future of AI and Cybersecurity
    Section 13.5: Building a Secure and Resilient AI-Driven Future: A Call to Action for Cybersecurity Leaders and Professionals
    Chapter 13 Conclusion

14. Chapter 14: Final Thoughts   207

About the author   209

ONE

— ❖ —

CHAPTER 1: INTRODUCTION TO AI AND CYBERSECURITY

Section 1.1: The Intersection of AI and Cybersecurity

The world of cybersecurity is facing an unprecedented challenge. As digital technologies become more integrated into every aspect of our lives, the surface area for potential cyber attacks has expanded exponentially. Simultaneously, the sophistication of these threats has grown by leaps and bounds. Today's cyber criminals are leveraging cutting-edge tools and techniques, including artificial intelligence (AI), to launch increasingly complex and damaging attacks.

In the face of this evolving threat landscape, traditional cybersecurity approaches are struggling to keep pace. Conventional security tools, which rely heavily on rule-based detection and signature matching, are ill-equipped to identify and respond to the advanced threats of today. Malware that can morph its code to evade detection, social engineering attacks that exploit human vulnerabilities, and insider threats that operate under the guise of legitimate users - these are just a few examples of the challenges that cybersecurity professionals are grappling with.

This is where AI comes into the picture. With its ability to process vast amounts of data, identify patterns and anomalies, and learn and adapt over time, AI has the potential to revolutionize cybersecurity as we know it. By leveraging AI technologies such as machine learning, deep learning, and natural language processing, organizations can develop security systems that are more proactive, adaptive, and autonomous.

Real-world examples of AI in action are already emerging. For instance, machine learning algorithms are being used to detect anomalous network behavior that could indicate a breach. By training on normal network activity, these algorithms can identify deviations that might be missed by human analysts or rule-based systems. Similarly, deep learning models are being applied to malware analysis, enabling the detection of previously unseen malware variants based on their underlying code structure and behavior.

The intersection of AI and cybersecurity represents a critical frontier in the battle against cyber threats. As attacks become more sophisticated, so too must our defenses. AI provides a powerful tool in this fight, enabling organizations to stay one step ahead of the adversaries. However, the integration of AI into cybersecurity is not without its challenges and considerations, as we will explore throughout this book.

Section 1.2: The Benefits of AI for Cybersecurity

The application of AI in cybersecurity offers a multitude of benefits that can help organizations strengthen their security posture and better protect against the advanced threats of today. Let's explore some of the key advantages that AI brings to the table.

Firstly, AI can significantly enhance threat prevention capabilities. Through techniques like predictive analytics, AI systems can identify potential vulnerabilities and risks before they can be exploited. By analyzing vast amounts of data from network logs, security events, and threat intelligence feeds, AI algorithms can spot patterns and correlations that might indicate an impending attack. This proactive approach allows organizations to take preventive measures, such as patching vulnerabilities or adjusting security policies, to mitigate risks preemptively.

Secondly, AI can dramatically improve threat detection. One of the biggest challenges in cybersecurity is the sheer volume of data that security teams need to analyze. With the proliferation of devices and the increasing complexity of network environments, manually sifting through security logs to identify threats is like finding a needle in a haystack. AI can automate this process, using machine learning algorithms to analyze massive datasets in real-time and flag potential threats. This not only reduces the burden on human analysts but also enables much faster detection of threats, minimizing the window of opportunity for attackers.

Thirdly, AI can streamline and optimize incident response. When a security incident does occur, speed is of the essence. The longer an attacker remains undetected within a network, the more damage they can inflict. AI can help automate and orchestrate the incident response process, ensuring that the right actions are taken swiftly and effectively. For example, AI can be used to automatically isolate infected devices, cut off malicious traffic, and initiate forensic analysis. By reducing the mean time to detect (MTTD) and mean time to respond (MTTR), AI can significantly limit the impact of a breach.

Moreover, AI can bring significant cost and efficiency benefits to cybersecurity operations. By automating routine tasks and enabling faster, more accurate threat detection, AI can allow security teams to do more with less. This is particularly important in the context of the ongoing cybersecurity skills shortage. With a limited pool of qualified security professionals, organizations need to find ways to maximize the efficiency and effectiveness of their existing teams. AI can be a force multiplier, augmenting the capabilities of human analysts and enabling them to focus on higher-value tasks.

Real-world examples of AI's benefits in cybersecurity are numerous. For instance, a leading financial institution implemented an AI-powered threat detection system that was able to identify and block a series of advanced persistent threat (APT) attacks that had evaded traditional security controls. By analyzing network traffic in real-time and identifying subtle anomalies, the AI system was able to flag the malicious activity and enable the security team to respond quickly, preventing a potentially damaging breach.

Similarly, a global telecommunications company used AI to automate and optimize its vulnerability management process. By leveraging machine learning to prioritize vulnerabilities based on risk level and likelihood of exploitation, the company was able to patch the most critical vulnerabilities 50% faster than before. This not only improved their security posture but also freed up time for the security team to focus on more strategic initiatives.

The benefits of AI in cybersecurity are clear and compelling. However, realizing these benefits requires careful planning, execution, and consideration of the unique challenges and risks associated with AI-driven security, as we will explore in the following section.

Section 1.3: The Challenges of AI in Cybersecurity

While the potential of AI in cybersecurity is immense, it's not without its challenges. Implementing AI in security operations comes with a unique set of hurdles that organizations need to be aware of and plan for. Let's dive into some of the key challenges.

One of the biggest challenges is the "black box" nature of many AI models. Unlike traditional rule-based systems, where the decision-making process is transparent and explainable, AI models can be opaque. Deep learning models, in particular, can involve millions of parameters and complex neural network architectures that make it difficult to understand how they arrive at specific conclusions. This lack of explainability can be problematic in a cybersecurity context, where understanding why a particular event was flagged as malicious or benign is critical for investigation and response.

Another challenge is the potential for AI models to inherit biases from their training data. AI systems learn from the data they are fed. If this data contains biases, whether explicit or implicit, the resulting models can perpetuate these biases. In a cybersecurity context, this could lead to skewed risk scores, false positives, or missed threats. For example, if an AI model is trained on a dataset that primarily includes attacks from certain geographic regions, it may be less effective at identifying threats originating from other locations.

Adversarial attacks pose another significant challenge. Just as organizations can use AI to defend against threats, attackers can use AI to defeat these defenses. Adversarial attacks involve crafting inputs specifically designed to fool AI models. By making subtle changes to malware code or network traffic patterns, attackers can potentially bypass AI-based detection systems. This highlights the need for robust and resilient AI models that can withstand adversarial attempts.

Data quality and quantity is another hurdle. AI models require vast amounts of high-quality, labeled data to learn effectively. In cybersecurity, obtaining this data can be challenging. Threat data is often sensitive and closely guarded, and labeling data requires significant time and expertise. Moreover, the constantly evolving nature of the threat landscape means that data can quickly become outdated. Ensuring a steady stream of fresh, relevant data to train and update AI models is a continuous challenge.

Finally, there's the skills gap. Cybersecurity is already facing a significant workforce shortage, and the rise of AI is exacerbating this challenge. Building and maintaining AI systems for cybersecurity requires a rare combination of skills in data science, machine learning, and cybersecurity. Finding professionals with this blend of expertise is difficult, and competition for these talents is fierce. Organizations need to invest in training and upskilling their existing workforce while also developing strategies to attract and retain AI talent.

Despite these challenges, the potential benefits of AI in cybersecurity far outweigh the hurdles. By understanding and proactively addressing these challenges, organizations can set themselves up for success in their AI cybersecurity journey. This requires a strategic and holistic approach that considers not just the technical aspects but also the ethical, organizational, and human factors, as we will discuss in the next section.

Section 1.4: The Ethical Implications of AI in Cybersecurity

As AI becomes more deeply integrated into cybersecurity, it raises a host of ethical questions and considerations. The decisions made by AI systems can have significant real-world consequences, and it's crucial that these decisions are made in a way that is fair, unbiased, and aligned with human values. Let's explore some of the key ethical implications of AI in cybersecurity.

One major concern is privacy. AI systems for cybersecurity often involve the collection and analysis of vast amounts of data, much of which can be sensitive personal information. The use of AI to monitor network traffic, analyze user behavior, and detect threats can easily cross the line into surveillance if not implemented with proper safeguards and oversight. There's a delicate balance to be struck between security and privacy, and organizations need to be transparent about how they are using AI and what data they are collecting.

Another ethical consideration is the potential for AI to be used for harmful purposes. Just as AI can be a powerful tool for defense, it can also be weaponized by malicious actors. The development of AI-powered malware, deepfakes, and social engineering attacks is a real and present danger. There's also the risk of AI systems being used for offensive purposes by nation-states or other groups. The cybersecurity community has a responsibility to consider the dual-use potential of AI and to develop safeguards against misuse.

Bias and fairness are also critical ethical concerns. As mentioned earlier, AI models can inherit biases from their training data, leading to skewed or discriminatory outcomes. In a cybersecurity context, this could mean certain groups or individuals being unfairly targeted or profiled as threats. It's crucial that AI systems for cybersecurity are designed and trained in a way that is fair and unbiased, and that there are mechanisms in place to detect and mitigate bias when it occurs.

Accountability and explainability are also key ethical considerations. When an AI system makes a decision in a cybersecurity context, such as blocking a user's access or initiating an incident response, there needs to be clarity around who is responsible for that decision. Is it the AI system itself, the developers who trained it, or the organization deploying it? There also needs to be a way to explain and justify the decision, especially if it has significant consequences for individuals or organizations.

Finally, there's the overarching question of human agency and oversight. As AI systems become more autonomous and capable, there's a risk of over-reliance and a loss of human control. It's important that AI is seen as a tool to augment and assist human decision-making, not replace it entirely. There needs to be human oversight and the ability to override AI decisions when necessary.

Addressing these ethical implications requires a proactive and thoughtful approach. Organizations need to develop robust ethical frameworks for their use of AI in cybersecurity, and there needs to be ongoing dialogue and collaboration between the cybersecurity, AI, and ethics communities. By considering these issues upfront and designing AI systems with ethics in mind, we can harness the power of AI for good while mitigating the potential for harm.

Chapter 1 Conclusion

In this chapter, we've explored the critical intersection of AI and cybersecurity. We've seen how the increasing sophistication of cyber threats is necessitating a new approach to security, one that leverages the power of AI to detect, prevent, and respond to attacks. We've discussed the many benefits that AI can bring to cybersecurity, from enhancing threat prevention and detection to streamlining incident response and improving efficiency.

However, we've also seen that implementing AI in cybersecurity is not without its challenges. The black box nature of AI models, the potential for bias, the risk of adversarial attacks, the need for quality data, and the skills gap are all significant hurdles that organizations need to overcome. Moreover, the use of AI in cybersecurity raises important ethical questions around privacy, fairness, accountability, and human agency that must be carefully considered.

Despite these challenges, the potential of AI to revolutionize cybersecurity is immense. By enabling more proactive, adaptive, and autonomous defenses, AI can help organizations stay one step ahead of the ever-evolving threat landscape. However, realizing this potential requires a strategic and holistic approach that addresses not just the technical aspects but also the organizational, human, and ethical factors.

In the chapters to come, we will dive deeper into the specific applications of AI in cybersecurity, exploring use cases, best practices, and real-world examples. We will also further examine the challenges and considerations associated with AI in security, and provide practical guidance on how to navigate them. By the end of this book, you will have a comprehensive understanding of how AI is transforming cybersecurity and how to leverage it effectively in your own organization.

The intersection of AI and cybersecurity represents a critical frontier in the fight against cyber threats. As we move into this new era of intelligent security, it's crucial that we approach it with a blend of optimism and caution, harnessing the power of AI for good while carefully managing the risks and challenges. With the right knowledge, strategies, and principles, AI can be a game-changer for cybersecurity, enabling a more secure and resilient digital future.

Two

— • —

Chapter 2: AI Fundamentals for Cybersecurity

Section 2.1: Understanding AI and Machine Learning

To effectively leverage AI in cybersecurity, it's essential to have a solid understanding of the fundamental concepts and techniques that underpin AI and machine learning. In this section, we'll provide a primer on these key concepts, laying the foundation for the more advanced applications we'll discuss later in the book.

At its core, AI is about creating intelligent machines that can perform tasks that typically require human intelligence, such as visual perception, speech recognition, decision-making, and language translation. Machine learning is a subset of AI that focuses on the development of computer programs that can access data and use it to learn for themselves.

The key idea behind machine learning is that instead of explicitly programming rules for a computer to follow, you feed it large amounts of data and let it learn from that data to make decisions or predictions. This is a paradigm shift from traditional software development, where programmers write explicit instructions for the computer to execute.

There are three main types of machine learning: supervised learning, unsupervised learning, and reinforcement learning. In supervised learning, the machine is trained on a labeled dataset, where the desired output is known. For example, you might train a model on a dataset of emails labeled as spam or not spam. The model learns to identify the features that distinguish spam from non-spam emails and can then use this knowledge to classify new, unseen emails.

In unsupervised learning, the machine is given an unlabeled dataset and must find structure and relationships in the data on its own. This is often used for tasks like clustering, where the aim is to group similar data points together, or anomaly detection, where the goal is to identify unusual data points that don't conform to the norm.

Reinforcement learning is a bit different. Here, the machine learns through trial and error interactions with a dynamic environment. It receives rewards or penalties for the actions it takes and learns to optimize its behavior to maximize the reward over time. This type of learning is often used in scenarios like game playing or robotics.

Another key concept in machine learning is the idea of features. Features are the individual measurable properties or characteristics of the phenomena being observed. In the context of cybersecurity, features might include things like network traffic volume, IP addresses, file sizes, or system log entries. The process of selecting and engineering the right features is crucial for building effective machine learning models.

Deep learning is a more advanced subset of machine learning that uses artificial neural networks with multiple layers to learn from vast amounts of data. Deep learning has revolutionized fields like image and speech recognition and is increasingly being applied in cybersecurity for tasks like malware detection and network anomaly detection.

Understanding these fundamental AI and machine learning concepts is critical for anyone looking to apply these technologies in a cybersecurity context. In the following sections, we'll build on these fundamentals to explore specific AI techniques and their applications in cybersecurity in more depth.

Section 2.2: Key AI Techniques for Cybersecurity

With a foundational understanding of AI and machine learning in place, let's now dive into some of the specific AI techniques that are most relevant for cybersecurity. These techniques form the toolkit that data scientists and security researchers use to build intelligent systems for threat detection, risk assessment, and automated response.

One of the most widely used techniques in cybersecurity is classification. Classification involves training a model on a labeled dataset to categorize new, unseen data into predefined classes. In a security context, this could mean classifying network traffic as malicious or benign, or categorizing malware samples into different families based on their behaviors and characteristics.

There are many different algorithms that can be used for classification, including logistic regression, decision trees, random forests, and support vector machines (SVM). Each has its own strengths and weaknesses, and the choice of algorithm often depends on the specific problem and the nature of the data.

Another key technique is anomaly detection. As the name suggests, anomaly detection is about identifying unusual or unexpected patterns in data that deviate from the norm. This is particularly useful in cybersecurity, where many threats, such as zero-day exploits or insider attacks, are often characterized by subtle abnormalities in system or user behavior.

Anomaly detection techniques can be broadly categorized into statistical methods, machine learning methods, and hybrid methods. Statistical methods, such as Gaussian distribution or Z-score, define a normal range based on historical data and flag any new data points that fall outside this range. Machine learning methods, like One-Class SVM or Isolation Forest, learn the characteristics of normal data and detect anomalies as deviations from this learned pattern. Hybrid methods combine both statistical and machine learning techniques.

Clustering is another unsupervised learning technique that is frequently used in cybersecurity. Clustering algorithms aim to group similar data points together based on their features or attributes. In a security context, this can be used for tasks like grouping similar types of network traffic, identifying clusters of users with similar behavioral patterns, or grouping malware samples based on their code similarities.

Popular clustering algorithms include K-means, DBSCAN (Density-Based Spatial Clustering of Applications with Noise), and hierarchical clustering. Each algorithm has its own method for determining similarity and forming clusters, and the choice of algorithm depends on factors like the size and structure of the data, the desired number of clusters, and the tolerance for noise or outliers.

Deep learning techniques, particularly deep neural networks (DNNs), are also increasingly being applied in cybersecurity. DNNs are capable of learning complex, hierarchical representations of data, making them well-suited for tasks like malware detection, where the distinguishing features may be subtle and hard to define manually.

Convolutional Neural Networks (CNNs), which are commonly used in image recognition, have been adapted for malware detection by treating malware binaries as images. Recurrent Neural Networks (RNNs), which are designed for processing sequential data, have been used for analyzing network traffic and system logs to identify threats.

Generative Adversarial Networks (GANs), which pit two neural networks against each other in a game-theoretic framework, have also shown promise in cybersecurity. GANs can be used to generate realistic decoy traffic to deceive attackers, or to create adversarial examples to test the robustness of machine learning models.

Natural Language Processing (NLP) techniques are also relevant for cybersecurity, particularly in the context of social engineering and phishing attacks. NLP can be used to analyze the content and sentiment of emails, social media posts, or chat messages to identify potential threats or manipulative content.

Techniques like word embeddings, which map words to high-dimensional vector spaces based on their context, and sequence models like Long Short-Term Memory (LSTM) networks, which can process and generate sequential text data, are commonly used in NLP for cybersecurity.

These are just a few examples of the many AI techniques that are relevant for cybersecurity. As the field advances, new techniques and applications are continually emerging. In the next section, we'll look at how these techniques are being applied to address specific cybersecurity challenges.

Section 2.3: Applications of AI in Cybersecurity

The techniques we've discussed are not just theoretical concepts; they are being actively applied to solve real-world cybersecurity problems. In this section, we'll explore some of the most promising and impactful applications of AI in cybersecurity.

One of the most significant applications is in the area of threat detection. Traditional signature-based detection methods, which rely on predefined rules and patterns, are no longer sufficient in the face of the rapidly evolving threat landscape. AI-based anomaly detection and machine learning classification can identify novel and unknown threats by learning the characteristics of normal and malicious activity.

For example, machine learning models can be trained on large datasets of network traffic to learn the normal patterns of communication for a given network. Any deviations from these learned patterns, such as unusual port activity or abnormal data volumes, can be flagged as potential threats for further investigation.

Similarly, AI can be applied to endpoint security to detect malicious activities on individual devices. By monitoring system processes, file activity, and user behavior, machine learning models can identify signs of malware infection, unauthorized access attempts, or insider threats.

Another key application area is in automated incident response. When a potential threat is detected, AI systems can automatically initiate containment and mitigation actions, such as isolating infected devices, blocking malicious IP addresses, or rolling back harmful changes. This can significantly reduce the response time and minimize the damage caused by an attack.

AI is also being used for vulnerability management. Machine learning models can be trained to predict which vulnerabilities are most likely to be exploited based on factors like the availability of exploit code, the ease of exploitation, and the potential impact. This risk-based prioritization helps organizations focus their patching and remediation efforts on the most critical vulnerabilities.

In the realm of fraud detection, AI is being applied to identify fraudulent transactions, insurance claims, or identity theft attempts. By learning the patterns of legitimate and fraudulent activity, machine learning models can flag suspicious cases for review, reducing false positives and catching more fraud.

AI is also transforming the way we perform security testing and code analysis. Machine learning models can be used to automatically identify coding errors, security vulnerabilities, and compliance issues in software code. This can help developers catch and fix issues early in the development process, reducing the risk of exploitation later on.

User and Entity Behavior Analytics (UEBA) is another area where AI is making a significant impact. By modeling the normal behavior patterns of users and entities (like devices or applications) within an organization, UEBA systems can detect anomalies that may indicate insider threats, compromised accounts, or data exfiltration attempts.

Finally, AI is being used to enhance threat intelligence and attribution. By analyzing the tactics, techniques, and procedures (TTPs) used by different threat actors, machine learning models can help attribute attacks to specific groups or nation-states. This attribution can inform defensive strategies and help organizations better understand their risk profile.

These are just a few examples of the many ways AI is being applied in cybersecurity. As the technology continues to advance, we can expect to see even more innovative and impactful applications emerge. However, the successful implementation of AI in cybersecurity also comes with its own set of challenges and considerations, which we will discuss in the next section.

Section 2.4: Challenges and Considerations for AI in Cybersecurity

While the potential of AI in cybersecurity is immense, it's not without its challenges.

Implementing AI in security operations comes with a unique set of considerations that organizations need to be aware of. In this section, we'll explore some of the key challenges and factors to consider when applying AI in a cybersecurity context.

One of the most significant challenges is data quality and quantity. AI systems, particularly machine learning models, are only as good as the data they are trained on. In cybersecurity, getting access to high-quality, labeled data can be difficult. Threat data is often sensitive and closely guarded, and labeling large datasets requires significant time and expertise.

Moreover, the dynamic nature of the threat landscape means that data can quickly become outdated. Models trained on historical data may not be effective against new and evolving threats. Ensuring a continuous supply of fresh, relevant data to train and update AI models is a key challenge.

Another consideration is the interpretability and explainability of AI models. Many machine learning models, particularly deep learning models, are essentially "black boxes". It can be difficult to understand how they arrive at their decisions or predictions. In a cybersecurity context, being able to explain why a particular activity was flagged as malicious or benign is crucial for incident response and forensic analysis.

There are techniques emerging to improve the interpretability of AI models, such as Local Interpretable Model-Agnostic Explanations (LIME) and Shapley Additive Explanations (SHAP), but this remains an ongoing area of research and development.

Adversarial attacks are another major concern. Just as organizations can use AI to defend against threats, attackers can use AI to try to evade or deceive these defenses. Adversarial machine learning involves crafting inputs specifically designed to fool AI models and cause them to make incorrect predictions or decisions.

For example, an attacker could slightly modify a malware sample in a way that is imperceptible to humans but causes a machine learning model to misclassify it as benign. Developing AI systems that are robust and resilient to these types of adversarial attacks is a significant challenge.

The integration of AI into existing security workflows and systems is another consideration. Organizations need to think about how AI tools will fit into their current security operations and incident response processes. This may require adapting these processes or redesigning them to effectively leverage AI capabilities.

It's also important to consider the human element. AI should be seen as a tool to augment and assist human security analysts, not replace them entirely. Analysts need to be trained on how to effectively use and interpret AI tools, and there needs to be clear processes for how to handle AI-generated alerts and recommendations.

Ethical considerations, as discussed in the previous chapter, are also crucial. Organizations need to ensure that their use of AI in cybersecurity is aligned with ethical principles and legal requirements around data privacy, non-discrimination, and transparency.

Finally, there's the challenge of keeping up with the rapid pace of change. The AI and cybersecurity landscapes are both evolving incredibly fast. New AI techniques and applications are emerging all the time, as are new types of cyber threats. Organizations need to have processes in place to continuously monitor these changes and adapt their AI strategies accordingly.

Addressing these challenges requires a holistic and proactive approach. Organizations need to invest in robust data management practices, develop strategies for explainable AI, implement rigorous testing and validation processes to ensure model robustness, foster close collaboration between AI and security teams, and maintain a strong focus on ethics and governance.

By understanding and proactively addressing these challenges, organizations can set themselves up for success in leveraging AI for cybersecurity. In the following chapters, we'll dive deeper into specific AI applications and use cases in cybersecurity, and provide practical guidance on how to effectively implement and manage AI in security operations.

Chapter 2 Conclusion

In this chapter, we've taken a deep dive into the fundamentals of AI and machine learning, and how these technologies are being applied in the context of cybersecurity. We've explored key techniques like classification, anomaly detection, clustering, deep learning, and natural language processing, and discussed how they can be used to address various security challenges.

We've seen that AI has the potential to transform nearly every aspect of cybersecurity, from threat detection and incident response to vulnerability management and security testing. By learning from vast amounts of data and adapting to new patterns, AI systems can help organizations stay ahead of the ever-evolving threat landscape.

However, we've also discussed the significant challenges and considerations that come with implementing AI in cybersecurity. Issues like data quality, model interpretability, adversarial attacks, workflow integration, and ethical considerations all need to be carefully addressed.

The key takeaway is that while AI offers immense potential for enhancing cybersecurity, it is not a silver bullet. Effective implementation requires a strategic and holistic approach that takes into account the unique challenges and considerations of applying AI in a security context.

As we move forward in this book, we'll build on these fundamental concepts to explore specific AI applications and use cases in more depth. We'll discuss how AI is being used for network security, endpoint protection, application security, and more, and provide practical guidance on how to integrate AI into your security operations.

Remember, the goal is not to replace human security experts with AI, but rather to augment and empower them. By leveraging the power of AI to automate routine tasks, detect hidden threats, and provide intelligent insights, security professionals can focus their efforts on higher-level strategic tasks and decision-making.

The future of cybersecurity undoubtedly involves AI. By understanding the fundamentals, keeping pace with the latest developments, and proactively addressing the challenges, organizations can position themselves to harness the power of AI to build a more secure and resilient digital future.

THREE

— · —

CHAPTER 3: AI FOR NETWORK SECURITY

Section 3.1: Introduction to Network Security

I n the vast and complex world of cybersecurity, network security stands as a critical pillar. As organizations increasingly rely on interconnected systems and data transfer over networks, securing these networks has become paramount. Network security involves a multitude of practices and tools designed to protect the usability, reliability, integrity, and safety of a network and data.

The main objective of network security is to protect the network infrastructure and the data that flows through it from unauthorized access, misuse, malfunction, modification, destruction, or improper disclosure. This includes protecting both the hardware, such as routers and switches, and the software, including the operating systems and applications.

Networks face a variety of threats, both from external attackers and insider threats. Some common network security threats include:

- Malware: Malicious software like viruses, worms, trojans, and ransomware that can infect network devices and spread across the network.

- Denial of Service (DoS) attacks: Attempts to make a network resource unavailable to its intended users by temporarily or indefinitely disrupting services of a host connected to the network.

- Unauthorized access: Attackers gaining access to the network and its resources without permission, often through stolen credentials or by exploiting vulnerabilities.

- Man-in-the-Middle (MitM) attacks: Attackers intercepting communication between two parties, allowing them to eavesdrop or alter the communication.

- Advanced Persistent Threats (APTs): Prolonged, targeted attacks where an unauthorized person gains access to a network and remains undetected for an extended period.

To counter these threats, network security employs a variety of measures and controls. These include:

- Firewalls: Network security devices that monitor incoming and outgoing network traffic and decide whether to allow or block specific traffic based on a defined set of security rules.

- Intrusion Detection and Prevention Systems (IDPS): Tools that monitor network traffic for suspicious activity and can take automated actions to block potential threats.

- Virtual Private Networks (VPNs): Encrypted connections between devices or networks over less secure networks, ensuring the privacy and integrity of transmitted data.

- Network Segmentation: Dividing a network into smaller, isolated subnetworks to limit the potential damage of a breach and to improve performance.

- Access Control: Controlling who and what can access network resources, often through user authentication and permission settings.

However, as network threats continue to evolve and become more sophisticated, traditional network security measures are struggling to keep up. This is where Artificial Intelligence (AI) comes into play. AI has the potential to revolutionize network security by enabling more proactive, adaptive, and automated defense mechanisms.

In the following sections, we'll explore how AI is being applied to enhance various aspects of network security, from threat detection and incident response to network analytics and behavioral monitoring. We'll discuss real-world use cases, emerging trends, and best practices for integrating AI into your network security strategy.

As we navigate this chapter, keep in mind that while AI offers immense potential for fortifying network defenses, it is not a replacement for human expertise and judgement. The most effective network security strategies will be those that leverage the power of AI to augment and empower human security teams, not replace them.

Section 3.2: AI for Network Threat Detection

One of the most significant applications of AI in network security is in the area of threat detection. Traditional signature-based detection methods, which rely on predefined rules and known threat patterns, are increasingly struggling to keep pace with the rapid evolution of network threats. Cybercriminals are constantly developing new attack techniques that can evade conventional detection mechanisms.

This is where AI, particularly machine learning, can make a profound difference. Machine learning algorithms can be trained on vast amounts of network data to learn the normal behaviors and patterns of a network. They can then use this learned baseline to identify anomalies and potential threats in real-time.

There are several approaches to using AI for network threat detection:

1. Supervised Learning: In this approach, the machine learning model is trained on a labeled dataset, where the data is pre-categorized as "normal" or "malicious". The model learns to classify new, unseen data based on the patterns it has learned. For example, a supervised learning model could be trained on a dataset of network traffic logs, where each log is labeled as either benign or associated with a specific type of attack. The model would then be able to classify new traffic logs as benign or malicious.

2. Unsupervised Learning: Here, the machine learning model is trained on an unlabeled dataset. It learns to identify patterns and structures in the data on its own, without being told what to look for. In the context of network security, unsupervised learning is often used for anomaly detection. The model learns what "normal" network behavior looks like and flags any deviations from this norm as potential threats. For example, an unsupervised learning model could be used to detect unusual spikes in network traffic, which could indicate a DoS attack.

3. Deep Learning: Deep learning models, particularly deep neural networks, are capable of learning complex, hierarchical representations of data. They can automatically identify relevant features from raw data, making them well-suited for detecting subtle and unknown threats. For instance, a deep learning model could be trained on raw network packet data to identify patterns associated with malware communication, even if the specific malware signature is unknown.

4. Ensemble Methods: Ensemble methods combine multiple machine learning models to improve the overall accuracy and robustness of threat detection. For example, a combination of supervised and unsupervised learning models could be used, where the supervised model identifies known threats and the unsupervised model flags anomalies for further investigation.

Real-world applications of AI for network threat detection are numerous and varied. For example:

- AI-powered Intrusion Detection Systems (IDS) can analyze network traffic in real-time, identifying patterns indicative of known attack vectors as well as spotting anomalies that could signal zero-day exploits.

- AI can be used to detect botnets by identifying patterns in network traffic that are characteristic of bot communication, even if the specific botnet is previously unknown.

- Machine learning can be applied to DNS logs to identify Domain Generation Algorithm (DGA) malware, which uses algorithmically generated domain names to evade detection.

- AI models can be trained to recognize the network footprints of specific threat actors or nation-state groups, aiding in attribution and threat intelligence.

However, it's important to note that AI-based threat detection is not foolproof. Adversarial machine learning techniques can be used to generate malicious inputs designed to deceive or evade AI detection models. Ensuring the robustness and resilience of these models to adversarial attacks is an ongoing area of research and development.

Moreover, the effectiveness of AI for threat detection is heavily dependent on the quality and quantity of the data used to train the models. Obtaining labeled data for supervised learning can be challenging, and even unsupervised models require a comprehensive baseline of normal network behavior.

Despite these challenges, the potential of AI to enhance network threat detection is immense. By learning from   vast quantities of data and adapting to new threat patterns in real-time, AI can provide a powerful supplement to traditional detection methods. When combined with human expertise and integrated into a comprehensive security strategy, AI can significantly improve an organization's ability to identify and respond to network threats.

Section 3.3: AI for Network Incident Response

Detecting threats is only half the battle in network security. Equally important is the ability to respond quickly and effectively when a potential incident is identified. This is where AI can also play a significant role, by automating and optimizing incident response processes.

Traditionally, incident response has been a largely manual process. When a potential threat is detected, security analysts must investigate the alert, determine if it represents a genuine security incident, and if so, take steps to contain and remediate the threat. This can be a time-consuming process, and in the fast-moving world of cybersecurity, every second counts.

AI can help to streamline and accelerate this process in several ways:

1. Alert Triage: One of the biggest challenges in incident response is dealing with the sheer volume of security alerts. Many of these alerts are false positives, but distinguishing genuine threats from noise can be a daunting task. AI can be used to automatically triage alerts, prioritizing them based on factors like severity, confidence level, and potential impact. This allows security teams to focus their efforts on the most critical threats.

2. Incident Investigation: AI can assist in the investigation process by automatically correlating data from multiple sources, such as network logs, endpoint data, and threat intelligence feeds. Machine learning models can be trained to recognize patterns and connections that might be missed by human analysts. For example, an AI system could identify that a series of failed login attempts on different systems are actually part of a coordinated brute-force attack.

3. Automated Containment: Once a threat is confirmed, AI can help to automate containment measures. For instance, if an AI system detects that a network device is behaving maliciously, it can automatically isolate that device from the network to prevent further damage. Or if a malware infection is detected, AI can initiate processes to quarantine affected files and roll back harmful changes.

4. Adaptive Response: AI systems can learn from each incident, becoming more effective at identifying and responding to similar threats over time. For example, if an AI system successfully identifies and contains a new type of malware, it can use that experience to more quickly detect and block similar malware in the future.

Real-world examples of AI in network incident response are emerging. For instance, some organizations are using AI-powered chatbots to automate the initial triage of security alerts. These chatbots can interact with security analysts, asking relevant questions and providing recommendations based on predefined playbooks.

Other companies are using machine learning to optimize the incident investigation process. By training models on historical incident data, these systems can learn to identify relevant patterns and suggest optimal response strategies.

However, there are challenges to consider. Automating incident response with AI requires a high degree of trust in the system's decision-making capabilities. Rigorous testing and human oversight are necessary to ensure that automated actions are appropriate and do not cause unintended consequences.

There are also potential risks associated with relying too heavily on AI for incident response. If an attacker is aware that an organization is using AI, they may attempt to manipulate the system, such as by gradually training it to accept malicious behavior as normal.

Despite these challenges, the potential benefits of AI for network incident response are significant. By automating routine tasks and providing intelligent recommendations, AI can help security teams to work more efficiently and effectively. This is particularly valuable in the context of the cybersecurity skills shortage, where many organizations struggle to find and retain enough qualified security personnel.

As with threat detection, the most effective approach is likely to be a combination of human expertise and AI capabilities. By leveraging AI to handle the repetitive and data-heavy aspects of incident response, human analysts can focus on higher-level tasks that require strategic thinking and creativity.

Section 3.4: AI for Network Behavior Analytics

Another promising application of AI in network security is in the area of behavior analytics. Network Behavior Analytics (NBA) is the process of using machine learning to model and analyze the behavior of users, devices, and applications on a network. The goal is to identify patterns and anomalies that could indicate security threats or performance issues.

Traditional network monitoring tools often rely on predefined rules and thresholds to identify issues. For example, a tool might alert if network traffic exceeds a certain level or if a particular port is accessed. While these rules can be effective for detecting known issues, they are less useful for identifying novel or subtle threats.

NBA takes a different approach. Instead of relying on predefined rules, NBA uses machine learning to create a baseline model of normal network behavior. This model is continuously updated as new data is collected, allowing it to adapt to changing network conditions.

There are several key areas where NBA can be applied:

1. User Behavior Analytics: NBA can be used to model the typical behavior patterns of individual users on a network. This includes factors like the devices they use, the applications they access, the times they are active, and the locations they connect from. By establishing a baseline of normal behavior for each user, NBA can identify anomalies that could indicate a compromised account or insider threat. For example, if a user suddenly starts accessing sensitive data that they have never accessed before, or if they log in from an unusual location, NBA can flag this as a potential threat.

2. Device Behavior Analytics: Similar to user behavior analytics, NBA can also be used to model the behavior of devices on a network. This includes monitoring factors like the type and volume of traffic each device generates, the protocols it uses, and the other devices it communicates with. Anomalies in device behavior, such as a printer suddenly sending out large amounts of data, can indicate that a device has been compromised and is being used for malicious purposes.

3. Application Behavior Analytics: NBA can also be applied at the application level, modeling the normal behavior of individual applications on a network. This includes monitoring factors like the users and devices that typically access each application, the volume of data it generates, and the external services it communicates with. Anomalies in application behavior, such as a sudden spike in data usage or communication with an unknown external server, can indicate a potential security issue.

The benefits of NBA are significant. By continuously monitoring network behavior and adapting to changing conditions, NBA can identify threats that might be missed by traditional security tools. This includes zero-day exploits, insider threats, and advanced persistent threats (APTs) that are designed to evade detection.

NBA can also help to reduce the burden on security teams by automatically prioritizing potential threats. Instead of manually sifting through large volumes of security alerts, analysts can focus their efforts on the anomalies identified by NBA as being the most likely to represent genuine security issues.

However, implementing NBA effectively can be challenging. It requires collecting and processing large volumes of network data in real-time, which can be computationally intensive. It also requires a deep understanding of machine learning techniques and how to apply them effectively to network security.

There are also potential privacy concerns to consider, particularly when it comes to user behavior analytics. Monitoring individual user behavior can be a sensitive issue, and organizations need to ensure that they have appropriate data protection measures in place and that they are transparent about their use of NBA.

Despite these challenges, the potential of NBA to transform network security is significant. By leveraging the power of machine learning to understand normal network behavior and identify anomalies, NBA can provide a powerful complement to traditional security tools and help organizations to stay one step ahead of evolving threats.

As the volume and complexity of network data continue to grow, the importance of NBA is only likely to increase. Organizations that are able to effectively leverage NBA as part of their overall network security strategy will be well-positioned to detect and respond to the sophisticated threats of today and tomorrow.

Section 3.5: AI for Network Forensics and Analysis

When a network security incident does occur, the ability to quickly and accurately investigate what happened is critical. Network forensics involves collecting, preserving, and analyzing network data to understand the nature and extent of a security incident. This can be a complex and time-consuming process, particularly in large and complex network environments.

AI can play a significant role in streamlining and enhancing network forensics. Machine learning techniques can be applied to automatically identify and extract relevant data from large volumes of network traffic, greatly reducing the time and effort required for manual analysis.

There are several key areas where AI can be applied in network forensics:

1. Data Triage: One of the first steps in network forensics is to identify which data is relevant to the investigation. AI can be used to automatically classify network data based on factors like file type, protocol, and content. This can help investigators to quickly zero in on the data that is most likely to be relevant, rather than having to manually sift through large volumes of irrelevant data.

2. Pattern Recognition: AI can be used to identify patterns in network data that might be indicative of malicious activity. For example, machine learning models can be trained to recognize the network signatures of specific types of malware or attack techniques. By automatically flagging these patterns, AI can help investigators to quickly identify the key indicators of compromise.

3. Anomaly Detection: As in network behavior analytics, AI can also be used in forensics to identify anomalies that deviate from normal network behavior. This can help investigators to spot unusual activities that might be related to the security incident, even if they don't match known malware signatures or attack patterns.

4. Data Visualization: AI can be used to automatically generate visual representations of network data, such as traffic flow diagrams or node-link graphs. These visualizations can make it easier for investigators to understand complex relationships and identify key patterns, without having to manually parse through large volumes of raw data.

5. Predictive Analysis: AI can also be used to make predictions based on historical

network data. For example, machine learning models can be trained on data from past security incidents to predict the likelihood of future incidents based on current network conditions. This can help organizations to proactively identify and mitigate potential threats.

Real-world applications of AI in network forensics are emerging. For instance, some tools use machine learning to automatically reconstruct the timeline of a security incident, stitching together data from multiple sources to create a comprehensive narrative of what happened.

Other tools use AI to automatically generate incident reports, summarizing the key findings of a forensic investigation in a format that is easy for non-technical stakeholders to understand.

However, there are also challenges to consider. The effectiveness of AI in network forensics is heavily dependent on the quality and relevance of the data used to train the models. If the training data is incomplete or not representative of real-world network conditions, the AI may not be effective at identifying relevant patterns or anomalies.

There are also potential legal and ethical considerations around the use of AI in forensics. The use of AI to analyze network data could raise privacy concerns, particularly if the data includes sensitive personal information. Organizations need to ensure that they have appropriate legal and ethical frameworks in place to govern the use of AI in forensic investigations.

Despite these challenges, the potential of AI to enhance network forensics is significant. By automating many of the time-consuming and repetitive tasks involved in forensic analysis, AI can free up investigators to focus on higher-level tasks that require human judgement and expertise.

As network environments continue to grow in size and complexity, the need for efficient and effective forensic tools will only increase. Organizations that are able to leverage AI to streamline their forensic processes will be better positioned to respond to security incidents quickly and minimize their impact.

However, it's important to remember that AI is not a replacement for human expertise in network forensics. The most effective approach is likely to be a combination of AI-powered tools and skilled human investigators who can interpret the findings and make informed decisions based on their knowledge and experience.

Chapter 3 Conclusion

In this chapter, we've explored the many ways in which AI is transforming the field of network security. From threat detection and incident response to behavior analytics and forensic analysis, AI is providing powerful new tools for defending against the ever-evolving landscape of network threats.

We've seen how machine learning can be used to identify anomalies and patterns that might indicate malicious activity, even if those patterns don't match known threat signatures. We've discussed how AI can automate and optimize incident response processes, helping security teams to work more efficiently and effectively. And we've explored how AI can streamline network forensics, making it easier to investigate and understand security incidents when they do occur.

The potential benefits of AI in network security are clear. By leveraging the power of machine learning to process and analyze vast amounts of network data in real-time, AI can help organizations to detect threats faster, respond more effectively, and gain deeper insights into the security of their networks.

However, we've also discussed the challenges and considerations involved in implementing AI for network security. The effectiveness of AI is heavily dependent on the quality and relevance of the data used to train the models. There are potential privacy and ethical concerns to navigate, particularly when it comes to monitoring user behavior. And there is always the risk that attackers could attempt to manipulate or evade AI-based defenses.

Despite these challenges, the integration of AI into network security is only likely to accelerate in the coming years. As the volume and complexity of network data continue to grow, and as the sophistication of network threats continues to evolve, the need for intelligent, automated security tools will become increasingly critical.

The most successful organizations will be those that are able to effectively leverage AI as part of a comprehensive network security strategy - one that combines the power of machine learning with the expertise and judgement of skilled human professionals.

As we've emphasized throughout this chapter, AI is not a silver bullet for network security. It is a powerful tool, but one that must be wielded with care and integrated into a broader framework of security policies, processes, and technologies.

Going forward, it will be essential for organizations to stay abreast of the latest developments in AI and network security, and to continually adapt their strategies as new threats and opportunities emerge. This will require ongoing investment in research and development, as well as a commitment to collaboration and knowledge-sharing across the cybersecurity community.

By working together to harness the power of AI in a responsible and effective way, we can build a future in which our networks are more secure, more resilient, and better able to support the needs of our digital society.

FOUR

— ◆ —

CHAPTER 4: AI FOR ENDPOINT PROTECTION

Section 4.1: Understanding Endpoint Security

In the vast landscape of cybersecurity, endpoint security stands as a critical frontier. As the name suggests, endpoint security focuses on securing the end-user devices that connect to a network, such as laptops, smartphones, tablets, and IoT devices. These endpoints represent potential entry points for cyber threats, making their protection crucial for overall network security.

Endpoints are attractive targets for attackers for several reasons. Firstly, they often represent the weakest link in an organization's security chain. While network perimeters are usually well-fortified with firewalls and intrusion detection systems, individual endpoints may have weaker security controls and more vulnerabilities.

Secondly, endpoints are used by humans, and humans are prone to making mistakes. An employee might click on a malicious link in a phishing email, download malware from an unsafe website, or use a weak password that can be easily guessed. These human errors can provide attackers with an easy path into the network.

Thirdly, the proliferation of mobile and remote work has greatly expanded the attack surface for endpoints. Employees are increasingly accessing corporate networks and data from personal devices and unsecured public networks, making it harder for organizations to maintain visibility and control over endpoint security.

The consequences of a compromised endpoint can be severe. An attacker who gains control of an endpoint device can use it as a foothold to move laterally through the network, steal sensitive data, deploy ransomware, or conduct other malicious activities.

To counter these threats, endpoint security employs a variety of tools and strategies.

These include:

- Antivirus and Anti-malware Software: These tools scan endpoint devices for known malware signatures and suspicious behaviors, helping to detect and block malicious software.

- Endpoint Detection and Response (EDR): EDR tools continuously monitor endpoints for signs of compromise, providing real-time visibility and enabling quick response to threats.

- Endpoint Encryption: Encrypting data on endpoints helps to protect sensitive information in case a device is lost or stolen.

- Patch Management: Keeping endpoints updated with the latest security patches helps to reduce vulnerabilities that attackers could exploit.

- Access Controls: Implementing strong authentication and access controls helps to ensure that only authorized users and devices can access the network.

However, as the number and complexity of endpoints continue to grow, traditional endpoint security approaches are struggling to keep pace. It's becoming increasingly difficult for security teams to manually monitor and manage the vast array of devices connecting to their networks.

This is where Artificial Intelligence (AI) comes into play. AI has the potential to revolutionize endpoint security by enabling more intelligent, automated, and scalable protection. By leveraging machine learning to understand normal endpoint behavior, identify anomalies, and respond to threats in real-time, AI can help organizations to secure their endpoints more effectively and efficiently.

In the following sections, we'll explore the specific applications of AI in endpoint security, from malware detection and behavioral analysis to threat hunting and automated response. We'll look at real-world use cases, emerging trends, and best practices for integrating AI into your endpoint security strategy.

As we navigate this chapter, it's important to remember that while AI offers immense potential for enhancing endpoint security, it is not a replacement for human expertise and oversight. The most effective endpoint security strategies will be those that combine the power of AI with the knowledge and judgement of skilled security professionals.

Section 4.2: AI-Powered Malware Detection

One of the most significant applications of AI in endpoint security is in the area of malware detection. Malware, short for malicious software, refers to any program or file that is harmful to a computer user. This includes viruses, worms, Trojan horses, ransomware, spyware, adware, and other types of threats.

Traditional antivirus software relies on signature-based detection, where the software compares files on a device to a database of known malware signatures. While this method can be effective for identifying known threats, it struggles to detect new or evolving malware that doesn't match existing signatures.

AI, particularly machine learning, offers a more proactive and adaptive approach to malware detection. Instead of relying on predefined signatures, machine learning models can be trained on vast datasets of malware and benign files to learn the distinguishing characteristics of malicious software. These models can then be used to classify new, unknown files as either malicious or benign based on their learned patterns.

There are several machine learning techniques that can be applied for malware detection:

1. Supervised Learning: In this approach, the machine learning model is trained on a labeled dataset, where each file is pre-classified as either malware or benign. The model learns to recognize the features and patterns that are associated with malware, such as specific API calls, file structures, or network behaviors. When presented with a new, unknown file, the model can then classify it based on its similarity to the malware examples it was trained on.

2. Unsupervised Learning: Here, the machine learning model is trained on an unlabeled dataset, without any pre-classified examples of malware or benign files. The model learns to identify patterns and anomalies in the data on its own. In the context of malware detection, unsupervised learning can be used to identify files that exhibit unusual or outlier behavior compared to the norm.

3. Deep Learning: Deep learning models, particularly deep neural networks, can be used for more advanced malware detection. These models can automatically learn hierarchical representations of data, enabling them to identify complex patterns and features that may be indicative of malware. For example, a deep learning model could be trained on raw bytecode from executable files, learning to identify malicious patterns at a granular level.

The advantages of AI-based malware detection are significant. Firstly, it can help to identify new and unknown malware that may evade traditional signature-based detection. By learning the general characteristics of malware rather than relying on specific signatures, AI models can potentially identify malicious files that have never been seen before.

Secondly, AI can help to reduce the burden on human analysts. With the vast number of new malware variants emerging every day, it's becoming increasingly difficult for humans to manually analyze and classify every file. AI can automate much of this process, flagging suspicious files for further investigation and freeing up analysts to focus on more strategic tasks.

However, there are also challenges to consider. One issue is the potential for false positives, where a benign file is incorrectly classified as malware. This can happen if the AI model isn't trained on a representative enough dataset, or if the malware exhibits characteristics that are very similar to benign software.

There's also the risk of adversarial attacks, where malware developers intentionally try to fool or evade AI-based detection. This could involve techniques like obfuscation, where the malware code is deliberately made difficult to analyze, or poisoning, where the training data for the AI model is contaminated with misleading examples.

To mitigate these risks, it's important to continually update and retrain AI models on the latest malware data, and to use AI as part of a layered security strategy rather than a sole line of defense. Human oversight and analysis will always be crucial for validating AI findings and making final determinations about the maliciousness of a file.

Real-world examples of AI-based malware detection are numerous. Many endpoint security products now incorporate machine learning as part of their malware detection engines. These products can analyze files in real-time as they enter the network, flagging suspicious ones for further investigation.

Some advanced AI-based malware detection tools can even identify malware that is specifically designed to evade AI detection. By analyzing not just the content of a file but also its context and metadata, these tools can spot anomalies and inconsistencies that may indicate a malware evasion attempt.

As malware continues to evolve and become more sophisticated, the role of AI in malware detection will only become more critical. By continually learning and adapting to new threats, AI can help organizations to stay one step ahead in the never-ending battle against malicious software.

However, it's important to remember that AI is not a silver bullet for malware detection. It should be used as part of a comprehensive endpoint security strategy that also includes traditional signature-based detection, behavioral analysis, threat intelligence, and human expertise. Only by combining the strengths of AI with other proven security methods can organizations mount the most effective defense against the ever-evolving malware landscape.

Section 4.3: AI for Endpoint Behavioral Analysis

While malware detection is a critical aspect of endpoint security, it's not the only area where AI can make a significant impact. Another key application is in the realm of endpoint behavioral analysis, which involves monitoring and analyzing the activities and behaviors of endpoint devices and users to identify potential security threats.

Traditional endpoint security tools often focus on preventing known malware and blocking specific, predefined actions. However, this approach can miss more subtle or unknown threats that don't follow expected patterns. That's where behavioral analysis comes in.

The concept behind behavioral analysis is that while the specific tools and tactics used by attackers may vary, the underlying behaviors and objectives often remain consistent. By establishing a baseline of normal activity for each endpoint and user, behavioral analysis tools can identify deviations that may indicate a security threat, even if the specific malware or attack method has never been seen before.

This is where AI, particularly machine learning, can be a game-changer. Machine learning models can be trained on vast amounts of endpoint data to learn the normal patterns of behavior for each device and user. This could include factors like:

- The processes and applications that typically run on the device
- The network resources and websites that the device usually accesses
- The login times and durations that are typical for the user
- The files and data that the user normally interacts with

By continuously monitoring endpoint activity and comparing it to these learned baselines, AI-powered behavioral analysis tools can identify anomalies that may indicate a security threat, such as:

- A device that starts communicating with an unknown external server
- A user who suddenly starts accessing sensitive files they've never touched before
- A process that begins consuming an abnormal amount of system resources
- A script that attempts to disable security tools or make system changes

When such anomalies are detected, the AI system can flag them for further investigation by security teams. Some advanced tools can even take automated actions, such as isolating the suspicious device from the network to prevent potential spread of an infection.

The advantages of AI-based behavioral analysis are numerous. Firstly, it can help to identify threats that may evade traditional signature-based detection, such as zero-day exploits or polymorphic malware that changes its code to avoid detection.

Secondly, it can provide a more comprehensive view of endpoint security by looking at the full context of device and user behavior, rather than just isolated events. This can help to identify more subtle or long-term threats, such as insider attacks or advanced persistent threats (APTs).

However, there are also challenges to consider. One issue is the potential for false positives, where normal but unusual behavior is flagged as a potential threat. This can happen if the AI model isn't trained on a diverse enough dataset, or if it's not given enough context to understand when certain behaviors are appropriate.

There's also the risk of alert fatigue, where security teams are overwhelmed by the volume of anomalies detected by the AI system. To mitigate this, it's important to carefully tune the sensitivity of the AI model and to provide tools for prioritizing and investigating the most significant alerts.

Privacy is another consideration. Monitoring user behavior, even for security purposes, can raise concerns about surveillance and data privacy. Organizations need to be transparent about their use of behavioral analysis and ensure that they have appropriate data protection measures in place.

Despite these challenges, the potential of AI for endpoint behavioral analysis is immense. By providing a more intelligent and adaptive approach to threat detection, it can help organizations to identify and respond to a wider range of security risks.

Real-world applications of AI-based behavioral analysis are growing. Many endpoint detection and response (EDR) and user and entity behavior analytics (UEBA) tools now incorporate machine learning to establish behavioral baselines and detect anomalies.

Some advanced tools even use deep learning techniques to analyze more complex behavioral patterns, such as the sequences of actions that a user takes or the relationships between different entities on the network.

As the complexity and volume of endpoint data continue to grow, the importance of AI for behavioral analysis will only increase. By automating the process of identifying unusual and potentially malicious activities, AI can help security teams to focus their efforts on the most significant threats and respond more quickly and effectively when incidents do occur.

However, it's crucial to remember that AI is not a replacement for human analysis and judgement. While AI can excel at identifying patterns and anomalies in vast amounts of data, it lacks the contextual understanding and intuition that human analysts bring to the table. The most effective endpoint security strategies will be those that leverage the strengths of both AI and human intelligence, using machine learning to surface potential threats and human expertise to validate and investigate them.

Moreover, as attackers become more aware of AI-based defenses, they are likely to adapt their tactics to evade detection. This could involve techniques like "living off the land," where attackers use legitimate system tools and processes to avoid triggering anomaly alerts, or "low and slow" attacks that make gradual, subtle changes over time to avoid detection.

To stay ahead of these evolving threats, it's essential for AI-based behavioral analysis tools to continually learn and adapt. This requires ongoing training on the latest endpoint data and attack techniques, as well as regular tuning and adjustment of detection algorithms.

It's also important to integrate behavioral analysis into a broader endpoint security strategy that includes other detection and prevention controls, such as antivirus, application whitelisting, and endpoint encryption. By layering multiple security mechanisms, organizations can create a more resilient defense against the wide range of threats facing endpoints today.

In conclusion, AI-powered behavioral analysis represents a significant advancement in endpoint security, enabling a more proactive and adaptive approach to threat detection. By learning the normal patterns of endpoint activity and identifying anomalies in real-time, AI can help organizations to catch threats that might otherwise slip through the cracks.

However, realizing the full potential of AI in this context requires careful planning, implementation, and ongoing management. Organizations need to select the right tools for their environment, ensure that they have the necessary data and computational resources to support machine learning, and invest in the skills and processes to investigate and respond to AI-generated alerts.

As the threat landscape continues to evolve, the role of AI in endpoint security will only become more critical. By embracing this technology and integrating it effectively into their security strategies, organizations can enhance their ability to protect against the advanced and persistent threats of today and tomorrow.

Section 4.4: AI for Autonomous Threat Hunting

As we've seen, AI can play a significant role in automating the detection of known and unknown threats at the endpoint level. However, threat detection is only part of the equation. To truly stay ahead of adversaries, organizations need to proactively hunt for threats that may be lurking in their environment undetected.

This is where autonomous threat hunting comes into play. Threat hunting is the practice of proactively searching for signs of compromise or malicious activity that have evaded initial detection. It's a more aggressive approach than traditional threat detection, which relies on triggers or alerts to initiate investigations.

Traditionally, threat hunting has been a largely manual process, requiring skilled security analysts to sift through vast amounts of endpoint data looking for anomalies and indicators of attack. However, as the volume and complexity of this data continues to grow, manual threat hunting is becoming increasingly difficult and time-consuming.

This is where AI can be a game-changer. By leveraging machine learning and data analytics, AI-powered tools can automate many of the repetitive and data-intensive tasks involved in threat hunting, enabling security teams to search for threats more efficiently and effectively.

One key application of AI in threat hunting is in the automated discovery of Indicators of Compromise (IoCs). IoCs are pieces of forensic data, such as virus signatures, IP addresses, or file hashes, that indicate a potential intrusion. AI models can be trained on vast datasets of endpoint activity to learn the characteristics of IoCs and automatically flag them for investigation.

For example, an AI system might analyze endpoint data looking for unusual process executions, suspicious network connections, or anomalous file access patterns. When it identifies an activity that matches the characteristics of an IoC, it can automatically trigger an alert for security teams to investigate.

Another application of AI in threat hunting is in the identification of Advanced Persistent Threats (APTs). APTs are sophisticated, long-term attacks where the adversary gains unauthorized access to a network and remains undetected for an extended period. These attacks are notoriously difficult to identify because the attackers often use legitimate credentials and tools to avoid triggering alerts.

AI can help to uncover APTs by analyzing endpoint behavior over time and identifying subtle patterns and anomalies that may indicate a long-term compromise. For example, an AI model might detect that a particular user account has been accessing sensitive files at unusual times or from unusual locations, potentially indicating that the account has been compromised.

Autonomous threat hunting can also leverage AI to prioritize and guide investigations. By analyzing the context and severity of different anomalies, AI systems can help security teams to focus their efforts on the most significant potential threats. Some advanced tools can even provide automated recommendations for containment and remediation based on the characteristics of the threat.

The benefits of AI-powered threat hunting are compelling. By automating the discovery of potential threats, it can help organizations to identify compromises that might otherwise go undetected for months or even years. This early detection can significantly reduce the impact and cost of a breach.

AI can also help to augment and empower human threat hunters. By handling much of the data analysis and anomaly detection, AI frees up security professionals to focus on higher-level tasks like investigating and responding to confirmed threats. This can help to improve the efficiency and effectiveness of security operations.

However, there are also challenges to consider. One issue is the potential for false positives. Because threat hunting involves looking for unknown threats, there's a risk that benign or unusual but legitimate activity could be flagged as malicious. This can lead to wasted time and resources investigating false alarms.

To mitigate this risk, it's important to carefully tune AI models and provide human oversight and validation of automated findings. Security teams need to work closely with data scientists to ensure that machine learning models are trained on representative data and that their outputs are interpreted appropriately.

There's also the challenge of data access and quality. AI-powered threat hunting requires access to large volumes of high-quality endpoint data. Organizations need to ensure that they have the necessary data collection and storage infrastructure in place, as well as the data governance and privacy controls to use this data appropriately.

Skills and knowledge are another consideration. While AI can automate many aspects of threat hunting, it still requires human expertise to investigate and respond to potential threats. Organizations need to invest in training and developing their security teams to work effectively with AI tools and interpret their outputs.

Despite these challenges, the potential of AI for autonomous threat hunting is significant. As the threat landscape continues to evolve and attackers become more sophisticated, proactive and automated approaches to threat detection will become increasingly critical.

Real-world examples of AI-powered threat hunting are already emerging. Many endpoint detection and response (EDR) and security information and event management (SIEM) tools now incorporate machine learning capabilities to automate the discovery of potential threats.

Some advanced tools even use unsupervised learning techniques to identify anomalies and outliers without relying on predefined threat signatures or indicators. This allows them to detect truly novel and unknown threats that might evade rule-based detection.

Looking to the future, we can expect AI to play an even greater role in autonomous threat hunting. As machine learning algorithms become more sophisticated and endpoint data becomes more granular, AI will be able to identify threats with greater speed and precision.

We may also see the emergence of more specialized AI threat hunting tools, designed to detect specific types of threats or attack techniques. For example, there could be AI models trained specifically to identify ransomware, fileless malware, or insider threats based on their unique behavioral fingerprints.

Ultimately, the goal of AI in threat hunting is not to replace human analysts, but to augment and empower them. By automating the tedious and time-consuming aspects of threat hunting, AI can help security teams to work more efficiently and effectively, focusing their efforts on the most significant risks.

However, to realize this potential, organizations will need to invest not just in AI technology, but in the people and processes to support it. This includes building strong partnerships between security and data science teams, developing governance frameworks for the ethical and responsible use of AI, and continually training and upskilling security professionals to work with AI tools.

As we navigate the future of endpoint security, the role of AI in autonomous threat hunting will only become more critical. By embracing this technology and integrating it effectively into their security strategies, organizations can proactively defend against the ever-evolving threat landscape and maintain a robust security posture in the face of increasingly sophisticated attacks.

Section 4.5: AI-Powered Endpoint Response and Remediation

Detecting and hunting threats is only half the battle in endpoint security. Once a potential compromise has been identified, organizations need to be able to quickly and effectively respond to mitigate the impact and prevent further damage. This is where AI can also play a significant role, by automating and optimizing the process of endpoint response and remediation.

Traditionally, endpoint response has been a largely manual process. When a security alert is triggered, it's up to human analysts to investigate the issue, determine the appropriate course of action, and execute the necessary steps to contain and remediate the threat. This can be a time-consuming and error-prone process, particularly in the face of advanced or fast-moving threats.

AI can help to streamline and accelerate this process in several ways. One key application is in the automated triage and prioritization of security alerts. In a typical enterprise environment, security teams can be inundated with a high volume of alerts from various security tools. Determining which alerts represent genuine threats that require immediate action can be a daunting task.

AI can assist by analyzing the context and characteristics of each alert and automatically assigning a risk score or priority level. Machine learning models can be trained on historical alert data to learn which factors are most predictive of a true positive, such as the type of asset involved, the severity of the anomaly, or the similarity to known attack patterns.

This automated triage can help security teams to quickly focus their efforts on the most significant threats, rather than wasting time chasing down false positives. Some advanced AI tools can even provide recommended actions for each alert based on predefined playbooks or best practices.

Another application of AI in endpoint response is in the automated containment of threats. When a genuine compromise is   detected, time is of the essence in preventing the attack from spreading or causing further damage. AI can help to automate the immediate steps needed to contain the threat, such as isolating the affected endpoint from the network, terminating malicious processes, or rolling back recent system changes.

For example, if an AI system detects that an endpoint has been infected with ransomware, it can automatically trigger a series of containment actions, such as disconnecting the device from the network to prevent the ransomware from spreading, and backing up critical data to prevent loss in case of encryption.

These automated containment capabilities can significantly reduce the mean time to respond (MTTR) to security incidents, minimizing the window of opportunity for attackers to cause damage. They can also help to ensure that containment actions are carried out consistently and effectively, reducing the risk of human error.

AI can also support the investigation and remediation phases of incident response. Machine learning can be used to automatically gather and analyze relevant data from affected endpoints, such as system logs, network traffic, and file activity. This can help to accelerate the forensic investigation process and pinpoint the root cause of the incident more quickly.

Some AI tools can even generate automated incident reports, summarizing the key findings and providing recommendations for remediation and prevention. This can help to streamline the post-incident review process and ensure that valuable lessons are learned and implemented.

In terms of remediation, AI can assist by automating the deployment of patches, updates, or configuration changes needed to address the underlying vulnerability that allowed the compromise to occur. Machine learning models can be used to prioritize remediation efforts based on the criticality of the asset and the risk of the vulnerability.

The benefits of AI-powered endpoint response are significant. By automating and accelerating the detection, containment, and remediation of threats, AI can help organizations to minimize the impact of security incidents and prevent minor compromises from turning into major breaches.

AI can also help to alleviate the burden on human security teams, who are often overworked and understaffed. By handling routine tasks and providing intelligent recommendations, AI can allow security professionals to focus their time and expertise on more strategic activities.

However, there are also challenges and considerations to keep in mind. One risk is the potential for automated actions to have unintended consequences. For example, automatically isolating a critical business system could disrupt operations if done unnecessarily or without proper precautions.

To mitigate this risk, it's important to carefully define and test the rules and playbooks used by AI response tools. There should always be human oversight and the ability to override automated actions if needed.

Another challenge is the need for integration and compatibility with existing security tools and processes. AI response tools need to be able to ingest data and trigger actions across the security stack, which can be complex in environments with multiple vendor solutions.

Organizations need to carefully plan their AI response deployments and ensure that they have the necessary APIs and integrations in place. They may also need to update their incident response playbooks and train their teams on how to effectively work with AI tools.

There are also potential adversarial risks to consider. As attackers become aware of AI-powered response capabilities, they may attempt to develop countermeasures or evasion techniques. For example, they could try to mislead or poison the machine learning models used for detection and response.

To stay ahead of these threats, it's essential for AI response tools to be continually updated and adapted based on the latest threat intelligence and attacker tactics. Organizations should also employ a multi-layered defense strategy that includes both AI and traditional security controls.

Despite these challenges, the potential of AI for transforming endpoint response is immense. As the volume and complexity of cybersecurity threats continue to grow, the speed and scale of AI will become increasingly critical for effective incident response.

Real-world examples of AI-powered response are already emerging, particularly in the realm of security orchestration, automation, and response (SOAR) platforms. These tools use machine learning to automate and optimize the incident response workflow, from initial alert to final remediation.

Some advanced SOAR platforms even incorporate chatbots or virtual assistants that can guide security analysts through the response process, providing contextual information and recommending actions at each step.

As AI technology continues to advance, we can expect to see even more sophisticated and autonomous response capabilities emerge. For example, self-healing endpoints that can automatically detect and repair damage from security incidents, or adaptive security policies that can dynamically adjust based on the current threat environment.

Ultimately, the goal of AI in endpoint response is to enable organizations to respond to threats at machine speed and scale, while still maintaining human oversight and control. By striking this balance, organizations can harness the power of AI to significantly improve their security posture and resilience.

However, achieving this will require ongoing investment and commitment. Organizations will need to continually assess and update their AI response tools and processes to keep pace with the evolving threat landscape. They will also need to invest in the skills and training of their security teams to work effectively with AI.

As we look to the future of endpoint security, the integration of AI into response and remediation will be a key factor in staying ahead of the curve. By proactively embracing this technology and adapting their strategies accordingly, organizations can position themselves for success in the face of ever-evolving cybersecurity challenges.

Chapter 4 Conclusion

Throughout this chapter, we've explored the many ways in which AI is revolutionizing the field of endpoint security. From malware detection and behavioral analysis to threat hunting and incident response, AI is providing powerful new capabilities for protecting endpoints against the full spectrum of cybersecurity threats.

We've seen how machine learning can be used to identify known and unknown malware based on its characteristics and behaviors, providing a more proactive and adaptive approach than traditional signature-based detection. We've discussed how behavioral analysis using AI can help to identify subtle signs of compromise that might evade rule-based security controls.

We've also delved into the world of autonomous threat hunting, where AI is helping security teams to proactively search for hidden threats across their endpoint landscape. And we've examined how AI can automate and optimize the incident response process, from initial triage to containment and remediation.

The potential benefits of AI in endpoint security are clear. By leveraging the speed, scale, and intelligence of machine learning, organizations can detect threats faster, respond more effectively, and adapt more quickly to new attack vectors. AI can also help to alleviate the burden on human security teams, allowing them to focus their efforts on higher-value activities.

However, we've also highlighted the challenges and considerations that come with deploying AI in an endpoint security context. Issues like data quality, model interpretability, algorithmic bias, and adversarial attacks all need to be carefully managed. Organizations need to approach AI as part of a holistic security strategy, not a silver bullet solution.

The successful integration of AI into endpoint security requires a collaborative effort between security teams, data scientists, and business stakeholders. It requires ongoing investment in skills, processes, and technology to ensure that AI tools are effectively deployed, monitored, and maintained over time.

As we've emphasized throughout this chapter, the role of human expertise remains crucial. While AI can automate and augment many aspects of endpoint security, it is not a replacement for human judgement and creativity. The most effective endpoint security strategies will be those that combine the strengths of both human and machine intelligence.

Looking to the future, we can expect the role of AI in endpoint security to continue to grow and evolve. As the volume and sophistication of cyber threats continue to escalate, the need for intelligent, adaptive, and autonomous defenses will only become more acute.

We're likely to see more advanced applications of AI emerge, such as self-learning endpoints that can automatically adapt their security posture based on the current threat environment, or predictive analytics that can forecast future attack vectors based on historical patterns.

At the same time, we can also expect to see more focus on the responsible and ethical use of AI in cybersecurity. As AI systems become more autonomous and influential, it will be critical to ensure that they are designed and deployed in a way that is transparent, accountable, and aligned with human values.

Ultimately, the journey of AI in endpoint security is still in its early stages. While the progress made so far is impressive, there is still much work to be done to fully realize the potential of this transformative technology.

By staying informed about the latest developments, investing in the necessary skills and capabilities, and proactively addressing the challenges and risks, organizations can position themselves to harness the power of AI for a more secure and resilient endpoint environment.

The future of endpoint security is inextricably linked with the advancement of AI. As we navigate this new frontier, it will be the organizations that can effectively bridge the gap between human and machine intelligence that will be best positioned for success. By embracing AI as a partner in endpoint protection, we can build a future where our digital assets are safer, our responses are swifter, and our defenses are smarter than ever before.

FIVE

— • —

CHAPTER 5: AI FOR APPLICATION SECURITY

Section 5.1: Introduction to Application Security

In the vast and complex landscape of cybersecurity, application security stands out as a critical area of focus. In today's digital age, software applications have become ubiquitous, powering everything from personal devices and business operations to critical infrastructure and government services. As our reliance on these applications grows, so too does the importance of ensuring their security.

At its core, application security is about protecting software applications from various types of threats throughout their lifecycle. These threats can manifest at different stages, from design and development to deployment and operation. They can also take many forms, ranging from common vulnerabilities like SQL injection and cross-site scripting to more sophisticated attacks like business logic abuse and API manipulation.

The consequences of application security breaches can be severe. A compromised application can lead to data theft, system disruption, reputational damage, financial losses, and in some cases, even physical harm. In an interconnected world, a single vulnerable application can provide an entry point for attackers to compromise an entire network or supply chain.

Despite its critical importance, application security has often been overshadowed by network and endpoint security in traditional cybersecurity strategies. This is partly because applications are complex and constantly evolving, making them difficult to secure using conventional methods. The rapid adoption of cloud computing, microservices architectures, and DevOps practices has further compounded these challenges.

To address these challenges, organizations are increasingly turning to Artificial Intelligence (AI) to enhance their application security posture. AI offers a powerful set of tools and techniques for identifying, preventing, and responding to application-level threats at scale. By leveraging the speed, accuracy, and adaptability of machine learning, organizations can significantly improve their ability to secure the applications that drive their business.

In the following sections, we'll explore the specific applications of AI in different aspects of application security, from code analysis and vulnerability detection to runtime protection and threat modeling. We'll look at real-world use cases, emerging trends, and best practices for integrating AI into your application security strategy.

As we navigate this chapter, it's important to keep in mind that while AI offers immense potential for enhancing application security, it is not a silver bullet. Effective application security requires a comprehensive approach that combines technical controls, secure development practices, and continuous monitoring and improvement. AI should be seen as a powerful tool in this toolkit, but one that must be wielded with skill and integrated into a broader strategy.

With that context in mind, let's dive into the exciting world of AI-powered application security and explore how this transformative technology is reshaping the way we protect the software that underpins our digital world.

Section 5.2: AI for Secure Software Development

One of the most promising applications of AI in application security is in the realm of secure software development. The development phase is a critical point in the application lifecycle where many security vulnerabilities are introduced, often due to coding errors, design flaws, or the use of insecure libraries and frameworks. Identifying and fixing these issues early in the development process can significantly reduce the risk and cost of application security incidents.

Traditionally, secure coding has relied on manual code reviews, static analysis tools, and developer training to catch potential vulnerabilities. While these methods can be effective, they are time-consuming, error-prone, and difficult to scale in today's fast-paced development environments. This is where AI can make a significant impact.

One key application of AI in secure software development is automated code analysis. Machine learning models can be trained on large codebases to learn the patterns and characteristics of secure and insecure code. These models can then be used to automatically scan new code for potential vulnerabilities, providing developers with immediate feedback and guidance on how to fix issues.

For example, AI-powered code analysis tools can identify common coding mistakes like buffer overflows, null pointer dereferences, and memory leaks. They can also spot more subtle issues like race conditions, improper input validation, and weak cryptographic implementations. By flagging these issues early in the development process, AI can help developers catch and fix vulnerabilities before they make it into production.

Another application of AI in secure development is intelligent threat modeling. Threat modeling is the process of identifying, quantifying, and addressing the potential security risks associated with an application. It involves analyzing the application's architecture, data flows, and trust boundaries to identify potential attack vectors and prioritize security controls.

AI can assist in threat modeling by automatically generating threat models based on the application's code and configuration. Machine learning models can be trained on historical threat data and attack patterns to identify the most likely threats for a given application. This can help development teams focus their security efforts on the areas of highest risk, rather than trying to defend against every possible threat.

AI can also be used to prioritize and triage security findings from code analysis and threat modeling. By analyzing the severity, exploitability, and potential impact of each finding, AI can help development teams focus on the most critical issues first. This can be particularly valuable in agile development environments where time and resources are often constrained.

Beyond code analysis and threat modeling, AI can also support secure development by providing intelligent recommendations and automated fixes for security issues. For example, some AI-powered tools can suggest secure coding patterns or provide automated remediation for common vulnerabilities. This can help developers to not only find security issues but also learn how to prevent them in the future.

Real-world examples of AI in secure development are emerging. For instance, some integrated development environments (IDEs) now incorporate AI-powered code analysis and vulnerability detection. These tools can provide real-time feedback to developers as they write code, helping them to identify and fix security issues on the spot.

Other tools use machine learning to analyze code changes and commits, automatically flagging potential security risks for further review. This can help development teams to catch issues that might be missed by traditional static analysis tools, particularly in large and complex codebases.

However, there are also challenges and considerations to keep in mind when applying AI to secure development. One risk is the potential for false positives and false negatives. No AI system is perfect, and there will always be some margin of error in its findings. Developers need to be able to understand and validate the results of AI-powered tools, and have processes in place to handle false alarms.

There's also the challenge of integrating AI into existing development workflows and tools. Developers are already using a wide range of languages, frameworks, and platforms, each with its own security considerations. AI-powered security tools need to be flexible and adaptable enough to work across these diverse environments.

Skills and training are another consideration. While AI can automate many aspects of secure development, it still requires human expertise to interpret results, make decisions, and implement fixes. Organizations need to invest in training their development teams on how to effectively use AI-powered security tools and interpret their outputs.

Despite these challenges, the potential of AI to transform secure software development is significant. By catching vulnerabilities early, prioritizing risks intelligently, and providing actionable guidance to developers, AI can help organizations to build more secure applications faster and at scale.

As the application threat landscape continues to evolve, the need for intelligent, automated, and scalable security solutions will only grow. Organizations that can effectively harness the power of AI in their secure development practices will be better positioned to innovate safely and stay ahead of emerging application security risks.

Section 5.3: AI for Application Vulnerability Detection

Once an application is developed and deployed, the focus of security efforts shifts to identifying and mitigating vulnerabilities that could be exploited by attackers. This is a daunting task in today's complex application environments, where a single organization might have hundreds or even thousands of applications running across multiple platforms and infrastructures.

Traditional vulnerability management relies on a combination of manual testing, automated scanning tools, and threat intelligence to identify potential security holes. While these methods can be effective, they often struggle to keep pace with the scale and speed of modern application deployments. They can also produce a high volume of alerts, many of which may be false positives or low-priority issues that distract from more critical risks.

This is where AI can make a significant impact. By leveraging machine learning and data analytics, AI-powered tools can automate and optimize many aspects of the vulnerability management process, from discovery and prioritization to remediation and reporting.

One key application of AI in vulnerability detection is in the automated discovery of application assets and their associated risks. In large enterprise environments, simply keeping track of all the applications in use can be a challenge. Applications may be deployed across multiple clouds, containers, and on-premises systems, often without centralized visibility or control.

AI can assist by automatically scanning network traffic, configuration files, and other data sources to identify application components and map their relationships. Machine learning models can be trained to recognize the signatures and behaviors of different application types, platforms, and protocols. This can provide security teams with a more complete and up-to-date inventory of their application landscape, which is a critical foundation for effective vulnerability management.

Another application of AI is in the intelligent prioritization of vulnerabilities based on risk. Not all vulnerabilities are created equal, and fixing every potential issue is often impractical or impossible given limited time and resources. AI can help security teams to focus their efforts on the vulnerabilities that pose the greatest risk to the organization.

Machine learning models can be trained on historical vulnerability and exploit data to predict the likelihood and potential impact of a given vulnerability being exploited. Factors like the vulnerability's severity score, its ease of exploitation, the value of the affected asset, and the availability of a patch or workaround can all be weighted to produce an overall risk score.

This risk-based prioritization can be particularly valuable in helping security teams to navigate the deluge of vulnerabilities that are disclosed on a daily basis. By focusing remediation efforts on the highest-risk issues, organizations can maximize the impact of their security resources and minimize their exposure to potential attacks.

AI can also support the actual process of vulnerability remediation. Some AI-powered tools can automatically generate remediation plans based   on the characteristics of the vulnerability and the affected application. These plans can include step-by-step guidance on how to patch or mitigate the issue, as well as estimates of the time and resources required.

Other tools use machine learning to automate the testing and validation of patches and fixes. By analyzing the code changes and their potential impact on the application's functionality and performance, these tools can help ensure that remediation efforts don't introduce new issues or break critical business processes.

Beyond discovery, prioritization, and remediation, AI can also enhance vulnerability reporting and communication. Traditional vulnerability reports can be lengthy, technical, and difficult for non-security audiences to understand. This can make it challenging to get buy-in and support for remediation efforts from business stakeholders and application owners.

AI can help by automatically generating more concise, actionable, and business-relevant vulnerability reports. Natural Language Processing (NLP) techniques can be used to translate technical vulnerability data into clear, plain-language summaries that highlight the business impact and recommended actions. Interactive data visualization and chatbots can also be used to make vulnerability data more accessible and engaging for different audiences.

Real-world examples of AI in vulnerability detection are numerous and varied. Many leading vulnerability scanning and management platforms now incorporate machine learning capabilities to improve the accuracy and efficiency of their results. These tools can leverage AI to reduce false positives, prioritize findings based on risk, and provide more actionable remediation guidance.

Some more advanced tools are using deep learning techniques to identify novel or "zero-day" vulnerabilities that haven't yet been publicly disclosed. By training on large datasets of code and configuration files, these tools can spot subtle patterns and anomalies that might indicate a previously unknown security flaw.

AI is also being applied to automate and scale application security testing. Tools like AI-powered dynamic application security testing (DAST) and interactive application security testing (IAST) can continuously scan live applications for vulnerabilities, learning and adapting their testing strategies based on the application's behavior and responses.

However, there are also challenges and considerations to keep in mind. As with any AI application, the quality and relevance of the training data is critical. Vulnerability detection AI needs to be trained on a diverse and representative set of application types, platforms, and vulnerability classes to be effective. It also needs to be continually updated as new threats and attack techniques emerge.

There's also the risk of attacker evasion and counterattacks. As AI becomes more widely used in vulnerability detection, attackers will likely develop new techniques to evade or fool these systems. This could include techniques like adversarial inputs, model poisoning, or exploitation of algorithmic biases. Keeping AI models robust and resilient to these evolving threats will require ongoing research and development.

Integration and interoperability are other key challenges. Most organizations have a complex patchwork of security tools and processes, often from multiple vendors. AI-powered vulnerability detection needs to be able to integrate smoothly into these existing workflows and share data and insights across different platforms and teams.

Despite these challenges, the potential of AI to transform application vulnerability detection is immense. By automating and optimizing the discovery, prioritization, and remediation of vulnerabilities at scale, AI can help organizations to dramatically improve their security posture and keep pace with the rapid evolution of application threats.

As the volume and velocity of application vulnerabilities continue to grow, the ability to leverage AI for smarter, faster, and more targeted vulnerability management will become increasingly critical. Organizations that can effectively harness this technology as part of a comprehensive application security strategy will be better positioned to protect their critical assets and maintain the trust of their customers and stakeholders.

Section 5.4: AI for Application Runtime Protection

While secure development practices and proactive vulnerability management are critical components of application security, they are not enough on their own. Even the most rigorously developed and thoroughly tested applications can still be vulnerable to attacks once they are deployed and running in production environments.

This is where runtime application protection comes into play. Runtime protection involves monitoring and securing applications as they execute, in real-time, to prevent or mitigate exploitation attempts. It's the last line of defense against attacks that have managed to circumvent other security controls.

Traditionally, runtime protection has relied on tools like web application firewalls (WAFs), runtime application self-protection (RASP), and application performance monitoring (APM) to detect and block malicious activity. While these tools can be effective, they often rely on predefined rules and signatures that can miss novel or sophisticated attacks. They can also generate a high volume of alerts, many of which may be false positives that create noise and distract from real threats.

This is where AI can make a significant difference. By leveraging machine learning and behavioral analytics, AI-powered runtime protection tools can provide more intelligent, adaptive, and automated defenses against application-level threats.

One key application of AI in runtime protection is in the detection of anomalous application behavior. Machine learning models can be trained on normal application traffic and user interactions to create a baseline of expected behavior. Any deviations from this baseline, such as unusual request patterns, abnormal resource consumption, or suspicious data access, can then be flagged as potential threats for further investigation.

For example, an AI-powered runtime protection tool might learn that a particular web application typically receives a certain volume and type of traffic from a specific set of IP addresses. If the tool suddenly detects a spike in traffic from a new IP range, or requests for resources that are not normally accessed, it can automatically flag this as a potential attack and take action to block or redirect the traffic.

Another application of AI in runtime protection is in the identification and prevention of specific attack types. Deep learning techniques can be used to analyze application traffic and identify patterns associated with known attack vectors, such as SQL injection, cross-site scripting (XSS), or remote code execution.

By training on large datasets of malicious and benign traffic, these models can learn to spot even subtle indicators of an attack, such as specific character sequences or payload structures. They can then automatically block or sanitize the malicious requests before they can reach the application, without relying on predefined signatures or rules.

AI can also be used to provide more context-aware and risk-based runtime protection. By analyzing factors like the user's identity, location, device, and behavior, AI models can assess the risk level of each request and adapt the protection measures accordingly.

For example, a request from an authenticated user on a corporate network might be treated as lower risk than an anonymous request from an untrusted IP address. An AI-powered protection tool could automatically apply more stringent security controls, like multi-factor authentication or request throttling, to the higher-risk traffic, while allowing the lower-risk traffic to proceed with fewer barriers.

Beyond detection and prevention, AI can also assist in the automated investigation and response to runtime security incidents. When a potential threat is detected, AI can help to quickly triage the alert, correlate it with other relevant data, and provide actionable recommendations for mitigation.

For example, if an AI tool detects a potential SQL injection attack, it could automatically gather related data like the IP address, user agent, and targeted database queries. It could then cross-reference this data with threat intelligence feeds and historical attack patterns to assess the severity and scope of the incident. Based on this analysis, the tool could then suggest specific actions, like blocking the attacker IP, resetting compromised passwords, or rolling back malicious database changes.

Real-world examples of AI in application runtime protection are emerging across a range of tools and platforms. Many leading WAF and RASP vendors now incorporate machine learning capabilities to improve the accuracy and efficiency of their threat detection. These tools can leverage AI to reduce false positives, identify novel attack patterns, and provide more granular and dynamic protection policies.

Some more advanced tools are using unsupervised learning techniques to build self-learning models of application behavior. Rather than relying on predefined rules or attack signatures, these tools continuously learn and adapt to the unique characteristics of each application, making them more effective at spotting subtle anomalies and zero-day threats.

AI is also being applied to provide more unified and correlated runtime protection across distributed application environments. With the rise of microservices architectures and multi-cloud deployments, applications are becoming more modular and decentralized. This can make it harder to get a cohesive view of application behavior and identify threats that span multiple components or platforms.

Some AI-powered tools are designed to provide cross-platform visibility and protection, ingesting data from multiple sources like application logs, network traffic, and infrastructure telemetry. By applying machine learning to this diverse dataset, these tools can identify complex attack patterns and provide more comprehensive and coordinated defenses.

However, there are also challenges and considerations to keep in mind when applying AI to application runtime protection. One issue is the potential performance impact. Analyzing every application request and response in real-time can introduce latency and consume significant computing resources. Organizations need to carefully balance the benefits of AI-powered protection with the performance requirements of their applications.

Another challenge is the explainability and transparency of AI models. When an AI tool blocks or flags a particular request as malicious, security teams need to be able to understand and trust the reasoning behind that decision. Black box models that provide no insight into their decision-making process can be difficult to audit and may not meet regulatory or compliance requirements.

There's also the risk of attacker evasion and countermeasures. As attackers become aware of AI-powered defenses, they may develop techniques to fool or bypass these systems, such as using adversarial inputs or mimicking normal application behavior. Keeping AI models robust and adaptive to these evolving threats will require continuous monitoring and retraining.

Despite these challenges, the potential of AI to revolutionize application runtime protection is significant. By providing more intelligent, automated, and adaptive defenses, AI can help organizations to keep pace with the increasing speed and sophistication of application-level attacks.

As the application threat landscape continues to evolve, the need for AI-powered runtime protection will only grow. Organizations that can effectively integrate this technology into their application security strategy will be better positioned to protect their critical assets, maintain the trust of their users, and drive their business forward securely.

Section 5.5: AI for Application Security Testing and Validation

Ensuring the security of applications is not a one-time event, but a continuous process that should be integrated throughout the software development lifecycle (SDLC). This is where application security testing and validation come into play. Security testing involves proactively assessing applications for potential vulnerabilities and weaknesses, while validation ensures that the application meets the required security standards and regulations.

Traditionally, application security testing has relied on a combination of manual and automated techniques, such as code reviews, penetration testing, and vulnerability scanning. While these methods can be effective, they can also be time-consuming, costly, and prone to human error. Moreover, with the increasing complexity and pace of modern application development, traditional testing methods often struggle to keep up.

This is where AI can make a significant impact. By leveraging machine learning and automation, AI-powered testing tools can help organizations to test their applications more efficiently, effectively, and continuously. AI can be applied across a range of testing techniques and phases, from static code analysis and dynamic testing to fuzzing and behavioral monitoring.

One key application of AI in security testing is in the automation of code analysis.

As discussed earlier in the context of secure development, machine learning models can be trained to identify coding patterns and practices that are indicative of security vulnerabilities. These models can then be applied to automatically scan source code or binaries for potential issues, without the need for manual review.

AI-powered code analysis tools can help to catch a wide range of security flaws, from simple coding errors like buffer overflows and SQL injection to more complex issues like race conditions and memory corruption. By analyzing code at scale and in real-time, these tools can provide developers with immediate feedback and guidance on how to fix issues, reducing the risk of vulnerabilities making it into production.

Another application of AI is in the generation of test cases and input data for dynamic testing. Dynamic testing involves running the application with different inputs and observing its behavior for potential security issues. However, manually generating comprehensive test cases that cover all possible scenarios can be a daunting task.

AI can assist by automatically generating test cases based on the application's code structure, input fields, and expected behaviors. Machine learning models can be trained on historical testing data and known vulnerability patterns to generate more targeted and effective test cases. This can help to uncover edge cases and corner conditions that might be missed by manual testing.

AI can also be used to enhance the efficiency and coverage of fuzz testing. Fuzz testing involves feeding the application with randomized or semi-randomized inputs to see if it crashes, hangs, or behaves unexpectedly. While fuzz testing can be a powerful technique for uncovering security issues, it can also be resource-intensive and time-consuming.

AI can help to optimize fuzz testing by learning from the application's responses and adapting the input generation strategy accordingly. For example, if the AI model detects that certain input patterns are more likely to trigger crashes or anomalies, it can prioritize those patterns in subsequent test runs. This can help to find more bugs faster, with fewer resources.

Beyond input generation, AI can also be used to automate the analysis and classification of testing results. In a typical testing cycle, security teams may be faced with a large volume of alerts and crash reports, many of which may be false positives or low-priority issues. Manually triaging these results can be a time-consuming and error-prone process.

AI can assist by automatically analyzing the testing outputs and classifying them based on their likely severity, exploitability, and impact. Machine learning models can be trained on historical testing data and vulnerability databases to recognize patterns and characteristics associated with high-risk issues. This can help security teams to quickly focus their attention on the most critical findings, rather than getting bogged down in noise.

Another area where AI can add value is in the validation of security controls and configurations. Many applications rely on external security controls, such as firewalls, intrusion prevention systems, and access management solutions, to protect against threats. However, ensuring that these controls are properly configured and effective can be a challenge.

AI can help by continuously monitoring the application's environment and comparing it against established security baselines and best practices. Machine learning models can be trained to recognize misconfigurations, policy violations, and other deviations that could introduce risk. This can provide security teams with real-time visibility into the state of their security controls and help them to proactively address issues before they can be exploited.

Real-world examples of AI in application security testing are numerous and varied. Many leading application security testing tools and platforms now incorporate machine learning capabilities to improve the efficiency and accuracy of their results. These tools can leverage AI to automate various testing tasks, from code analysis and test case generation to result classification and prioritization.

Some more advanced tools are using deep learning techniques to provide more comprehensive and intelligent testing coverage. For example, some tools use neural networks to model complex application behaviors and identify subtle deviations that could indicate a security flaw. Others use reinforcement learning to automatically explore the application's attack surface and find optimal testing strategies.

AI is also being applied to provide more continuous and integrated security testing throughout the SDLC. With the rise of DevOps and continuous integration/continuous deployment (CI/CD) practices, applications are being developed and updated at an ever-increasing pace. Traditional point-in-time testing methods can struggle to keep up with this velocity.

Some AI-powered tools are designed to provide continuous security testing, seamlessly integrating into the CI/CD pipeline and automatically testing each code change and deployment. By leveraging machine learning to adapt the testing strategies based on the application's risk profile and development cadence, these tools can help organizations to embed security into their development process without slowing down innovation.

However, there are also challenges and considerations to keep in mind when applying AI to application security testing. One issue is the potential for AI models to introduce their own biases and blind spots. If the training data used to build the models is not representative or comprehensive enough, the resulting tests may miss certain types of vulnerabilities or generate false positives.

Another challenge is the interpretability and explainability of AI-powered testing results. When an AI tool flags a particular code snippet or input as potentially malicious, security teams need to be able to understand the reasoning behind that decision. Opaque or "black box" models that provide no clear explanation can be difficult to trust and act upon.

There's also the risk of attacker evasion and gaming of AI-based testing tools. As attackers become aware of the testing strategies and models used by these tools, they may develop techniques to evade detection or exploit weaknesses in the AI itself. Keeping the testing models robust and adaptive to these evolving threats will require ongoing monitoring, tuning, and retraining.

Despite these challenges, the potential of AI to transform application security testing is immense. By automating and optimizing various testing tasks, AI can help organizations to test their applications more thoroughly, frequently, and efficiently. This can lead to the discovery of more vulnerabilities earlier in the development process, when they are cheaper and easier to fix.

Moreover, by providing more continuous and integrated testing capabilities, AI can help organizations to embed security into their development culture and workflows. Rather than being seen as a separate and burdensome activity, security testing can become a natural and integral part of the development process, helping to build more secure applications from the ground up.

As the complexity and pace of application development continue to accelerate, the need for AI-powered testing solutions will only grow. Organizations that can effectively harness this technology as part of their overall application security strategy will be better positioned to deliver secure, reliable, and innovative applications in the face of ever-evolving threats and business demands.

However, it's important to remember that AI is not a silver bullet for application security testing. While it can significantly enhance and automate many testing tasks, it is not a replacement for human expertise and judgment. The most effective testing strategies will be those that combine the power of AI with the knowledge and creativity of skilled security professionals.

Going forward, the successful adoption of AI in application security testing will require close collaboration between security teams, developers, and data scientists. It will require investments in the right tools, talent, and processes to build, validate, and maintain effective AI testing models. And it will require a commitment to continuous learning and adaptation as the technology and threat landscape continue to evolve.

By embracing these challenges and opportunities, organizations can unlock the full potential of AI to drive more secure, resilient, and successful applications in the digital age.

Chapter 5 Conclusion

Throughout this chapter, we've explored the critical role of AI in enhancing application security across the software development lifecycle. From enabling more secure coding practices and intelligent threat modeling to automating vulnerability detection and run-time protection, AI is proving to be a powerful tool in the fight against application-level threats.

We've seen how machine learning   can be used to analyze vast amounts of code, traffic, and behavior data to identify patterns and anomalies that may indicate security weaknesses or attacks. We've discussed how deep learning techniques can be applied to generate more effective test cases, fuzz inputs, and attack simulations. And we've highlighted how AI can provide more context-aware, risk-based, and adaptive security controls based on the unique characteristics of each application and environment.

The potential benefits of AI in application security are significant. By automating and optimizing various security tasks, AI can help organizations to develop, deploy, and operate applications more securely and efficiently. It can reduce the burden on human security teams, freeing them up to focus on more strategic and creative work. And it can enable more continuous and integrated security testing and monitoring, helping to catch and fix vulnerabilities faster and earlier in the development process.

However, we've also emphasized that realizing these benefits requires careful planning, execution, and governance. Organizations need to be mindful of the potential limitations and risks of AI, such as biased or opaque models, performance overhead, and attacker evasion. They need to ensure that their AI tools and processes are transparent, auditable, and aligned with relevant security standards and regulations. And they need to cultivate the right skills and culture to effectively integrate AI into their application security practices.

As we've stressed throughout this chapter, AI is not a replacement for human expertise and responsibility in application security. While it can augment and scale many security tasks, it still requires human oversight, interpretation, and decision-making. The most successful organizations will be those that can leverage AI as part of a holistic and adaptive application security strategy, one that combines the strengths of both human and machine intelligence.

Looking ahead, the future of AI in application security is both exciting and challenging. As applications continue to grow in complexity, connectivity, and criticality, the need for more intelligent and automated security solutions will only intensify. At the same time, as attackers become more sophisticated and AI-savvy, the bar for effective AI-based defenses will keep rising.

To stay ahead of these trends, organizations will need to continuously invest in and innovate their AI application security capabilities. This may involve exploring new techniques and architectures, such as federated learning, homomorphic encryption, and AI-driven chaos engineering. It may require developing more explainable and auditable AI models that can earn the trust of both security teams and business stakeholders. And it may necessitate forging new partnerships and ecosystems to share threat intelligence, testing data, and best practices across the application security community.

Ultimately, the journey of AI in application security is still in its early stages. While the progress made so far is impressive, there is still much work to be done to fully realize the potential of this transformative technology. As we move forward, it will be crucial for organizations to approach AI with a blend of enthusiasm and caution, openness and diligence, creativity and discipline.

By doing so, we can harness the power of AI to build a future where our applications are not just more functional and innovative, but also more secure, resilient, and trustworthy. A future where the benefits of digital transformation can be fully realized without compromising the safety and privacy of our data and users. A future where humans and machines can work together seamlessly to protect the lifeblood of our digital economy and society.

This is the promise and the challenge of AI in application security. It's a journey that will require ongoing learning, collaboration, and adaptation from all of us. But it's a journey that we must embark on if we want to seize the opportunities and mitigate the risks of the ever-evolving application threat landscape.

As security professionals, developers, and business leaders, we all have a role to play in shaping this future. By staying informed, engaged, and proactive, we can collectively drive the responsible and effective adoption of AI in application security. And by doing so, we can not only safeguard our applications, but also unleash their full potential to transform our world for the better.

So let us embrace this challenge with curiosity, courage, and commitment. Let us learn from each other, push each other, and support each other in this shared mission. And let us never lose sight of the ultimate goal: to create a digital future that is not just more innovative and productive, but also more secure, trustworthy, and beneficial for all.

The road ahead may be complex and uncertain, but the destination is clear and worthy. With AI as our ally and human ingenuity as our guide, we can navigate this journey with confidence and purpose. Together, we can build a new era of application security - one that is smarter, faster, and more resilient than ever before.

Six

— • —

Chapter 6: AI for Cloud Security

Section 6.1: Introduction to Cloud Security

The advent of cloud computing has revolutionized the way organizations approach IT infrastructure and services. By leveraging the cloud, businesses can achieve greater scalability, flexibility, and cost-efficiency compared to traditional on-premises solutions. However, this shift to the cloud also introduces new security challenges and considerations that must be addressed to protect data, applications, and systems in this dynamic and shared environment.

At its core, cloud security refers to the set of policies, controls, procedures, and technologies that work together to protect cloud-based systems, data, and infrastructure from threats. It is a shared responsibility between the cloud provider and the customer, with the distribution of responsibilities varying depending on the specific cloud service model being used (e.g., Infrastructure as a Service (IaaS), Platform as a Service (PaaS), or Software as a Service (SaaS)).

The main goals of cloud security are to:

1. Protect data: Ensuring the confidentiality, integrity, and availability of data stored and processed in the cloud.

2. Secure applications: Protecting cloud-based applications and services from unauthorized access, tampering, and other threats.

3. Ensure compliance: Meeting regulatory and industry-specific security standards and requirements.

4. Manage access: Controlling who can access what resources in the cloud and under what conditions.

5. Detect and respond to threats: Identifying and mitigating security incidents and breaches in a timely manner.

Achieving these goals in the cloud requires addressing a range of security challenges and risks, such as:

- Data breaches: Unauthorized access to or disclosure of sensitive data in the cloud.

- Insecure interfaces and APIs: Vulnerabilities in the cloud service provider's interfaces and APIs that can be exploited by attackers.

- Shared technology vulnerabilities: Threats that arise from the shared, multi-tenant nature of the cloud infrastructure.

- Account hijacking: Unauthorized access to and misuse of cloud accounts and resources.

- Malicious insiders: Threats posed by malicious actors within the cloud provider or customer organization.

- Compliance and legal issues: Challenges in meeting various security and privacy regulations across different jurisdictions.

To address these challenges, cloud security employs a variety of controls and best practices, such as:

- Encryption: Protecting data at rest and in transit using strong encryption algorithms and key management processes.

- Access control: Implementing robust authentication, authorization, and accounting (AAA) mechanisms to control access to cloud resources.

- Network security: Securing communication between cloud resources and the internet using firewalls, intrusion detection/prevention systems (IDS/IPS), and virtual private networks (VPNs).

- Monitoring and logging: Continuously monitoring cloud environments for security events and maintaining detailed audit logs for forensics and compliance purposes.

- Vulnerability management: Regularly assessing cloud systems and applications for vulnerabilities and promptly patching or mitigating identified issues.

- Incident response: Establishing processes and procedures for detecting, investigating, and responding to security incidents in the cloud.

However, as the complexity and scale of cloud environments continue to grow, traditional security approaches are struggling to keep pace. Manual processes, signature-based detection, and rule-based policies are no longer sufficient to secure the dynamic and ephemeral nature of cloud workloads and data.

This is where Artificial Intelligence (AI) comes into play. AI offers a powerful set of technologies and techniques that can help organizations to automate, optimize, and enhance various aspects of cloud security. By leveraging the speed, scale, and intelligence of AI, organizations can more effectively identify, protect against, detect, and respond to threats in the cloud.

In the following sections, we'll explore the specific applications of AI in cloud security, from threat detection and response to access control and compliance monitoring. We'll examine real-world use cases, emerging trends, and best practices for integrating AI into your cloud security strategy.

As we navigate this chapter, it's important to keep in mind that while AI offers immense potential for strengthening cloud security, it is not a silver bullet. Effective cloud security requires a comprehensive and multi-layered approach that combines AI with other proven security controls, processes, and human expertise.

With that context in mind, let's dive into the exciting world of AI-powered cloud security and discover how this transformative technology is reshaping the way we protect our most vital and valuable assets in the cloud era.

Section 6.2: AI for Cloud Threat Detection and Response

One of the most significant applications of AI in cloud security is in the area of threat detection and response. The cloud presents a unique set of security challenges due to its dynamic, distributed, and multi-tenant nature. Traditional security tools and processes that were designed for static, on-premises environments often struggle to keep pace with the speed and scale of cloud-based threats.

This is where AI can make a profound difference. By leveraging machine learning, behavioral analytics, and automation, AI-powered security tools can help organizations to more effectively detect, investigate, and respond to threats in the cloud.

One key application of AI in cloud threat detection is in the analysis of vast amounts of security data generated by cloud environments. Cloud infrastructures and applications produce a staggering volume and variety of logs, events, and telemetry data, including network traffic, user activities, resource configurations, and more. Manual analysis of this data is simply not feasible, and even traditional rule-based security information and event management (SIEM) systems can struggle to identify sophisticated or novel threats.

AI can help by automatically processing and analyzing this data in real-time, using machine learning algorithms to identify patterns and anomalies that may indicate a security threat. For example, unsupervised learning techniques like clustering and anomaly detection can be used to spot unusual resource usage patterns, suspicious network connections, or atypical user behaviors. These anomalies can then be flagged for further investigation by security teams.

Supervised learning techniques can also be used to train AI models on known examples of malicious and benign activities in the cloud. These models can then be used to classify new events and behaviors as either threats or false positives, helping to prioritize alerts and reduce alert fatigue for security analysts.

Another application of AI in cloud threat detection is in the identification of advanced and emerging attack techniques. As adversaries become more sophisticated and cloud-savvy, they are increasingly using techniques like serverless attacks, container escapes, and cloud-native malware to evade traditional defenses. AI can help by continuously learning and adapting to these evolving threats.

For example, deep learning techniques like recurrent neural networks (RNNs) and long short-term memory (LSTM) networks can be used to model complex, sequential patterns in cloud data. These models can learn to recognize the subtle indicators of an advanced attack, such as the specific sequence of API calls used in a serverless attack or the unique communication patterns of a cloud-native botnet.

Once a threat is detected, AI can also assist in the automated investigation and response process. By correlating alerts and events across multiple cloud services and data sources, AI can help to quickly determine the scope and severity of an incident. It can also recommend or automatically initiate appropriate response actions, such as isolating affected resources, blocking malicious IP addresses, or escalating high-priority incidents to human analysts.

For example, if an AI system detects an unusual spike in S3 bucket access patterns coming from a previously unseen IP address, it could automatically correlate this with other factors like the geolocation of the IP, the IAM permissions of the accessing user, and any recent vulnerabilities in the S3 service. Based on this analysis, the AI could determine that the activity represents a potential data exfiltration attempt and automatically quarantine the affected bucket while alerting security teams for further investigation.

Real-world examples of AI-powered cloud threat detection and response are numerous and varied. Many leading cloud security platforms and services now incorporate machine learning and AI capabilities to enhance their detection and response capabilities.

For instance, Amazon GuardDuty is a threat detection service that continuously monitors for malicious activity and unauthorized behavior in AWS accounts. It uses machine learning to analyze billions of events across multiple AWS data sources, identifying threats like unusual API calls, unauthorized deployments, and compromised instances. When a potential threat is detected, GuardDuty delivers detailed security findings to AWS CloudWatch Events and AWS Security Hub for easy integration with existing event management and workflow systems.

Similarly, Microsoft Azure Security Center uses AI to provide advanced threat protection across hybrid cloud workloads. It collects and analyzes security data from a variety of sources, including network traffic, user activity, and resource configurations, to identify potential threats and vulnerabilities. Azure Security Center also provides automated response capabilities, such as adaptive application controls and just-in-time VM access, to help organizations quickly mitigate identified risks.

Google Cloud Security Command Center is another example of an AI-powered cloud security platform. It provides a centralized view of security and risk across Google Cloud Platform (GCP) resources, using machine learning to identify misconfigurations, compliance violations, and potential threats. Security Command Center also integrates with Google's Event Threat Detection (ETD) service, which uses advanced analytics and threat intelligence to detect suspicious activities like cryptocurrency mining, data exfiltration, and command-and-control communication.

Other cloud-native AI security solutions are emerging from startups and niche vendors. For example, Lacework is a cloud security platform that uses unsupervised machine learning to build behavioral models of cloud entities and their interactions. By continuously learning what normal activity looks like for each unique cloud environment, Lacework can identify anomalous behaviors and zero-day threats that evade rule-based detection.

Similarly, Darktrace's Enterprise Immune System uses self-learning AI to detect and respond to cloud-based threats. It works by creating a dynamic, evolving understanding of normal activity for every user, device, and application in a cloud environment. When the AI identifies a deviation from this learned pattern of life, it can take autonomous response actions to neutralize the threat, like interrupting suspicious connections or enforcing step-up authentication.

However, implementing AI for cloud threat detection and response also comes with challenges and considerations. One challenge is the potential for false positives and alert fatigue. While AI can help to reduce the noise of traditional rule-based detection, poorly tuned or overly sensitive AI models can still generate a high volume of false alarms. This can overwhelm security teams and lead to real threats being missed among the noise.

To mitigate this risk, it's important to carefully train and validate AI models on representative cloud data, and to continuously monitor and tune their performance over time. Human oversight and expertise are also critical for investigating and verifying AI-generated alerts before taking action.

Another challenge is the explainability and transparency of AI models. When an AI system flags a particular activity as malicious, security teams need to be able to understand and trust the reasoning behind that decision. Black box models that provide no insight into their decision-making process can be difficult to audit and may not meet regulatory or compliance requirements for cloud security.

To address this, there is a growing emphasis on developing explainable AI (XAI) techniques for cloud security. These techniques aim to make the inner workings of AI models more transparent and interpretable, without sacrificing their accuracy or performance. Examples include attention mechanisms that highlight the specific features or behaviors that contributed to a threat detection, and counterfactual explanations that show how a different input would have changed the AI's decision.

A third challenge is the potential for adversarial attacks against AI-based cloud security systems. As attackers become more aware of the use of AI in cloud defenses, they may attempt to exploit weaknesses or blind spots in the AI models themselves. For example, they could try to poison the training data used to build the models, or craft adversarial inputs that are designed to evade or mislead the AI's detection capabilities.

To defend against these threats, it's important to incorporate adversarial robustness and resilience into the design and training of AI models for cloud security. This can involve techniques like adversarial training, where the AI is explicitly trained on malicious examples to learn to recognize and resist them, and defensive distillation, which aims to make the AI more resistant to small perturbations in its inputs.

Despite these challenges, the potential of AI for transforming cloud threat detection and response is immense. As the volume, velocity, and sophistication of cloud-based threats continue to grow, the speed and scale of AI will become increasingly essential for staying ahead of adversaries.

Going forward, we can expect to see even more advanced and autonomous applications of AI emerge in this space. For instance, self-healing cloud infrastructures that can automatically detect and remediate security issues without human intervention, or predictive threat intelligence that can forecast and proactively block emerging attack vectors based on global trends and patterns.

At the same time, as AI becomes more deeply embedded into cloud security workflows and decision-making processes, it will be crucial to ensure that it is being used in a responsible, ethical, and accountable manner. This will require ongoing collaboration and dialogue among cloud providers, security vendors, researchers, policymakers, and customers to develop best practices and standards for the safe and effective use of AI in cloud security.

Ultimately, the successful integration of AI into cloud threat detection and response will require a balance of technological innovation, human expertise, and organizational process and culture. By combining the power of AI with the knowledge and judgment of skilled security professionals, organizations can build a more intelligent, adaptive, and resilient security posture for the cloud era.

Section 6.3: AI for Cloud Access Control and Identity Management

Access control and identity management are critical components of cloud security. In the shared, multi-tenant environment of the cloud, it's essential to ensure that only authorized users and services can access sensitive resources and data. At the same time, the dynamic and elastic nature of cloud computing requires access controls that are flexible, scalable, and adaptable to changing business needs.

Traditionally, cloud access control has relied on role-based access control (RBAC) models, where permissions are assigned to users based on their job functions or organizational roles. While RBAC can be effective for relatively   static and predictable access patterns, it can struggle to keep pace with the complexity and fluidity of modern cloud environments. As organizations adopt more cloud services, containers, serverless functions, and ephemeral resources, managing access based on predefined roles becomes increasingly challenging.

This is where AI can offer significant benefits. By leveraging machine learning and behavioral analytics, AI-powered access control systems can provide more granular, context-aware, and adaptive access decisions based on real-time user and resource attributes.

One key application of AI in cloud access control is in the development of attribute-based access control (ABAC) models. ABAC goes beyond traditional RBAC by considering a wider range of attributes when making access decisions, such as the user's location, device, time of day, resource sensitivity, and more. AI can be used to automatically learn and assign these attributes based on patterns in user and resource behavior, rather than relying on manual configuration.

For example, an AI-powered ABAC system might observe that a particular user typically accesses a specific set of cloud resources during business hours from a corporate office location. If the same user attempts to access those resources outside of their normal patterns, such as from a foreign country at 2am, the AI could flag this as an anomaly and require additional authentication or block the access attempt altogether.

Another application of AI in cloud access control is in the continuous monitoring and adjustment of access policies based on changing risk factors. Traditional access control policies are often relatively static and based on periodic reviews of user roles and permissions. However, in the fast-moving world of the cloud, access risks can change rapidly based on factors like new vulnerabilities, changes in user behavior, or shifts in the threat landscape.

AI can help by continuously analyzing access patterns and risk signals across the cloud environment, and dynamically adjusting access policies to mitigate emerging threats. For instance, if an AI system detects a newly disclosed vulnerability in a particular cloud service, it could automatically restrict access to that service for all but the most critical users and applications until a patch is available.

AI can also be used to enhance user authentication and identity management in the cloud. One emerging area is the use of biometric and behavioral analytics for continuous, risk-based authentication. Rather than relying solely on static credentials like passwords or access keys, AI can analyze a user's typing patterns, mouse movements, and other behavioral factors to continuously verify their identity and detect potential account compromises.

For example, if an AI system detects that a user's typing speed and rhythm suddenly change in the middle of a session, it could trigger a re-authentication prompt or even block access entirely if the behavior is deemed high-risk. This kind of continuous, adaptive authentication can provide an additional layer of security beyond traditional point-in-time login controls.

Real-world examples of AI-powered cloud access control and identity management are emerging from both cloud providers and third-party security vendors. AWS, for instance, offers Amazon Cognito, a service that provides authentication, authorization, and user management for web and mobile apps. Cognito uses machine learning to provide advanced security features like adaptive authentication, which adjusts the authentication requirements based on the assessed risk level of each login attempt.

Microsoft Azure Active Directory (Azure AD) also incorporates AI and machine learning to enhance access control and identity protection. Azure AD Identity Protection uses machine learning to detect risky user behaviors and potential identity compromises, such as sign-ins from unfamiliar locations or devices. It can then automatically apply risk-based conditional access policies, like requiring multi-factor authentication or blocking access from untrusted networks.

Google Cloud's Context-Aware Access is another example of an AI-powered access control solution. It uses machine learning to analyze a variety of signals, like the user's identity, location, and device security posture, to make granular access decisions in real-time. For instance, it can grant access to low-risk resources like public websites without requiring authentication, while enforcing stricter controls for sensitive data or high-risk contexts.

Third-party vendors are also developing AI-based solutions for cloud access control and identity management. For example, Okta's Advanced Server Access uses machine learning to provide granular, contextual access to cloud infrastructure based on factors like the user's role, location, and device posture. It can automatically grant and revoke access to servers and resources as needed, reducing the risk of standing privileges.

Another example is Idaptive (formerly Centrify), which uses machine learning to provide adaptive multi-factor authentication (MFA) for cloud and on-premises applications. Idaptive's AI engine analyzes user behavior and context to determine the appropriate level of authentication required for each access attempt. For low-risk requests, it may only require a single factor like a password, while higher-risk attempts may trigger additional factors like a biometric scan or hardware token.

However, implementing AI for cloud access control and identity management also comes with challenges and considerations. One challenge is the potential for bias and fairness issues in AI-based access decisions. If the training data used to build the AI models contains biases, such as over-representing certain user groups or access patterns, the resulting access policies may be discriminatory or unfair.

To mitigate this risk, it's important to ensure that the data used to train AI access control models is diverse, representative, and free from historical biases. It's also important to regularly audit and test the models for fairness and non-discrimination, and to provide mechanisms for users to appeal or override AI-based access decisions when necessary.

Another challenge is the explainability and transparency of AI-based access decisions. When an AI system grants or denies access to a particular resource, it's important for both users and administrators to understand the reasoning behind that decision. Opaque or "black box" AI models that provide no insight into their decision-making process can be difficult to trust and may not meet regulatory or compliance requirements for access control.

To address this, there is a growing emphasis on developing explainable AI (XAI) techniques for access control, similar to those discussed for threat detection. These techniques can help to make the factors and weights behind AI access decisions more transparent and auditable, without compromising the privacy or security of the underlying data.

A third challenge is the integration and interoperability of AI-based access control with existing identity and access management (IAM) systems and processes. Many organizations have already invested heavily in IAM solutions and workflows, and introducing AI-based access control can require significant changes and disruptions to these established practices.

To minimize these disruptions, it's important to choose AI access control solutions that can integrate smoothly with existing IAM platforms and standards, such as SAML, OAuth, and OpenID Connect. It's also important to provide clear guidance and training to users and administrators on how to work with AI-based access policies and decisions within their familiar IAM workflows.

Despite these challenges, the potential benefits of AI for enhancing cloud access control and identity management are significant. By providing more granular, context-aware, and adaptive access decisions, AI can help organizations to strike a better balance between security and productivity in the cloud. It can reduce the risk of unauthorized access and data breaches, while still enabling users to access the resources they need to do their jobs effectively.

Moreover, as the complexity and scale of cloud environments continue to grow, the need for more intelligent and automated access control solutions will only intensify. Manual, rule-based approaches to access management simply won't be able to keep pace with the speed and dynamism of the cloud.

Going forward, we can expect to see more advanced and integrated applications of AI emerge in this space. For example, AI-powered access control systems that can automatically discover and classify sensitive data across multiple cloud services, and dynamically adjust access policies based on the data's risk level and business value. Or self-learning authentication systems that can continuously adapt to each user's unique behavioral patterns and risk profile, providing a more personalized and secure access experience.

At the same time, as AI becomes more deeply embedded into access control decisions and processes, it will be crucial to ensure that it is being used in a responsible, ethical, and accountable manner. This will require ongoing collaboration and dialogue among cloud providers, security vendors, privacy advocates, regulators, and users to develop best practices and standards for the fair and transparent use of AI in access control.

Ultimately, the journey of AI in cloud access control and identity management is still in its early stages. While the progress made so far is promising, there is still much work to be done to fully realize the potential of this transformative technology. As we move forward, it will be essential to approach AI with a mindset of continuous learning, adaptation, and improvement, always keeping the end goal of secure and seamless cloud access at the forefront.

By doing so, we can harness the power of AI to build a future where the cloud is not only more accessible and productive, but also more secure and trustworthy for all. A future where the right people can access the right resources at the right time, while still protecting the confidentiality, integrity, and privacy of our most sensitive data and systems. A future where AI and human intelligence work together seamlessly to enable the full potential of the cloud, without compromising on the fundamental principles of security and trust.

This is the promise and the challenge of AI in cloud access control and identity management. It's a journey that will require ongoing commitment, collaboration, and innovation from all of us. But it's a journey that we must undertake if we want to truly unlock the benefits of the cloud in a secure and sustainable way.

Section 6.4: AI for Cloud Security Posture Management

As organizations continue to expand their use of cloud services and infrastructures, maintaining a strong and consistent security posture has become increasingly challenging. With the rapid pace of change, the distributed nature of cloud resources, and the shared responsibility model of cloud security, it's all too easy for misconfigurations, policy violations, and vulnerabilities to slip through the cracks.

This is where Cloud Security Posture Management (CSPM) comes into play. CSPM refers to the continuous process of identifying and remediating security risks across an organization's cloud environment. It involves monitoring cloud resources for misconfigurations, compliance violations, and exposure to potential threats, and providing actionable recommendations for mitigating these risks.

Traditionally, CSPM has relied on rule-based policies and manual reviews to assess cloud security posture. Security teams would define a set of best practices and benchmarks, such as the CIS AWS Foundations Benchmark or the Azure Security Benchmark, and periodically scan their cloud environment to check for deviations from these standards.

However, this approach has several limitations. First, it's reactive rather than proactive. By the time a misconfiguration or policy violation is detected, it may have already been exploited by attackers. Second, it's static and inflexible. As cloud environments change and new services are adopted, the predefined rules and policies may quickly become outdated or irrelevant. Third, it's manual and time-consuming. With the scale and complexity of modern cloud deployments, manually reviewing every resource and configuration is simply not feasible.

This is where AI can make a significant impact. By leveraging machine learning, natural language processing, and automation, AI-powered CSPM tools can provide more proactive, adaptive, and scalable security posture management for the cloud.

One key application of AI in CSPM is in the continuous discovery and classification of cloud resources. In a typical enterprise cloud environment, there can be thousands of resources spread across multiple regions, accounts, and services. Keeping track of all these resources and their configurations is a daunting task for human analysts.

AI can help by automatically scanning cloud environments and cataloging all the resources and their metadata. Machine learning algorithms can be used to classify resources based on their type, purpose, sensitivity, and other attributes. This can provide security teams with a more comprehensive and up-to-date inventory of their cloud assets, which is a critical foundation for effective CSPM.

Another application of AI in CSPM is in the identification and prioritization of security risks. With the vast amount of configuration and activity data generated by cloud environments, manually sifting through this data to identify potential issues is like finding a needle in a haystack.

AI can assist by analyzing this data in real-time and flagging configurations or activities that deviate from established baselines or best practices. Machine learning models can be trained on historical cloud security data to learn the patterns and indicators of high-risk misconfigurations, such as open S3 buckets, overly permissive security groups, or unencrypted data stores.

These models can then be used to continuously scan cloud environments for similar risks, and rank them based on their potential impact and likelihood of exploitation. This risk-based prioritization can help security teams to focus their remediation efforts on the most critical issues first.

AI can also be used to provide more intelligent and context-aware recommendations for remediating identified risks. Rather than simply flagging a misconfiguration and leaving it up to the security team to figure out how to fix it, AI-powered CSPM tools can suggest specific remediation steps based on the unique characteristics of each resource and its environment.

For example, if an AI system detects an EC2 instance with an open SSH port exposed to the internet, it could recommend a series of graduated responses based on the instance's purpose and criticality. For a development or test instance, it might suggest simply closing the port or restricting access to a specific IP range. For a production instance hosting sensitive data, it might recommend additional steps like enabling multi-factor authentication, encrypting the attached storage, and logging all access attempts.

These AI-generated remediation recommendations can be particularly valuable for organizations with complex or rapidly changing cloud environments, where a one-size-fits-all approach to security is no longer sufficient. By providing more nuanced and adaptive guidance, AI can help security teams to strike the right balance between security and agility in the cloud.

Real-world examples of AI-powered CSPM are growing rapidly, as more organizations look to automate and optimize their cloud security posture. Many leading cloud providers and security vendors now offer CSPM solutions that incorporate machine learning and AI capabilities.

For example, Amazon GuardDuty, which we mentioned earlier in the context of threat detection, also provides CSPM functionality for AWS environments. It uses machine learning to analyze API calls and resource configurations across multiple AWS accounts, and identifies potential security issues like unauthorized access attempts, suspicious API activity, and risky resource configurations. GuardDuty also integrates with AWS Security Hub to provide a centralized view of security and compliance across all AWS services.

Microsoft Azure Security Center, also discussed previously, provides similar CSPM capabilities for Azure environments. It uses AI to continuously assess the security state of Azure resources, and provides prioritized recommendations for remediation based on the Azure Security Benchmark. Azure Security Center also offers automated remediation options, such as applying default security policies or configurations to new resources as they are deployed.

Google Cloud Security Command Center is another AI-powered CSPM solution, focused on Google Cloud Platform (GCP) environments. It provides a unified view of security and compliance across GCP services, using machine learning to identify misconfigurations, vulnerabilities, and threats. Security Command Center also integrates with other Google Cloud security tools, like Event Threat Detection and Cloud DLP, to provide a more comprehensive and integrated security management experience.

Beyond the major cloud providers, there are also many third-party CSPM solutions that leverage AI and machine learning. For example, Palo Alto Networks' Prisma Cloud (formerly RedLock) uses AI to provide continuous security and compliance monitoring for multi-cloud environments. It can automatically discover and map cloud resources across AWS, Azure, and GCP, and identify misconfigurations, policy violations, and compliance risks. Prisma Cloud also provides risk scores and remediation recommendations based on industry standards and best practices.

Another example is Fugue, a cloud infrastructure security and compliance platform that uses AI to automate the detection and remediation of cloud misconfigurations. Fugue's AI engine continuously scans cloud environments for policy violations and deviations from baseline configurations, and can automatically revert unauthorized changes to maintain a consistent and compliant state.

However, implementing AI for CSPM also comes with challenges and considerations. One challenge is the potential for false positives and alert fatigue. While AI can help to identify more subtle and complex security risks, it can also generate a high volume of low-priority or irrelevant alerts if not properly tuned. This can overwhelm security teams and lead to real issues being missed or ignored.

To mitigate this, it's important to carefully train and validate AI models on representative cloud security data, and to provide mechanisms for users to fine-tune the sensitivity and specificity of the AI's detection capabilities. It's also important to integrate AI-powered CSPM with other security tools and processes, like incident response platforms and ticketing systems, to ensure that high-priority issues are properly triaged and addressed.

Another challenge is the explainability and auditability of AI-based CSPM recommendations. When an AI system suggests a particular remediation action, security and compliance teams need to be able to understand and validate the reasoning behind that recommendation. Black box models that provide no insight into their decision-making process can be difficult to trust, especially in heavily regulated industries with strict compliance requirements.

To address this, there is a growing emphasis on developing explainable AI (XAI) techniques for CSPM, similar to those discussed for other cloud security use cases. These techniques can help to expose the key factors and logic behind AI-generated recommendations, allowing human analysts to review and approve them before implementation.

A third challenge is the integration and customization of AI-powered CSPM for each organization's unique cloud environment and security policies. While many CSPM solutions come with pre-built rulesets and benchmarks based on industry standards, these may not always align with an organization's specific requirements or risk tolerance.

To ensure that AI-based CSPM is providing relevant and actionable insights, it's important to be able to customize and extend the AI models based on each organization's own security policies, compliance obligations, and business priorities. This may require close collaboration between security teams, cloud operations, and data scientists to define appropriate training data, feature sets, and success metrics for the AI.

Despite these challenges, the potential of AI to transform cloud security posture management is immense. By providing more continuous, comprehensive, and adaptive monitoring and remediation of cloud security risks, AI can help organizations to maintain a strong security posture even as their cloud environment grows and evolves.

Moreover, by automating many of the manual and repetitive tasks involved in CSPM, AI can free up security teams to focus on more strategic and proactive security measures. This can include threat hunting, incident response planning, security training and awareness, and more.

As the complexity and pace of cloud adoption continue to accelerate, the need for AI-powered CSPM solutions will only intensify. Organizations that can effectively leverage AI to automate and optimize their cloud security posture will be better positioned to reap the benefits of the cloud without exposing themselves to undue risk.

Going forward, we can expect to see even more sophisticated and integrated applications of AI emerge in this space. For instance, self-healing cloud infrastructures that can automatically detect and remediate misconfigurations and policy violations without human intervention. Or predictive CSPM that can forecast potential security risks based on patterns in resource provisioning, configuration changes, and user behavior.

At the same time, as AI becomes more deeply embedded into cloud security posture management, it will be crucial to ensure that it is being used in a responsible, ethical, and governable manner. This will require ongoing collaboration and dialogue among cloud providers, security vendors, regulators, and customers to develop standards and best practices for the transparent and accountable use of AI in CSPM.

Ultimately, the journey of AI in cloud security posture management is about enabling organizations to embrace the full potential of the cloud with confidence and control. By providing intelligent, automated, and adaptive tools for managing the complex security challenges of the cloud, AI can help us to build a future where innovation and security go hand in hand.

However, this future won't arrive on its own. It will require sustained investment, experimentation, and collaboration from all stakeholders in the cloud ecosystem. It will require a willingness to learn from both successes and failures, and to continuously adapt our approaches as the technology and threat landscape evolve.

But if we can rise to this challenge, the rewards will be significant. We'll be able to harness the power of the cloud to drive our businesses and societies forward, while ensuring that our most critical assets and infrastructures remain safe, resilient, and trustworthy.

So let us embrace this opportunity with curiosity, courage, and commitment. Let us work together to advance the state of the art in AI-powered cloud security posture management, and to build a future where the cloud is a source of both innovation and assurance for all.

The road ahead may be complex and uncertain, but the destination is clear and worthy. With AI as our guide and human ingenuity as our driving force, we can navigate this journey with confidence and purpose. Together, we can build a new era of cloud security - one that is smarter, more agile, and more adaptive than ever before.

Section 6.5: AI for Cloud Compliance and Governance

Compliance and governance are critical aspects of cloud security that ensure an organization's cloud usage aligns with relevant laws, regulations, industry standards, and internal policies. With the increasing adoption of cloud services, the scope and complexity of compliance and governance have also grown, making it challenging for organizations to keep up using traditional manual approaches.

This is where AI can play a significant role. By leveraging machine learning, natural language processing, and automation, AI can help organizations to more effectively manage their cloud compliance and governance obligations, reducing risk and freeing up resources for more strategic tasks.

One key application of AI in cloud compliance is in the automated mapping of regulatory requirements to specific cloud controls and configurations. Many regulations and standards, such as HIPAA, PCI-DSS, and GDPR, have detailed requirements for how data must be protected in the cloud. Manually translating these requirements into specific technical controls can be a time-consuming and error-prone process.

AI can assist by using natural language processing to analyze the text of regulations and standards, and automatically extract the relevant security and privacy requirements. Machine learning models can then be used to map these requirements to the corresponding cloud controls and settings, based on patterns learned from previous manual mappings or best practice guides.

For example, if a particular regulation requires data to be encrypted at rest, an AI system could automatically identify the relevant cloud services (such as storage buckets or databases) and check that they have encryption enabled with appropriate key management. If any gaps are found, the AI could flag them for remediation and suggest specific actions to bring the configuration into compliance.

Another application of AI in cloud compliance is in the continuous monitoring and auditing of cloud environments for compliance violations. With the dynamic and elastic nature of the cloud, ensuring ongoing compliance can be a challenge. Resources can be rapidly provisioned and deprovisioned, configurations can be changed with a few clicks, and data can be moved across regions and services.

AI can help by continuously analyzing cloud logs, configurations, and activity data to identify potential compliance issues in real-time. Machine learning models can be trained on historical compliance data to learn the patterns and indicators of non-compliant behavior, such as unauthorized access attempts, unencrypted data transfers, or deviations from approved configurations.

When a potential violation is detected, the AI system can automatically trigger alerts and remediation workflows, such as blocking the non-compliant activity, quarantining the affected resources, or notifying the appropriate compliance and security teams for further investigation. This continuous, automated monitoring can help organizations to catch and address compliance issues much faster than periodic manual audits.

AI can also assist in the generation and maintenance of compliance documentation and evidence. Many regulations and standards require organizations to maintain detailed records of their compliance activities, such as risk assessments, control implementations, and audit trails. Manually creating and updating this documentation can be a significant burden, especially in complex multi-cloud environments.

AI can help automate this process by generating compliance reports and evidence packs based on the real-time state of the cloud environment. Natural language generation techniques can be used to translate technical configuration and activity data into human-readable narratives that satisfy the documentation requirements of different regulations and standards.

For example, an AI system could automatically generate a HIPAA compliance report by analyzing the security controls and data handling practices across all cloud services that process protected health information (PHI). The report could include details on access controls, encryption, logging, and incident response procedures, with references to specific evidence and artifacts collected by the AI.

This AI-generated documentation can not only save time and effort for compliance teams, but also provide a more comprehensive and up-to-date view of an organization's compliance posture. By automating the collection and presentation of compliance evidence, AI can help organizations to be better prepared for audits and regulatory inquiries.

Real-world examples of AI in cloud compliance and governance are emerging from both cloud providers and third-party vendors. Many cloud providers now offer native tools and services that leverage AI to help customers manage their compliance obligations.

For instance, Amazon Web Services (AWS) offers a service called AWS Config, which uses machine learning to continuously monitor and assess the compliance of AWS resources against desired configurations. AWS Config can automatically evaluate resource configurations against a set of predefined or custom rules, and generate compliance reports and notifications based on the results.

Microsoft Azure provides a similar service called Azure Policy, which uses AI to enforce and monitor compliance across Azure subscriptions and resources. Azure Policy can automatically detect non-compliant resources and apply remediation actions, such as modifying configurations or deploying pre-approved templates. It also integrates with Azure Compliance Manager to provide a unified view of compliance status across different regulations and standards.

Google Cloud Platform (GCP) offers a service called Cloud Security Command Center, which uses machine learning to provide real-time compliance monitoring and risk assessment for GCP resources. Cloud SCC can automatically detect misconfigurations, vulnerabilities, and threats, and map them to relevant compliance standards such as PCI-DSS, HIPAA, and ISO 27001. It also provides recommendations for remediation and integrates with other GCP security tools for a more comprehensive compliance management experience.

In addition to these native cloud provider tools, there are also many third-party solutions that leverage AI for cloud compliance and governance. For example:

- Palo Alto Networks' Prisma Cloud (formerly RedLock) uses machine learning to provide continuous compliance monitoring and enforcement across AWS, Azure, and GCP environments. It can automatically assess cloud configurations against industry standards and best practices, and provide risk scores and remediation guidance.

- Symantec's Cloud Workload Protection (CWP) platform uses AI to automate the discovery, protection, and compliance of cloud workloads and data. It can map regulatory requirements to specific cloud controls, monitor for compliance violations, and provide actionable insights for remediation.

- IBM's Cloud Pak for Security uses AI to provide integrated compliance management across hybrid, multi-cloud environments. It can automatically discover and classify regulated data, assess compliance risks, and recommend actions to align with relevant standards and frameworks.

However, implementing AI for cloud compliance and governance also comes with challenges and considerations. One challenge is ensuring the accuracy and reliability of AI-generated compliance assessments and recommendations. Compliance is a high-stakes area where mistakes or false positives can have serious legal and financial consequences. Organizations need to carefully validate and test their AI compliance models to ensure they are providing trustworthy and actionable insights.

Another challenge is keeping AI compliance models up-to-date with the constantly evolving landscape of regulations, standards, and cloud services. As new compliance requirements emerge or existing ones change, the AI models need to be quickly updated to reflect these changes. This requires close collaboration between compliance experts, who understand the regulatory requirements, and data scientists, who can translate these requirements into machine-readable rules and models.

There are also potential privacy and security risks to consider when using AI for compliance. Compliance-related data often includes sensitive personal information or confidential business records. When this data is processed by AI systems, especially those provided by third-party vendors, it's critical to ensure appropriate data protection and access controls are in place. Organizations need to carefully review the security and privacy practices of their AI compliance vendors, and ensure they meet relevant regulatory and contractual obligations.

Despite these challenges, the potential benefits of AI for streamlining and automating cloud compliance and governance are significant. By providing more comprehensive, continuous, and evidence-based compliance management, AI can help organizations to reduce compliance risks, costs, and burdens. This can free up compliance teams to focus on more strategic and value-added activities, such as developing compliance policies, training employees, and engaging with regulators and auditors.

Moreover, by embedding compliance into the fabric of cloud operations, AI can help to foster a culture of continuous compliance and shared responsibility across the organization. Rather than treating compliance as a periodic checkbox exercise, AI-powered compliance tools can make it an integral and transparent part of everyday cloud usage. This can help to build trust with customers, partners, and regulators, and demonstrate an organization's commitment to responsible and ethical cloud practices.

Looking ahead, we can expect to see even more advanced and integrated applications of AI in cloud compliance and governance. For example:

- Predictive compliance that uses machine learning to forecast potential compliance risks based on patterns in resource configurations, user behavior, and external events. This could help organizations to proactively address compliance issues before they occur, rather than reacting after the fact.

- Autonomous compliance remediation that uses AI to automatically correct non-compliant configurations or behaviors without human intervention. This could help to significantly reduce the mean time to remediation for compliance issues, and ensure a more consistent and reliable compliance posture.

- Conversational compliance assistants that use natural language processing to provide interactive guidance and support for cloud users on compliance-related questions and tasks. These AI-powered chatbots or voice assistants could help to democratize compliance knowledge and make it easier for everyone to do the right thing in the cloud.

Of course, realizing this vision will require ongoing research, investment, and collaboration across the cloud compliance community. It will require developing new standards and best practices for the responsible and transparent use of AI in compliance, and ensuring that AI systems are designed and governed in an ethical and accountable manner.

But if we can rise to this challenge, the potential rewards are great. By harnessing the power of AI, we can build a future where compliance is not a barrier to cloud innovation, but an enabler of it. A future where organizations can embrace the full potential of the cloud with confidence, knowing that they are operating within the bounds of the law and serving the best interests of their stakeholders.

So let us seize this opportunity with both hands. Let us work together to shape the future of AI-powered cloud compliance and governance, and to build a more trusted and sustainable digital world for all.

Chapter 6 Conclusion

Throughout this chapter, we've explored the multifaceted role of AI in enhancing cloud security across different domains - from threat detection and response, to access control and identity management, to security posture management, compliance, and governance.

We've seen how the unique characteristics of the cloud - its scale, complexity, dynamism, and shared responsibility model - create both new security challenges and new opportunities for AI-powered solutions. We've discussed how machine learning, natural language processing, and automation can help to provide more intelligent, adaptive, and efficient security controls and processes for the cloud era.

Some key themes and takeaways have emerged from this exploration:

1. AI is not a silver bullet for cloud security, but rather a powerful tool that must be used in combination with other security best practices, technologies, and human expertise. The most effective cloud security strategies will be those that leverage AI to augment and optimize human decision-making, not replace it entirely.

2. Realizing the full potential of AI in cloud security requires careful planning, design, and governance. Organizations need to be thoughtful about the data they use to train their AI models, the explainability and auditability of AI decisions, the performance and scalability of AI systems, and the potential risks and ethical implications of AI-powered security automation.

3. Collaboration and integration are critical for success. Cloud security is a shared responsibility that spans multiple stakeholders, including cloud providers, security vendors, developers, operations teams, compliance officers, and end-users. AI solutions need to be able to work seamlessly across these different stakeholders and integrate with existing security tools, processes, and frameworks.

4. Continuous learning and adaptation are essential. The cloud security landscape is constantly evolving, with new threats, technologies, and regulatory requirements emerging all the time. AI systems need to be able to continuously learn and adapt to these changes, leveraging new data and insights to improve their accuracy and effectiveness over time.

5. Trust and transparency are paramount. As AI becomes more deeply embedded in cloud security decision-making and automation, it's critical to ensure that it is being used in a way that is transparent, accountable, and aligned with human values and ethics. Building and maintaining trust in AI-powered cloud security solutions will require ongoing dialogue, education, and oversight across all stakeholders.

Looking ahead, the future of AI in cloud security is both exciting and challenging. As the volume and velocity of cloud data continue to grow, and as the sophistication and impact of cloud threats continue to escalate, the need for AI-powered security solutions will only become more pressing.

We can expect to see more advanced and autonomous applications of AI emerge across all aspects of cloud security - from self-learning threat detection and response systems, to dynamic and risk-adaptive access control policies, to predictive and proactive compliance management.

At the same time, we can also expect to see more focus on the responsible and ethical development and deployment of AI in cloud security. This will require new standards, guidelines, and governance frameworks to ensure that AI systems are transparent, fair, accountable, and resilient to adversarial attacks and manipulation.

Ultimately, the journey of AI in cloud security is still in its early stages. While the progress made so far is impressive, there is still much work to be done to fully realize the potential of this transformative technology. As we move forward, it will be critical to approach AI with a spirit of openness, collaboration, and continuous learning - always keeping in mind the end goal of creating a more secure, trustworthy, and innovative cloud environment for all.

The cloud has become the foundation for the digital transformation of our economy and society. It is enabling new ways of working, learning, playing, and connecting that were once unimaginable. But this digital promise can only be fulfilled if we can ensure the security and resilience of the cloud against an ever-evolving landscape of cyber threats and risks.

AI offers us a powerful tool to meet this challenge - to create a cloud that is not only more agile and scalable, but also more intelligent, adaptive, and secure. By harnessing the power of AI responsibly and effectively, we can build a future where the benefits of the cloud can be realized without compromising the safety, privacy, and trust of our digital lives.

So let us embrace this opportunity with enthusiasm and responsibility. Let us work together across disciplines and borders to advance the state of the art in AI-powered cloud security, and to create a digital world that is more open, connected, and secure for all.

The road ahead may be uncertain and complex, but the destination is clear and worthwhile. With AI as our partner and human ingenuity as our guide, we can navigate this journey with confidence and purpose. Together, we can build a new era of cloud security - one that is smarter, faster, and more resilient than ever before.

SEVEN

— · —

CHAPTER 7: AI FOR IOT SECURITY

Section 7.1: Introduction to IoT Security

The Internet of Things (IoT) has been a transformative force in our digital landscape, connecting billions of devices and enabling innovative applications across industries. From smart homes and wearables to industrial control systems and autonomous vehicles, IoT has the potential to revolutionize the way we live, work, and interact with our environment.

However, this vast network of connected devices also introduces new security risks and challenges. IoT devices often have limited computing power, memory, and battery life, which can make it difficult to implement traditional security controls. They also operate in diverse and distributed environments, making it harder to monitor and manage their security posture.

Moreover, many IoT devices are designed and deployed with minimal security features, often prioritizing functionality and time-to-market over security. This has led to numerous high-profile IoT security incidents, such as the Mirai botnet attack that hijacked millions of poorly secured IoT devices to launch massive distributed denial-of-service (DDoS) attacks.

The consequences of IoT security breaches can be severe, ranging from the loss of sensitive data and privacy to the disruption of critical infrastructure and even physical harm. As the number and diversity of IoT devices continue to grow, securing the IoT ecosystem has become a top priority for organizations and individuals alike.

IoT security encompasses a wide range of practices and technologies aimed at protecting IoT devices, networks, and data from unauthorized access, tampering, and other malicious activities. This includes:

1. Device security: Ensuring that IoT devices are designed, manufactured, and configured with appropriate security features, such as secure boot, firmware updates, and strong authentication.

2. Network security: Protecting the communication channels and protocols used by IoT devices, such as Wi-Fi, Bluetooth, and Zigbee, from eavesdropping, tampering, and other attacks.

3. Data security: Safeguarding the confidentiality, integrity, and availability of data collected, processed, and transmitted by IoT devices, both at   rest and in transit.

4. Identity and access management: Controlling who and what can access IoT devices and their data, using techniques such as device authentication, user authentication, and access control policies.

5. Monitoring and incident response: Continuously monitoring IoT devices and networks for security events and anomalies, and having processes in place to quickly detect, investigate, and mitigate security incidents.

However, implementing effective IoT security is a complex and multifaceted challenge. Traditional security approaches that were designed for enterprise IT environments often fall short in the IoT context, due to the unique characteristics and constraints of IoT devices and deployments.

This is where Artificial Intelligence (AI) comes into play. AI offers a powerful set of tools and techniques that can help to address many of the challenges of IoT security, from device vulnerability management to threat detection and response. By leveraging the ability of AI to learn from vast amounts of data, adapt to changing conditions, and automate complex tasks, we can create smarter, more resilient, and more scalable IoT security solutions.

In the following sections, we will explore some of the key applications of AI in IoT security, including:

- AI for IoT device security and vulnerability management
- AI for IoT network security and anomaly detection
- AI for IoT data security and privacy protection
- AI for IoT authentication and access control
- AI for IoT security monitoring and incident response

As we dive into each of these areas, we will examine the unique security challenges of IoT, the limitations of traditional security approaches, and the potential of AI to provide more intelligent, adaptive, and automated solutions. We will also discuss real-world examples, emerging trends, and best practices for integrating AI into your IoT security strategy.

It's important to note that while AI offers immense potential for enhancing IoT security, it is not a silver bullet. Effective IoT security requires a comprehensive and multidisciplinary approach that combines AI with other security best practices, such as secure device design, network segmentation, encryption, and human oversight.

Moreover, the use of AI in IoT security also raises important ethical and societal questions, such as data privacy, algorithmic bias, and the potential for AI-powered attacks. As we explore the applications of AI in IoT security, we will also touch on these broader implications and the need for responsible and inclusive AI development and deployment.

With that context in mind, let's dive into the exciting world of AI-powered IoT security and discover how this transformative technology can help us to secure the ever-expanding universe of connected devices.

Section 7.2: AI for IoT Device Security and Vulnerability Management

One of the fundamental challenges in IoT security is ensuring the security of the devices themselves. IoT devices are often resource-constrained, with limited processing power, memory, and storage. This makes it difficult to implement traditional security controls, such as antivirus software or intrusion detection systems, directly on the devices.

Moreover, many IoT devices are designed with minimal attention to security, often using default or hardcoded passwords, insecure protocols, and outdated software components. This leaves them vulnerable to a wide range of attacks, from password guessing and man-in-the-middle attacks to buffer overflows and code injection.

Managing the security of a large and diverse fleet of IoT devices is a daunting task for any organization. Manual processes for asset discovery, vulnerability assessment, and patch management simply cannot keep pace with the scale and velocity of IoT deployments.

This is where AI can make a significant impact. By leveraging machine learning and automation, AI-powered tools can help organizations to more effectively identify, assess, and mitigate vulnerabilities across their IoT device ecosystem.

One key application of AI in IoT device security is automated device discovery and profiling. In a typical enterprise IoT environment, there can be thousands of connected devices, many of which may be unknown or unmanaged by the IT or security teams. Manually keeping track of all these devices and their characteristics is nearly impossible.

AI can assist by continuously scanning the network and using machine learning to automatically identify and classify IoT devices based on their network behavior, communication patterns, and other attributes. For example, an AI system might observe that a particular device is sending data over the MQTT protocol, has a specific MAC address range, and communicates with a known IoT platform. Based on these characteristics, the AI can infer that the device is likely a certain model of smart sensor and add it to the device inventory with the appropriate categorization.

This kind of automated device discovery and profiling can give organizations a more complete and up-to-date view of their IoT asset landscape, which is a critical foundation for effective vulnerability management. By understanding what devices they have, where they are located, and what they are doing, organizations can make more informed decisions about which devices need to be patched, upgraded, or replaced based on their risk profile.

Another application of AI in IoT device security is automated vulnerability assessment. Traditional vulnerability scanning tools that are designed for enterprise IT environments often struggle in the IoT context, due to the heterogeneity and proprietary nature of many IoT devices. They may not have the appropriate plugins or configurations to accurately identify vulnerabilities in specific IoT devices or protocols.

AI can help overcome these limitations by learning the unique characteristics and behaviors of different IoT devices and using this knowledge to identify potential vulnerabilities more accurately. For example, an AI-powered vulnerability assessment tool might analyze the firmware of an IoT device using machine learning techniques like anomaly detection or natural language processing. By comparing the firmware code to known vulnerabilities and coding patterns, the AI can identify potential security flaws, such as hardcoded passwords, unpatched libraries, or insecure API calls, even if they are not included in traditional vulnerability databases.

AI can also be used to prioritize and automate the remediation of IoT device vulnerabilities based on their risk level and potential impact. Machine learning models can be trained on historical vulnerability and exploit data to predict the likelihood and severity of different types of IoT vulnerabilities. This risk-based prioritization can help organizations to focus their limited resources on the most critical vulnerabilities first.

Furthermore, AI can assist in the automated deployment of security patches and firmware updates to IoT devices. One of the biggest challenges in IoT device management is ensuring that devices are running the latest and most secure version of their software. Many IoT devices lack the ability to automatically update themselves, and manually pushing updates to a large fleet of devices can be time-consuming and error-prone.

AI can help automate this process by intelligently scheduling and orchestrating firmware updates based on factors like device type, location, network conditions, and business criticality. For example, an AI-powered device management platform might use machine learning to analyze the historical performance and reliability of different firmware versions on different types of devices. Based on this analysis, the AI can recommend the optimal firmware version and update schedule for each device, balancing the need for security with the potential for service disruption.

The AI system can then automatically push the firmware updates to the devices at the scheduled time, monitoring the update process and rolling back any failed or problematic updates. This kind of automated and intelligent update management can significantly reduce the time and effort required to keep IoT devices secure and up-to-date.

Real-world examples of AI-powered IoT device security and vulnerability management are emerging from a variety of vendors and research institutions. For instance:

- Armis is an IoT security platform that uses machine learning to automatically discover and profile IoT devices, identify vulnerabilities and behavioral anomalies, and enforce security policies. Armis claims to have the world's largest device knowledge base, with over 280 million device profiles and 1,500 behavioral models.

- Forescout is another IoT security platform that leverages AI and automation for device discovery, classification, and compliance. Forescout's eyeInspect product uses machine learning to analyze firmware images and identify vulnerabilities, misconfigurations, and compliance violations, without requiring access to the device itself.

- Microsoft's Azure Security Center for IoT uses AI to provide end-to-end security for IoT devices and services, including device discovery, threat detection, and incident response. Azure Security Center uses machine learning to profile IoT devices based on their network behavior and identify anomalies that could indicate a security breach or malfunction.

- Researchers at the University of Michigan and Johns Hopkins University have developed an AI-based system called Capture that can automatically analyze the security of IoT firmware at scale. Capture uses natural language processing and machine learning to extract security-related information from firmware images and identify potential vulnerabilities, such as outdated software components or insecure configuration options.

However, implementing AI for IoT device security and vulnerability management also comes with challenges and considerations. One challenge is the potential for false positives and negatives in AI-based vulnerability detection. While AI can help identify more complex and subtle vulnerabilities that might be missed by traditional scanning tools, it can also generate incorrect or irrelevant results if not properly trained and validated. Organizations need to carefully test and tune their AI models to ensure they are providing accurate and actionable vulnerability intelligence.

Another challenge is the explainability and transparency of AI-based vulnerability assessment and prioritization. When an AI system flags a particular device or firmware component as high-risk, security teams need to be able to understand and verify the reasoning behind that assessment. Black-box AI models that provide no insight into their decision-making process can be difficult to trust and act upon, particularly in mission-critical IoT environments.

To address this, there is a growing emphasis on developing explainable AI (XAI) techniques for IoT security, such as rule extraction, feature importance analysis, and counterfactual explanations. These techniques aim to make the logic and evidence behind AI-based vulnerability assessments more transparent and interpretable to human analysts, without sacrificing the accuracy and scalability benefits of AI.

A third challenge is the potential for adversarial attacks against AI-based IoT security systems. As attackers become more aware of the use of AI in IoT security, they may attempt to exploit weaknesses or blind spots in the AI models themselves. For example, they could try to poison the training data used to build the vulnerability assessment models, or craft malicious firmware that is designed to evade or mislead the AI's detection capabilities.

To defend against these threats, it's important to incorporate adversarial robustness and resilience techniques into the design and operation of AI-based IoT security solutions. This can include techniques like adversarial training, ensemble learning, and runtime monitoring and adaptation.

Despite these challenges, the potential of AI to transform IoT device security and vulnerability management is significant. By providing more comprehensive, automated, and intelligent vulnerability assessment and remediation capabilities, AI can help organizations to better understand and mitigate the risks associated with their IoT devices, even as the scale and complexity of IoT deployments continue to grow.

Moreover, by integrating AI-based device security with other aspects of IoT security, such as network monitoring, threat detection, and incident response, organizations can build a more holistic and adaptive security posture that can evolve with the changing IoT threat landscape.

As we move forward, it will be crucial for IoT device manufacturers, security vendors, and standards bodies to work together to incorporate AI and machine learning capabilities into the design and lifecycle management of secure IoT devices. This may involve developing new device architectures that are more amenable to AI-based security monitoring and control, as well as creating shared datasets and benchmarks for training and validating IoT security AI models.

Ultimately, the successful application of AI to IoT device security will require a collaborative and multidisciplinary effort that brings together expertise in AI, cybersecurity, IoT systems engineering, and domain-specific knowledge. By working together to advance the state of the art in AI-powered IoT device security, we can build a future where the benefits of ubiquitous device connectivity can be realized without compromising the safety, reliability, and privacy of our critical IoT infrastructures.

Section 7.3: AI for IoT Network Security and Anomaly Detection

While securing individual IoT devices is crucial, it's only one part of the IoT security equation. Equally important is ensuring the security of the networks that connect and enable communication between these devices. IoT devices typically operate in complex and dynamic network environments, using a variety of wireless and wired communication protocols, such as Wi-Fi, Bluetooth, Zigbee, and Ethernet.

Securing IoT networks presents several unique challenges compared to traditional IT networks. First, the sheer scale and heterogeneity of IoT networks make it difficult to apply conventional network security controls, such as firewalls and intrusion detection systems, uniformly across all devices and segments. Second, many IoT communication protocols were designed for simplicity and efficiency rather than security, lacking built-in features like encryption and authentication. Third, the distributed and often remote nature of IoT deployments makes it harder to physically secure and monitor IoT networks for potential breaches or anomalies.

Traditional approaches to network security, such as signature-based detection and rule-based access control, struggle to keep pace with the volume and variety of threats facing IoT networks. Attackers are constantly evolving their tactics, exploiting new vulnerabilities and using evasive techniques to bypass conventional network defenses.

This is where AI can provide a significant advantage. By leveraging machine learning and behavioral analysis, AI-powered network security solutions can automatically learn the normal patterns of activity for IoT devices and networks, and quickly identify deviations that could indicate a potential security threat or operational issue.

One key application of AI in IoT network security is anomaly detection. Anomaly detection involves building a baseline model of what "normal" looks like for a given IoT network or device, and then continuously monitoring for any activities or behaviors that deviate significantly from this baseline.

For example, an AI-based anomaly detection system for an IoT network might learn that a particular smart thermostat typically communicates with a specific set of IP addresses using the MQTT protocol, and exchanges a certain volume and type of data at regular intervals. If the system suddenly observes the thermostat communicating with an unknown IP address, using an unencrypted protocol, or transferring large amounts of data at odd hours, it would flag these activities as anomalous and potentially indicative of a security breach.

The power of AI in anomaly detection lies in its ability to learn and adapt to the unique characteristics and context of each IoT network, without relying on predefined rules or signatures. By training on historical network data and device telemetry, AI models can capture the subtle patterns and relationships that define normal behavior for a specific IoT environment, and spot deviations that might be missed by human analysts or traditional rule-based systems.

This adaptive learning capability is particularly valuable in IoT networks, where the definition of "normal" can vary significantly depending on the type of devices, their intended use case, and the operational environment. What might be considered anomalous behavior for a fleet of industrial sensors in a factory setting could be perfectly normal for a network of smart home devices in a residential context.

AI-based anomaly detection can be applied at various levels of an IoT network, from individual devices and sensors to gateway nodes and cloud services. At the device level, AI models can be trained to detect anomalies in sensor readings, actuator commands, and local data processing that could indicate a compromised or malfunctioning device. At the network level, AI can monitor traffic flows and communication patterns between devices, identifying unusual connections, protocols, or payloads that could signify an attack in progress.

Another key application of AI in IoT network security is threat intelligence and hunting. Threat intelligence involves collecting, analyzing, and sharing information about current and emerging threats facing IoT networks, such as new malware variants, vulnerability exploits, and attack vectors. Threat hunting is the proactive practice of searching for hidden or unknown threats that may have evaded initial detection by security controls.

AI can significantly enhance both threat intelligence and hunting in IoT networks by enabling the automated analysis of vast amounts of security data from multiple sources, such as network logs, device telemetry, and external threat feeds. Machine learning techniques like clustering, classification, and natural language processing can be used to identify patterns and correlations in this data that may indicate a new or previously unknown threat.

For example, an AI-powered threat intelligence platform for IoT might continuously scan the dark web and underground forums for mentions of new IoT exploits or attack tools. By training on the language and context of these discussions, the AI can automatically extract relevant information, such as the targeted devices, vulnerabilities, and potential impact of the threat. This intelligence can then be used to proactively update IoT network defenses and hunting strategies to detect and mitigate the threat before it can cause harm.

Similarly, AI can be used to automate and guide the threat hunting process in IoT networks. By learning the typical patterns and indicators of compromise for different types of IoT threats, AI models can help security analysts to prioritize and investigate potential hunting leads more efficiently. The AI can also continuously learn and adapt its hunting strategies based on the outcomes and feedback from each hunt, becoming more effective over time.

Real-world examples of AI-powered IoT network security and anomaly detection solutions are emerging from a range of vendors and research institutions, such as:

- Cisco's IoT Threat Defense is an AI-powered security solution that combines network segmentation, anomaly detection, and policy enforcement to protect IoT devices and networks. It uses machine learning to automatically profile IoT devices and detect abnormal behavior, such as unauthorized connections or malware activity.

- Darktrace's Industrial Immune System is an AI-based network security platform specifically designed for industrial IoT environments, such as manufacturing plants, power grids, and transportation systems. It uses unsupervised machine learning to build a self-learning model of normal network behavior, and can detect and respond to anomalies in real-time without relying on predefined rules or signatures.

- Researchers at the University of New South Wales have developed an AI-based anomaly detection system for IoT networks that uses a combination of autoencoder neural networks and density-based clustering. The system can learn the normal patterns of IoT network traffic and identify outliers that may represent potential security threats, even in the presence of concept drift and evolving attack tactics.

- Vectra's Cognito platform uses AI to provide real-time threat detection and response for IoT and industrial control system networks. It leverages machine learning to analyze network metadata and detect hidden threats, such as command-and-control communications, lateral movement, and data exfiltration attempts.

Despite the promise of AI for IoT network security and anomaly detection, there are also several challenges and considerations to keep in mind. One challenge is the potential for high false positive rates, especially in dynamic and noisy IoT network environments. Not all anomalies   are necessarily indicative of a security threat, and an overly sensitive AI system could generate a high volume of false alarms that overwhelm security teams and lead to alert fatigue.

To mitigate this risk, it's important to carefully tune and validate AI anomaly detection models using representative IoT network data, and to incorporate domain expertise and contextual information to help distinguish between benign and malicious anomalies. Techniques like unsupervised learning, one-class classification, and ensemble modeling can also help to reduce false positives by learning the unique characteristics of normal and abnormal behavior for each IoT environment.

Another challenge is the potential for adversarial attacks against AI-based IoT network security systems. Skilled attackers may attempt to evade or mislead anomaly detection models by manipulating the input data or exploiting weaknesses in the learning algorithms. For example, an attacker could gradually introduce malicious behavior into an IoT network over time, in a way that appears statistically similar to normal traffic, to avoid triggering anomaly alerts.

To defend against these threats, it's important to incorporate adversarial robustness and resilience techniques into the design and operation of AI-based IoT network security solutions. This can include techniques like adversarial training, where the AI models are explicitly trained on examples of adversarial attacks, as well as runtime monitoring and adaptation, where the models are continuously updated and validated based on new data and feedback from security analysts.

A third challenge is the scalability and efficiency of AI-based anomaly detection in large and complex IoT networks. Training and running sophisticated machine learning models can be computationally expensive, especially when dealing with high-volume, high-velocity data streams from thousands or millions of IoT devices. This can create performance bottlenecks and limit the real-time responsiveness of the anomaly detection system.

To address this challenge, there is ongoing research into distributed and edge-based architectures for AI-powered IoT network security, where the machine learning computation is divided and optimized across multiple nodes and layers of the network. This can involve techniques like federated learning, where the AI models are trained collaboratively by multiple edge devices without sharing raw data, as well as fog computing, where the AI inference and decision-making is performed closer to the data sources to reduce latency and bandwidth requirements.

Despite these challenges, the potential benefits of AI for IoT network security and anomaly detection are significant. By providing more adaptive, scalable, and automated threat detection and response capabilities, AI can help organizations to better protect their IoT networks from the ever-evolving landscape of cyber threats.

As the number and diversity of IoT devices and networks continue to grow, the need for AI-powered security solutions will only become more acute. Traditional signature-based and rule-based approaches simply won't be able to keep pace with the speed and sophistication of IoT attacks.

Going forward, it will be crucial for IoT device manufacturers, network operators, and security vendors to collaborate and innovate to build the next generation of AI-driven IoT network security solutions. This will require advances in areas like machine learning architectures, data preprocessing and feature engineering, explainable AI, and human-machine teaming for security operations.

It will also require the development of new standards and best practices for the responsible and ethical use of AI in IoT security, to ensure that these powerful technologies are deployed in a way that is transparent, accountable, and aligned with societal values and expectations.

Ultimately, the successful application of AI to IoT network security and anomaly detection will depend on a multidisciplinary effort that brings together experts in cybersecurity, machine learning, network engineering, and IoT domain knowledge. By working together to push the boundaries of what's possible with AI-powered security, we can create a future where the transformative benefits of the IoT can be realized without compromising the safety, privacy, and resilience of our digital infrastructure.

Section 7.4: AI for IoT Data Security and Privacy

The Internet of Things (IoT) is generating an unprecedented amount of data, from sensor readings and device telemetry to user interactions and personal information. This data is the lifeblood of many IoT applications and services, enabling everything from predictive maintenance and energy optimization to personalized healthcare and smart city services.

However, the massive scale and distributed nature of IoT data also create significant security and privacy risks. IoT data is often collected and transmitted over untrusted and resource-constrained networks, making it vulnerable to interception, tampering, and unauthorized access. IoT devices themselves may have limited storage and computing power, making it difficult to implement strong cryptography and access control mechanisms.

Moreover, many IoT applications involve the collection and processing of sensitive personal data, such as health metrics, location information, and behavioral patterns. The improper disclosure or misuse of this data can have serious consequences for individual privacy and trust in IoT systems.

Traditional approaches to data security and privacy, such as perimeter-based access control and deterministic encryption, often fall short in the dynamic and heterogeneous IoT environment. They struggle to keep pace with the volume and variety of IoT data flows, and lack the flexibility and granularity to enforce fine-grained data protection policies across diverse devices and platforms.

This is where AI can provide a powerful tool for enhancing IoT data security and privacy. By leveraging machine learning, data analytics, and cryptographic techniques, AI-powered solutions can enable more adaptive, context-aware, and scalable data protection for IoT systems.

One key application of AI in IoT data security is data classification and risk assessment. In a typical IoT deployment, not all data is equally sensitive or valuable from a security and privacy perspective. Some data may be public or low-risk, such as generic environmental sensor readings, while other data may be highly confidential or regulated, such as personal health information or financial transactions.

Manually classifying and labeling every data point generated by an IoT system is simply not feasible at scale. However, AI can automate this process by learning the patterns and characteristics of different types of IoT data and assigning appropriate sensitivity levels and protection policies.

For example, an AI-powered data classification system for a smart city IoT platform might analyze various data streams from traffic sensors, public transit systems, and utility meters. By training on historical data and domain knowledge, the AI can learn to recognize and categorize different data types based on factors like the source device, format, content, and metadata. It can then automatically apply predefined security and privacy labels to each data point, such as "public," "confidential," or "restricted," and trigger the appropriate encryption, access control, and retention policies.

This kind of AI-driven data classification and risk assessment can help organizations to better understand and manage the security and privacy implications of their IoT data flows, and to prioritize their data protection efforts based on the sensitivity and criticality of each data type.

Another key application of AI in IoT data security is anomaly detection and threat intelligence. As discussed in the previous section, AI-based anomaly detection can be a powerful tool for identifying unusual or suspicious patterns in IoT network traffic and device behavior. However, it can also be applied more specifically to the content and flow of IoT data itself, to detect potential security and privacy breaches.

For example, an AI-powered IoT data security system might continuously monitor the data exchanged between IoT devices and cloud services, looking for anomalies such as:

- Unusually large or frequent data transfers that could indicate data exfiltration or tampering

- Encrypted data flows to/from untrusted or unknown endpoints that could signify malware communication

- Inconsistencies or deviations in data format, structure, or content that could suggest data corruption or injection attacks

- Access patterns or queries that violate predefined data usage policies or privacy regulations

By training on normal IoT data flows and leveraging unsupervised learning techniques like clustering and outlier detection, the AI system can automatically flag these anomalies for further investigation and response by security teams. It can also correlate the anomalies with other threat intelligence feeds and knowledge bases to provide more context and guidance on the potential risks and mitigation actions.

This kind of AI-driven anomaly detection and threat intelligence can help organizations to more proactively identify and respond to data security and privacy incidents in their IoT environments, reducing the impact and likelihood of data breaches and compliance violations.

A third key application of AI in IoT data security is privacy-preserving analytics and machine learning. Many IoT applications rely on the aggregation and analysis of large amounts of IoT data to extract valuable insights and train machine learning models for tasks like predictive maintenance, demand forecasting, and personalized recommendations.

However, the centralized collection and processing of raw IoT data can create significant privacy risks, especially when the data contains sensitive personal information. Traditional encryption techniques can help to protect the data in transit and at rest, but they often require the data to be decrypted before it can be analyzed or used for machine learning, creating a potential point of vulnerability.

AI-powered privacy-preserving analytics and machine learning techniques can help to mitigate these risks by enabling the computation and learning on encrypted or obfuscated IoT data, without requiring access to the raw data itself. Some examples of these techniques include:

- Homomorphic encryption: This is a type of encryption that allows certain mathematical operations to be performed directly on encrypted data, without first decrypting it. Using homomorphic encryption, an IoT data analytics platform can perform aggregations, statistics, and even machine learning on encrypted IoT data from multiple sources, without ever seeing the underlying data in plaintext.

- Federated learning: This is a distributed machine learning approach where the training data is kept locally on each IoT device or edge node, and only the model updates are shared and aggregated centrally. This allows for collaborative learning across multiple IoT data silos, without requiring the raw data to be pooled or exposed.

- Differential privacy: This is a mathematical framework for quantifying and bounding the privacy risk of data analysis and publishing. By adding carefully calibrated noise to the IoT data or query results, differential privacy can provide strong guarantees on the privacy of individual data records, while still allowing for useful aggregate insights to be derived.

By leveraging these and other AI-powered privacy-preserving techniques, organizations can enable more secure and privacy-compliant analytics and intelligence on their IoT data, without sacrificing the utility and value of the data.

Real-world examples of AI-powered IoT data security and privacy solutions are emerging from both academic research and industry innovation. For instance:

- IBM's IoT Security solution includes an AI-powered "Data Shield" component that automatically discovers, classifies, and encrypts sensitive IoT data at rest and in motion, based on predefined policies and risk levels. It uses machine learning to continuously monitor IoT data flows for anomalies and threats, and can dynamically adjust the encryption and access control settings based on the changing risk landscape.

- Intel's IoT Platform includes a "Secure Device Onboard" (SDO) service that uses AI to automate the secure provisioning and management of IoT devices at scale. SDO uses machine learning to establish a unique "fingerprint" for each device based on its hardware and software characteristics, and can detect and prevent unauthorized or compromised devices from joining the IoT network.

- Researchers at MIT and Harvard have developed a privacy-preserving analytics platform called "Honeycrisp" that uses a combination of homomorphic encryption and secure multi-party computation to enable privacy-preserving queries and machine learning on distributed IoT data. Honeycrisp has been applied to various smart city and healthcare IoT use cases, demonstrating the feasibility and benefits of AI-powered privacy-enhancing technologies.

However, implementing AI for IoT data security and privacy also comes with challenges and considerations. One challenge is the computational and communication overhead of some AI-powered privacy-preserving techniques, especially when dealing with resource-constrained IoT devices and networks. Homomorphic encryption and secure multi-party computation, for example, can be orders of magnitude slower than plaintext computation, and may require significant bandwidth and storage for the encrypted data and intermediate results.

To address this challenge, there is ongoing research into more lightweight and efficient cryptographic primitives and protocols that can enable privacy-preserving AI on IoT data at scale. There are also efforts to develop hybrid architectures that combine edge computing, fog computing, and cloud computing to optimize the trade-off between privacy, performance, and cost in IoT data analytics pipelines.

Another challenge is the potential for bias and fairness issues in AI-based IoT data security and privacy solutions. If the training data used to build the AI models is not representative or contains historical biases, the resulting data protection decisions and actions may be discriminatory or unfair to certain individuals or groups.

For example, an AI-based IoT data risk assessment system that is trained primarily on data from affluent and tech-savvy users may underestimate the privacy risks and sensitivities of data from underrepresented or marginalized communities. Similarly, an AI-based anomaly detection system that is biased towards certain types of devices, protocols, or behaviors may generate more false positives or negatives for certain IoT data flows.

To mitigate these risks, it's important to ensure that the IoT data used to train and validate AI models for security and privacy is diverse, representative, and free from historical biases. It's also critical to continuously monitor and audit the fairness and accountability of AI-driven data protection decisions, and to provide mechanisms for human oversight and redress when necessary.

A third challenge is the interoperability and compatibility of AI-powered IoT data security and privacy solutions with existing IoT standards, protocols, and platforms. The IoT ecosystem is highly fragmented and heterogeneous, with a wide variety of devices, networks, and data formats that may not be fully compatible with each other or with new AI-based security and privacy technologies.

To enable the widespread adoption and effectiveness of AI for IoT data protection, it's important to develop and promote open, interoperable, and standards-based approaches that can work across different IoT domains and use cases. This may involve collaborating with IoT standards bodies, such as the International Organization for Standardization (ISO), the Institute of Electrical and Electronics Engineers (IEEE), and the Internet Engineering Task Force (IETF), to incorporate AI and privacy-enhancing technologies into existing or new IoT standards and best practices.

Despite these challenges, the potential benefits of AI for IoT data security and privacy are significant and far-reaching. By providing more intelligent, adaptive, and scalable data protection capabilities, AI can help organizations to harness the full value of their IoT data while preserving the privacy and trust of their users and stakeholders.

Looking ahead, we can expect to see more research and innovation in areas like privacy-preserving IoT data analytics, AI-powered IoT data governance, and human-centered IoT data privacy. Some promising future directions include:

- Federated deep learning for IoT data analytics, which can enable more powerful and expressive machine learning models to be trained on decentralized IoT data without compromising privacy.

- Blockchain-based IoT data marketplaces, which can use AI and cryptography to enable secure and fair data sharing and monetization across IoT ecosystems, while preserving data ownership and privacy rights.

- Explainable AI for IoT data privacy, which can provide more transparent and interpretable explanations of how IoT data is being collected, used, and protected by AI systems, empowering users to make more informed decisions about their data.

Ultimately, the success of AI in IoT data security and privacy will depend on a multidisciplinary and collaborative effort that engages technologists, policymakers, ethicists, and end-users in the design and governance of these powerful new technologies. By working together to advance the state of the art in AI-powered IoT data protection, while also grappling with the complex social and ethical implications, we can build a future where the IoT can reach its full potential as a driver of innovation, efficiency, and human well-being, without compromising the fundamental rights and values of privacy and trust.

Section 7.5: AI for IoT Security Operations and Incident Response

The sheer scale and complexity of IoT systems makes it challenging for security teams to effectively monitor, manage, and respond to the diverse range of threats and incidents that can arise. With millions or even billions of connected devices, generating vast amounts of data and logs, traditional manual approaches to security operations and incident response simply cannot keep pace.

This is where AI can play a vital role in augmenting and automating IoT security operations and incident response. By leveraging machine learning, data analytics, and automated reasoning, AI-powered solutions can help security teams to more quickly detect, investigate, and mitigate IoT security incidents, while also reducing the workload and cognitive burden on human analysts.

One key application of AI in IoT security operations is alert triage and prioritization. In a typical IoT environment, security monitoring tools and sensors can generate a huge volume of alerts and notifications, many of which may be false positives or low-priority issues that don't require immediate attention. Manually sifting through these alerts to identify the most critical and actionable ones can be a time-consuming and error-prone process.

AI can assist by automatically analyzing and scoring each alert based on various factors such as the severity, confidence, and context of the underlying event or anomaly. Machine learning models can be trained on historical alert data and incident reports to learn the patterns and characteristics of high-priority and low-priority alerts, and to predict the likelihood and impact of each new alert.

For example, an AI-powered alert triage system for an IoT-enabled manufacturing plant might prioritize alerts based on factors such as:

- The criticality and vulnerability of the affected device or system (e.g., a PLC controlling a safety-critical process vs. a non-critical environmental sensor)

- The rarity and severity of the detected anomaly or threat (e.g., a known malware signature vs. a novel or zero-day attack)

- The correlation and consistency with other alerts and data sources (e.g., multiple devices showing similar anomalies vs. an isolated event)

- The potential impact and consequences of the alert (e.g., a data breach vs. a device performance issue)

By automatically prioritizing alerts in this way, the AI system can help security teams to focus their attention and resources on the most important and urgent incidents, while filtering out or deprioritizing the noise and false positives.

Another application of AI in IoT security operations is automated incident investigation and forensics. When a high-priority IoT security alert is detected, security analysts need to quickly investigate the scope, root cause, and impact of the incident, in order to determine the appropriate response and remediation   actions.

Traditionally, this incident investigation process involves manual tasks such as collecting and analyzing relevant data from various sources (e.g., device logs, network traffic, threat intelligence feeds), interviewing stakeholders and experts, and piecing together the timeline and details of the incident. This can be a complex and time-consuming process, especially for IoT incidents that may involve multiple devices, protocols, and data streams.

AI can help to automate and accelerate this incident investigation process by leveraging techniques such as data fusion, pattern recognition, and knowledge representation. For example, an AI-powered IoT incident investigation system might:

- Automatically collect and correlate relevant data from across the IoT environment, using machine learning to identify key entities, events, and relationships

- Apply natural language processing and information extraction to unstructured data sources such as device logs, chat logs, and incident reports, to identify relevant keywords, phrases, and sentiments

- Use graph analytics and link analysis to visualize and explore the connections and dependencies between different devices, users, and data flows involved in the incident

- Apply probabilistic reasoning and causal inference to build and test hypotheses about the likely root cause, impact, and timeline of the incident

- Generate interactive incident reports and dashboards that summarize the key findings and recommendations for security analysts and stakeholders

By automating these incident investigation tasks, AI can help security teams to more quickly and comprehensively understand the scope and nature of IoT security incidents, reducing the mean time to respond and the risk of missed or incomplete analyses.

AI can also be applied to automate and guide the incident response and remediation process for IoT security incidents. Once an incident has been investigated and characterized, security teams need to take appropriate actions to contain and mitigate the impact, recover any affected systems or data, and prevent similar incidents from occurring in the future.

In traditional incident response, these actions are often guided by predefined playbooks or runbooks that specify the steps and procedures to follow for different types of incidents. However, these static playbooks may not always be well-suited for the dynamic and diverse nature of IoT incidents, which can involve novel attack vectors, complex system dependencies, and evolving compliance requirements.

AI-powered incident response systems can provide more adaptive and context-aware guidance for IoT security incidents, by leveraging techniques such as case-based reasoning, reinforcement learning, and automated planning. For example, an AI-powered IoT incident response system might:

- Use machine learning to automatically classify and map the incident to the most relevant response playbook or workflow, based on the specific characteristics and context of the incident

- Apply case-based reasoning to identify and retrieve similar past incidents and their successful response strategies, adapting them to the current incident as needed

- Use reinforcement learning to continuously optimize the response actions based on feedback and outcomes from past incidents, learning from both successes and failures

- Apply automated planning and scheduling techniques to generate and execute the most effective sequence of response actions, taking into account resource constraints, dependencies, and priorities

- Provide interactive decision support and recommendations to human responders, explaining the rationale and evidence behind each suggested action

By automating and optimizing incident response in this way, AI can help IoT security teams to more quickly and effectively contain and recover from security incidents, while also improving the consistency and auditability of the response process.

Real-world examples of AI-powered IoT security operations and incident response solutions are emerging from a range of vendors and research institutions. For instance:

- IBM's Watson for Cyber Security is an AI-powered security analytics platform that can ingest and analyze structured and unstructured data from various IoT security tools and sources, using natural language processing and machine learning to automatically identify and prioritize threats and incidents. It can also generate dynamic incident reports and response recommendations based on past incidents and best practices.

- Darktrace's Cyber AI Analyst is an automated threat investigation and response system that uses unsupervised machine learning to continuously learn the normal 'pattern of life' for IoT devices and networks, and can automatically detect and investigate anomalies that may indicate a security incident. It can also provide guided response actions and workflows for security analysts based on the specific details and context of each incident.

- Researchers at the Singapore University of Technology and Design have developed an AI-powered IoT security incident response system that uses case-based reasoning and reinforcement learning to automatically suggest and optimize response strategies based on similar past incidents and feedback from human experts. The system has been tested on various IoT security scenarios and has shown promising results in terms of response accuracy and efficiency.

However, implementing AI for IoT security operations and incident response also comes with challenges and considerations. One challenge is the need for large and diverse datasets to train and validate the AI models. IoT security incidents can be relatively rare and varied compared to traditional IT security incidents, making it difficult to collect sufficient data to cover the full range of possible scenarios and responses.

To address this challenge, researchers and vendors are exploring techniques such as data augmentation, transfer learning, and simulation to generate synthetic or adapted incident data that can be used to train AI models. There are also efforts to create shared IoT security incident databases and benchmarks that can enable collaborative learning and evaluation across different organizations and domains.

Another challenge is the potential for bias and blindspots in AI-powered incident response systems. If the AI models are trained on a narrow or biased set of past incidents and responses, they may not generalize well to novel or unforeseen situations, leading to inappropriate or suboptimal recommendations.

To mitigate this risk, it's important to ensure that the training data and algorithms used for AI-powered incident response are diverse, representative, and explicitly tested for fairness and robustness. It's also critical to provide mechanisms for human oversight and intervention in the AI decision-making process, to catch and correct any errors or biases.

A third challenge is the explainability and accountability of AI-powered incident response actions. In many IoT security scenarios, the stakes can be high, involving potential impacts to safety, privacy, and critical infrastructure. Security analysts and stakeholders need to be able to understand and trust the reasoning behind AI-generated response recommendations, in order to make informed decisions and take appropriate actions.

To address this challenge, there is growing research into techniques for explainable AI and human-AI collaboration in incident response workflows. This includes developing user interfaces and interaction paradigms that enable humans to easily interpret and interact with AI-generated insights and recommendations, as well as incorporating human feedback and guidance into the AI learning process.

Despite these challenges, the potential benefits of AI for IoT security operations and incident response are significant. By providing more automated, adaptive, and intelligent support for security monitoring, investigation, and response, AI can help IoT security teams to better protect their critical assets and infrastructure from the ever-evolving threat landscape.

Moreover, AI-powered security operations can enable more proactive and preventative approaches to IoT security, by continuously learning and adapting to new threats and vulnerabilities, and by providing predictive insights and recommendations for risk mitigation and resilience.

As the scale and complexity of IoT systems continue to grow, the need for AI-powered security operations and incident response will only become more pressing. Manual and reactive approaches will simply not be able to keep pace with the speed and sophistication of IoT attacks and failures.

Going forward, it will be essential for IoT device manufacturers, security providers, and researchers to collaborate and innovate to advance the state of the art in AI for IoT security operations. This will require developing new AI architectures, algorithms, and interaction paradigms that can provide more robust, explainable, and accountable support for IoT security decision-making and automation.

It will also require deeper partnerships and knowledge sharing between the IoT security and AI research communities, to ensure that the latest advances in AI are being effectively applied to real-world IoT security challenges, and that the unique constraints and requirements of IoT systems are being considered in AI research and development.

Ultimately, the success of AI in IoT security operations and incident response will depend not only on technological progress, but also on the human factors and organizational processes that shape the adoption and use of these powerful tools. It will require cultivating a culture of collaboration, continuous learning, and responsible innovation in IoT security, where humans and AI systems can work together seamlessly to protect our critical IoT infrastructure and data.

By embracing this opportunity and rising to its challenges, we can harness the transformative potential of AI to build a more secure, resilient, and trustworthy IoT ecosystem for all. So let us continue to push forward on this exciting frontier, and work together to shape a future where the benefits of IoT can be realized without compromising our core values of security, privacy, and trust.

Chapter 7 Conclusion

In this chapter, we have explored the critical role of AI in enhancing IoT security across various aspects - from device and network security to data protection and incident response. We have seen how the unique characteristics and challenges of IoT systems, such as their scale, heterogeneity, resource constraints, and attack surfaces, demand new and innovative approaches to security that go beyond traditional IT security paradigms.

We have discussed how AI, with its capabilities for learning, adaptation, and automation, can provide powerful tools and techniques for addressing these IoT security challenges in a more effective, efficient, and scalable way. By leveraging machine learning, anomaly detection, threat intelligence, and other AI techniques, we can build IoT security solutions that are more proactive, context-aware, and resilient to the ever-evolving threat landscape.

Some key themes and takeaways have emerged from this exploration:

1. AI is not a panacea for IoT security, but rather a key enabler that must be integrated with other security best practices, frameworks, and technologies. The most effective IoT

security strategies will be those that combine the strengths of AI with human expertise, governance, and collaboration.

2. Realizing the full potential of AI in IoT security requires addressing key challenges and considerations, such as data quality and diversity, algorithmic bias and fairness, explainability and accountability, performance and resource efficiency, and adversarial robustness and resilience.

3. Successful adoption of AI in IoT security demands close collaboration and knowledge sharing across various stakeholders, including IoT device manufacturers, security providers, researchers, policymakers, and end-users. It requires breaking down silos and fostering a culture of openness, trust, and continuous learning.

4. As AI becomes more pervasive and autonomous in IoT security, it is crucial to consider the broader social, ethical, and legal implications, such as privacy, transparency, liability, and human agency. We need to ensure that the development and deployment of AI in IoT security aligns with human values and promotes the responsible and beneficial use of these powerful technologies.

Looking ahead, the future of AI in IoT security is both exciting and challenging. As the IoT continues to grow and evolve, with billions of new devices and use cases emerging every year, the need for AI-powered security solutions will only become more critical and urgent.

We can expect to see more advanced and integrated applications of AI across the entire IoT security lifecycle, from secure device design and development to real-time threat detection and autonomous incident response. Some promising future directions include:

- Collaborative and federated learning approaches that enable IoT devices and edge nodes to collectively train and update security models without sharing raw data, preserving privacy and efficiency.

- Hybrid AI architectures that combine the strengths of different AI techniques, such as deep learning, reinforcement learning, and symbolic reasoning, to provide more robust and explainable IoT security decisions and actions.

- Human-centered AI interfaces and interaction paradigms that enable security analysts and end-users to more easily understand, trust, and guide AI-powered IoT security systems, promoting transparency and accountability.

- Adversarial AI techniques that can proactively identify and mitigate potential vulnerabilities and threats in IoT systems, by simulating and learning from the tactics and strategies of malicious actors.

- AI-powered digital twins and simulation environments that can provide realistic and scalable testbeds for evaluating and certifying the security and resilience of IoT systems and components, before and during deployment.

Of course, realizing this vision will require sustained investment, experimentation, and collaboration from all stakeholders in the IoT security ecosystem. It will require tackling hard problems and making difficult trade-offs, such as balancing security with privacy, efficiency, and usability.

But if we can rise to this challenge and harness the transformative potential of AI responsibly and effectively, the benefits for IoT security could be immense. We could build a future where our critical IoT infrastructures, from smart homes and cities to connected vehicles and industrial systems, are not only more functional and efficient, but also more secure, resilient, and trustworthy.

So let us embrace this opportunity with determination and care. Let us work together across disciplines and sectors to advance the state of the art in AI-powered IoT security, while also grappling with the complex social and ethical implications. Let us strive to create a future where the power of AI and IoT can be leveraged for the greater good, without compromising our fundamental values and rights.

The road ahead may be long and uncertain, but the destination is clear and worthy. With AI as our partner and human wisdom as our guide, we can navigate this journey with confidence and purpose. Together, we can build a new era of IoT security - one that is smarter, more adaptive, and more humane than ever before.

EIGHT

— • —

CHAPTER 8: QUANTUM COMPUTING AND AI SECURITY

Section 8.1: Introduction to Quantum Computing and its Implications for Cybersecurity

T he field of quantum computing has been making rapid advancements in recent years, with the potential to revolutionize various aspects of our digital world. While still in its early stages, quantum computing promises to solve certain problems much faster than classical computers, with significant implications for fields such as cryptography, optimization, and machine learning.

At its core, quantum computing leverages the principles of quantum mechanics to perform computations. Unlike classical computers, which use bits that can be either 0 or 1, quantum computers use quantum bits, or qubits, which can exist in multiple states simultaneously (a phenomenon known as superposition). This allows quantum computers to perform certain calculations exponentially faster than classical computers.

One of the most significant potential applications of quantum computing is in the field of cryptography. Many of the current encryption methods that secure our online communications and transactions, such as RSA and elliptic curve cryptography, rely on the difficulty of factoring large numbers or solving discrete logarithm problems. These problems are believed to be intractable for classical computers, providing the foundation for modern cryptography.

However, in 1994, mathematician Peter Shor developed a quantum algorithm (now known as Shor's algorithm) that can factor large numbers exponentially faster than the best-known classical algorithms. This means that a sufficiently powerful quantum computer could potentially break many of the encryption methods that we rely on today, rendering them ineffective.

The implications of this for cybersecurity are significant. If quantum computers become powerful enough to break current encryption methods, it could jeopardize the security of everything from personal emails and financial transactions to government and military communications. This has led to a surge of interest in developing new, quantum-resistant encryption methods that can withstand attacks from quantum computers.

Another potential application of quantum computing in cybersecurity is in the development of quantum key distribution (QKD) systems. QKD is a method of securely exchanging encryption keys using the principles of quantum mechanics, such as the no-cloning theorem and the uncertainty principle. Unlike classical key distribution methods, QKD can detect any attempt at eavesdropping or tampering, providing a theoretically unbreakable method of secure communication.

However, the development of quantum computers also poses significant challenges for the field of cybersecurity. In addition to the potential threat to current encryption methods, quantum computers could also be used to develop new and more powerful cyber attacks. For example, quantum computers could be used to quickly search through large databases of passwords or to optimize the delivery of malware and phishing attempts.

Moreover, the very nature of quantum computing makes it difficult to detect and defend against quantum-based attacks. Because quantum computers can exist in multiple states simultaneously and can perform certain calculations without leaving a classical trace, it may be much harder to detect and attribute quantum-based cyber attacks.

This has led to a growing interest in the development of quantum-resistant cybersecurity measures, such as post-quantum cryptography and quantum-safe security protocols. Post-quantum cryptography refers to cryptographic algorithms that are designed to be secure against both classical and quantum computers, using mathematical problems that are believed to be hard for both types of computers to solve. Quantum-safe security protocols, on the other hand, aim to leverage the principles of quantum mechanics itself to provide secure communication and computation, even in the presence of quantum computers.

The development of these quantum-resistant cybersecurity measures is still in its early stages, and there are many open research questions and challenges to be addressed. For example, there is still uncertainty about which mathematical problems will prove to be the most secure and practical for post-quantum cryptography, and how to efficiently implement and deploy these new algorithms in practice.

Moreover, the development of quantum computers and quantum-resistant cybersecurity measures is not just a technical challenge, but also a geopolitical and economic one. There is a global race underway to develop quantum computing capabilities, with major investments being made by governments, tech giants, and startups around the world. Whoever gains a significant advantage in quantum computing could potentially gain a major strategic advantage in fields such as cryptography, drug discovery, and financial modeling.

As such, the development of quantum computing and quantum-resistant cybersecurity measures is not just a matter of technical innovation, but also of international cooperation and governance. There is a need for global standards and protocols to ensure the peaceful and responsible development of quantum technologies, and to prevent their misuse for malicious purposes.

Despite these challenges, the potential benefits of quantum computing for cybersecurity are significant. In addition to providing new methods for secure communication and computation, quantum computing could also be used to enhance the development of artificial intelligence and machine learning models for cybersecurity.

For example, quantum machine learning algorithms could potentially be used to more efficiently train and optimize AI models for tasks such as anomaly detection, threat classification, and risk assessment. Quantum-enhanced AI could also be used to develop more sophisticated and adaptive cybersecurity systems that can learn and evolve in response to new threats and vulnerabilities.

Moreover, the intersection of quantum computing and AI could lead to the development of entirely new paradigms for cybersecurity, such as quantum-secured AI systems that are resistant to both classical and quantum-based attacks, or hybrid quantum-classical AI architectures that combine the strengths of both approaches.

Of course, the realization of these potential benefits will require significant research and development efforts, as well as close collaboration between   the quantum computing, AI, and cybersecurity communities. It will also require careful consideration of the ethical and societal implications of these powerful new technologies, to ensure that they are developed and used in a responsible and beneficial manner.

In this chapter, we will explore the current state of the art in quantum computing and its implications for cybersecurity and AI. We will discuss the key concepts and technologies underlying quantum computing, such as qubits, quantum gates, and quantum algorithms. We will also examine the potential impact of quantum computing on current and future cybersecurity measures, such as encryption, key exchange, and post-quantum cryptography.

Furthermore, we will delve into the intersection of quantum computing and AI, exploring how quantum technologies could be used to enhance the development and performance of AI models for cybersecurity. We will discuss current research efforts and future directions in this area, such as quantum machine learning, quantum neural networks, and quantum-enhanced cybersecurity systems.

Throughout this chapter, we will also consider the broader societal and ethical implications of quantum computing and AI for cybersecurity. We will discuss the potential risks and benefits of these technologies, as well as the need for responsible development and governance frameworks to ensure their safe and beneficial use.

As we explore this exciting and rapidly evolving field, it is important to keep in mind that the development of quantum computing and its applications for cybersecurity and AI is still in its early stages. There are many open questions and challenges to be addressed, and the full impact of these technologies on our digital world is still uncertain.

Nevertheless, the potential of quantum computing to revolutionize cybersecurity and AI is clear, and it is crucial that we engage with these technologies proactively and responsibly. By working together across disciplines and sectors, we can shape the future of quantum computing and its applications in a way that benefits society as a whole, while also safeguarding our digital security and privacy.

So let us embark on this fascinating journey into the world of quantum computing and its implications for cybersecurity and AI. Let us explore the possibilities and challenges of this transformative technology, and work together to build a future that is not only more secure and intelligent, but also more equitable and beneficial for all.

Section 8.2: Quantum Computing Basics and Key Concepts

To understand the implications of quantum computing for cybersecurity and AI, it is important to first grasp the fundamental concepts and principles underlying this transformative technology. In this section, we will provide an overview of the key concepts and building blocks of quantum computing, and how they differ from classical computing.

At the heart of quantum computing is the concept of the quantum bit, or qubit. Unlike classical bits, which can only exist in one of two states (0 or 1), qubits can exist in a superposition of multiple states simultaneously. This means that a single qubit can represent a combination of 0 and 1 at the same time, allowing for exponentially more information to be encoded and processed compared to classical bits.

Mathematically, the state of a qubit can be represented as a linear combination of two basis states, typically denoted as $|0\rangle$ and $|1\rangle$. The coefficients of these basis states, known as amplitudes, determine the probability of measuring the qubit in each state. For example, a qubit in the state $|\psi\rangle = \alpha|0\rangle + \beta|1\rangle$ has a probability of $|\alpha|^2$ of being measured in the $|0\rangle$ state and a probability of $|\beta|^2$ of being measured in the $|1\rangle$ state, where $|\alpha|^2 + |\beta|^2 = 1$.

Another key concept in quantum computing is quantum entanglement, which refers to the phenomenon where two or more qubits become correlated in such a way that the state of one qubit cannot be described independently of the state of the other(s). Entanglement allows for the creation of complex, multi-qubit states that exhibit non-classical correlations and can be used to perform certain computations more efficiently than classical computers.

To perform computations on qubits, quantum computers use quantum gates, which are analogous to the logic gates used in classical computing. However, unlike classical gates, which operate on classical bits, quantum gates operate on qubits and can perform operations that are not possible with classical gates, such as creating superposition and entanglement.

Some of the most common quantum gates include the Hadamard gate (H), which creates an equal superposition of $|0\rangle$ and $|1\rangle$ states, the Pauli-X gate (X), which flips the state of a qubit from $|0\rangle$ to $|1\rangle$ or vice versa, and the controlled-NOT gate (CNOT), which flips the state of a target qubit conditional on the state of a control qubit.

By applying sequences of quantum gates to qubits, quantum computers can perform complex computations that are intractable for classical computers. However, the design and implementation of quantum circuits is a significant challenge, as qubits are highly sensitive to noise and errors, and require careful control and error correction techniques to maintain their coherence and fidelity.

One of the most promising applications of quantum computing is in the development of quantum algorithms, which are designed to solve specific computational problems faster than the best-known classical algorithms. Some of the most well-known quantum algorithms include Shor's algorithm for integer factorization, Grover's algorithm for unstructured search, and the Harrow-Hassidim-Lloyd (HHL) algorithm for solving linear systems of equations.

The development of these and other quantum algorithms has significant implications for fields such as cryptography, optimization, and machine learning, as they could potentially provide exponential speedups over classical algorithms for certain tasks. However, the practical implementation of these algorithms on real quantum hardware is still a significant challenge, due to the limitations of current quantum devices and the need for error correction and fault tolerance.

Another important concept in quantum computing is quantum error correction, which refers to the techniques used to detect and correct errors that occur during quantum computations. Due to the fragility of quantum states and the sensitivity of qubits to noise and decoherence, quantum error correction is essential for building reliable and scalable quantum computers.

There are various approaches to quantum error correction, such as the use of redundant qubits to encode logical qubits, the implementation of error-correcting codes, and the use of fault-tolerant quantum gates and circuits. However, the overhead required for quantum error correction is significant, and the development of practical and efficient error correction schemes is an active area of research.

Despite these challenges, there has been significant progress in the development of quantum computing hardware and software in recent years. Companies such as IBM, Google, Microsoft, and Intel, as well as academic institutions and government labs around the world, are investing heavily in the development of quantum computers and quantum algorithms.

Some notable milestones in the field include:

- The demonstration of quantum supremacy by Google in 2019, using a 53-qubit quantum processor to perform a specific task in 200 seconds that would take the world's most powerful classical supercomputer over 10,000 years.

- The development of IBM's quantum computing platform, IBM Q, which provides access to quantum computers and quantum simulators over the cloud, allowing researchers and developers to experiment with quantum algorithms and applications.

- The establishment of the National Quantum Initiative in the United States in 2018, which provides $1.2 billion in funding over five years for quantum research and development, as well as the creation of quantum research centers and a quantum industry consortium.

As quantum computing continues to advance, it is likely to have significant implications for cybersecurity and AI. On the one hand, quantum computers could potentially break many of the encryption methods that currently secure our online communications and transactions, requiring the development of new, quantum-resistant cryptographic protocols and algorithms.

On the other hand, quantum computers could also be used to enhance the development and performance of AI models for cybersecurity, by providing new ways to efficiently process and analyze large datasets, optimize complex functions, and simulate complex systems.

Moreover, the intersection of quantum computing and AI could lead to the development of entirely new paradigms for cybersecurity, such as quantum machine learning algorithms that can learn and adapt to new threats in real-time, or quantum-secured communication protocols that are resistant to both classical and quantum attacks.

Of course, the realization of these potential applications will require significant research and development efforts, as well as close collaboration between the quantum computing, cybersecurity, and AI communities. It will also require careful consideration of the ethical and societal implications of these powerful new technologies, to ensure that they are developed and used in a responsible and beneficial manner.

But if we can rise to this challenge, the potential benefits of quantum computing for cybersecurity and AI could be immense. By harnessing the power of quantum technologies to secure our digital infrastructure and enhance our AI capabilities, we can build a future that is not only more secure and intelligent, but also more resilient and adaptive to the ever-evolving threats and challenges of the 21st century.

So let us continue to explore the exciting possibilities of quantum computing, and work together to shape its development and application in a way that benefits society as a whole. With dedication, collaboration, and a commitment to the responsible and ethical use of these transformative technologies, we can create a quantum future that is brighter, safer, and more prosperous for all.

Section 8.3: Post-Quantum Cryptography and Quantum-Safe Security

One of the most significant potential impacts of quantum computing on cybersecurity is the threat it poses to current encryption methods. Many of the cryptographic algorithms that are widely used today, such as RSA and elliptic curve cryptography (ECC), rely on the difficulty of certain mathematical problems, such as integer factorization and the discrete logarithm problem, for their security.

However, as we discussed in the previous section, quantum computers have the potential to solve these problems much faster than classical computers, using algorithms such as Shor's algorithm. This means that a sufficiently powerful quantum computer could potentially break many of the encryption methods that currently secure our online communications and transactions, rendering them vulnerable to attacks.

To address this threat, researchers and cybersecurity experts are working to develop new cryptographic methods that are resistant to attacks from both classical and quantum computers, a field known as post-quantum cryptography (PQC).

Post-quantum cryptography refers to cryptographic algorithms and protocols that are designed to be secure against attacks by quantum computers. Unlike current cryptographic methods, which rely on the hardness of certain mathematical problems, post-quantum cryptography is based on mathematical problems that are believed to be difficult for both classical and quantum computers to solve.

Some of the most promising approaches to post-quantum cryptography include:

- Lattice-based cryptography: This approach is based on the hardness of certain problems in lattices, which are mathematical structures that can be used to represent and solve various computational problems. Lattice-based cryptographic schemes, such as the Learning with Errors (LWE) and Ring Learning with Errors (RLWE) problems, are believed to be resistant to attacks by quantum computers, and have been used to construct various post-quantum cryptographic primitives, such as public-key encryption, digital signatures, and key exchange protocols.

- Code-based cryptography: This approach is based on the hardness of decoding certain types of error-correcting codes, such as the McEliece cryptosystem and its variants. Code-based cryptography has been studied for several decades, and is believed to be resistant to attacks by quantum computers. However, code-based schemes typically have large key sizes and high computational complexity, which can make them less practical for certain applications.

- Multivariate cryptography: This approach is based on the hardness of solving systems of multivariate polynomial equations over finite fields. Multivariate cryptographic schemes, such as the Unbalanced Oil and Vinegar (UOV) and Hidden Field Equations (HFE) systems, are believed to be resistant to attacks by quantum computers, and have been used to construct various post-quantum cryptographic primitives, such as digital signatures and key exchange protocols.

- Hash-based cryptography: This approach is based on the security of cryptographic hash functions, which are mathematical functions that take an input of arbitrary size and produce an output of fixed size, and are designed to be difficult to invert or find collisions. Hash-based cryptographic schemes, such as the Merkle signature scheme and its variants, are believed to be resistant to attacks by quantum computers, and have been used to construct various post-quantum cryptographic primitives, such as digital signatures and one-time signature schemes.

In addition to these approaches, there are also other post-quantum cryptographic primitives and protocols that are being developed and studied, such as supersingular isogeny-based cryptography, quantum key distribution (QKD), and quantum-resistant random number generation.

The development of post-quantum cryptography is an active area of research, and there are ongoing efforts to standardize and implement these new cryptographic methods. In 2016, the National Institute of Standards and Technology (NIST) in the United States initiated a process to solicit, evaluate, and standardize quantum-resistant public-key cryptographic algorithms, known as the Post-Quantum Cryptography Standardization Process.

The NIST PQC process is currently in its third round, with several candidate algorithms being evaluated for their security, performance, and implementation characteristics. The goal of the process is to select one or more algorithms for standardization by the end of 2021, which will then be recommended for use in various applications and protocols.

In addition to the development of post-quantum cryptographic algorithms, there are also efforts to develop quantum-safe security protocols and architectures that can provide end-to-end security for communications and transactions in the presence of quantum computers.

Quantum-safe security refers to the design and implementation of security systems that are resistant to attacks by both classical and quantum computers, and that can provide provable security guarantees based on the laws of quantum mechanics.

One approach to quantum-safe security is the use of quantum key distribution (QKD), which is a method for securely exchanging cryptographic keys using the principles of quantum mechanics, such as the no-cloning theorem and the uncertainty principle. Unlike classical key exchange methods, which rely on the assumed hardness of certain mathematical problems, QKD provides a theoretically unbreakable method for secure key exchange, as any attempt to intercept or measure the quantum states used in the protocol will be detectable by the communicating parties.

Another approach to quantum-safe security is the use of quantum-resistant cryptographic protocols and architectures, which combine post-quantum cryptographic primitives with classical security techniques, such as secure multiparty computation, homomorphic encryption, and zero-knowledge proofs, to provide end-to-end security for various applications and use cases.

For example, the Quantum-Safe Hybrid (QSH) framework is a proposed architecture for quantum-safe security that combines post-quantum cryptography with QKD to provide a layered approach to security. The QSH framework uses post-quantum cryptographic primitives for key exchange and authentication, and QKD for secure key distribution and renewal, providing a high level of security against both classical and quantum attacks.

Other examples of quantum-safe security protocols and architectures include the Quantum-Resistant Ledger (QRL) project, which is a blockchain platform that uses post-quantum cryptography to secure transactions and smart contracts, and the Quantum-Safe VPN (QSVPN) project, which is a virtual private network (VPN) protocol that uses post-quantum cryptography and QKD to provide secure and private communication over untrusted networks.

The development and deployment of quantum-safe security protocols and architectures is an important area of research and innovation, as it will be critical for ensuring the long-term security and resilience of our digital infrastructure in the face of advances in quantum computing.

However, the transition to quantum-safe security will also require significant efforts in terms of standardization, interoperability, and backward compatibility, as well as education and awareness-raising among developers, users, and policymakers.

Moreover, the development of quantum-safe security will also require careful consideration of the trade-offs between security, performance, and usability, as well as the potential risks and unintended consequences of these new technologies.

For example, the use of post-quantum cryptography may require larger key sizes and more computational resources compared to classical cryptography, which could impact the performance and scalability of certain applications and systems. Similarly, the use of QKD may require specialized hardware and infrastructure, which could limit its practicality and cost-effectiveness for certain use cases.

Additionally, the development of quantum-safe security may also raise new challenges and risks in terms of privacy, trust, and governance, as the use of these technologies may require the sharing of sensitive data and the reliance on trusted third parties or infrastructures.

To address these challenges and ensure the responsible and effective development and deployment of quantum-safe security, it will be important to engage in multistakeholder collaboration and dialogue, involving researchers, industry, governments, and civil society.

This may involve the creation of new standards, best practices, and governance frameworks for quantum-safe security, as well as the development of tools and methodologies for assessing and mitigating the risks and impacts of these technologies.

Ultimately, the goal of post-quantum cryptography and quantum-safe security is to ensure that our digital infrastructure remains secure and resilient in the face of the potential threats posed by quantum computing, and to enable the continued growth and innovation of the digital economy and society.

By working together to proactively address these challenges and opportunities, we can help to shape a quantum future that is not only more secure and advanced, but also more equitable, transparent, and accountable.

So let us continue to push the boundaries of what is possible with quantum-safe security, and work towards a future where the benefits of quantum technologies can be realized while also upholding our fundamental values and rights in the digital age.

Section 8.4: Quantum Machine Learning and its Applications in Cybersecurity

As we have discussed in the previous sections, quantum computing has the potential to revolutionize various aspects of cybersecurity, from cryptography and secure communication to threat detection and response. However, quantum computing is not just a tool for securing our digital infrastructure, but also a powerful enabler for the development of new and enhanced AI and machine learning techniques.

In particular, the intersection of quantum computing and machine learning has given rise to a new field of research known as quantum machine learning (QML), which aims to leverage the unique properties of quantum systems to   develop more efficient and effective algorithms for various machine learning tasks, such as classification, regression, clustering, and optimization.

Quantum machine learning is based on the idea that certain machine learning algorithms can be reformulated in terms of quantum operations and run on quantum computers, potentially providing exponential speedups over classical algorithms for certain types of problems.

For example, one of the most well-known quantum machine learning algorithms is the Harrow-Hassidim-Lloyd (HHL) algorithm, which is designed to solve linear systems of equations exponentially faster than classical algorithms. The HHL algorithm has been used to develop quantum versions of various machine learning algorithms, such as support vector machines (SVM), principal component analysis (PCA), and recommendation systems.

Another promising application of quantum machine learning is in the development of quantum neural networks (QNNs), which are artificial neural networks that are implemented using quantum circuits and quantum gates. Unlike classical neural networks, which are based on the computation of real-valued weights and activations, QNNs use quantum states and quantum operations to represent and process information, potentially providing more expressive and efficient models for certain types of data and tasks.

Some of the potential advantages of quantum neural networks include:

- Exponential speedup: QNNs can potentially provide exponential speedups over classical neural networks for certain types of problems, such as learning from high-dimensional or highly entangled data.

- Increased capacity: QNNs can potentially represent and learn more complex and expressive models than classical neural networks, due to the exponentially large state space of quantum systems.

- Noise resilience: QNNs can potentially be more resilient to certain types of noise and errors than classical neural networks, due to the inherent robustness of quantum error correction codes.

- Quantum feature extraction: QNNs can potentially learn and extract quantum features from data that are not accessible to classical neural networks, such as quantum correlations and entanglement.

However, the development and implementation of quantum neural networks also face significant challenges, such as the difficulty of designing and training quantum circuits, the limited size and quality of current quantum hardware, and the lack of clear theoretical and empirical evidence for the advantages of QNNs over classical neural networks.

Despite these challenges, there is growing interest and research in the application of quantum machine learning and quantum neural networks to various problems in cybersecurity, such as anomaly detection, malware classification, and network intrusion detection.

For example, some researchers have proposed using quantum machine learning algorithms, such as quantum support vector machines and quantum clustering, to detect and classify anomalous patterns in network traffic data, such as those caused by botnets, worms, or denial-of-service attacks. By leveraging the exponential speedup and increased capacity of quantum algorithms, these approaches could potentially provide more accurate and efficient detection of cyber threats than classical methods.

Other researchers have explored the use of quantum neural networks for malware classification and analysis, by training QNNs on large datasets of malware samples and benign files, and using the learned models to classify new and unknown malware samples. By leveraging the expressive power and noise resilience of QNNs, these approaches could potentially provide more robust and adaptive malware detection than classical machine learning methods.

Additionally, some researchers have proposed using quantum machine learning and quantum neural networks for network intrusion detection, by training models on network traffic data and using them to identify and classify potential intrusions and attacks. By leveraging the ability of QNNs to learn and extract complex patterns and correlations from high-dimensional data, these approaches could potentially provide more accurate and timely detection of network intrusions than classical methods.

Of course, the application of quantum machine learning and quantum neural networks to cybersecurity is still in its early stages, and there are many open questions and challenges to be addressed, such as the scalability and practicality of these approaches on real-world datasets and networks, the interpretability and explainability of the learned models, and the potential risks and unintended consequences of using quantum technologies for cybersecurity.

Moreover, the development and deployment of quantum machine learning and quantum neural networks for cybersecurity will also require significant advances in quantum hardware and software, as well as close collaboration between the quantum computing, machine learning, and cybersecurity communities.

Nevertheless, the potential of quantum machine learning and quantum neural networks to enhance and transform cybersecurity is significant, and it is an area of active research and innovation. By leveraging the unique properties and capabilities of quantum systems, we may be able to develop new and more powerful tools for detecting, understanding, and responding to cyber threats, and ultimately build a more secure and resilient digital future.

Some potential future directions for quantum machine learning and quantum neural networks in cybersecurity include:

- Quantum-enhanced threat intelligence: By leveraging quantum algorithms for data analysis and pattern recognition, we may be able to develop more accurate and timely methods for collecting, processing, and sharing threat intelligence data, such as indicators of compromise, attack vectors, and adversary tactics and techniques.

- Quantum-secured federated learning: By combining quantum cryptography and federated learning techniques, we may be able to enable the secure and privacy-preserving sharing and learning of cybersecurity models and data across multiple organizations and domains, without revealing sensitive information or exposing the models to attacks.

- Quantum-adaptive cybersecurity: By using quantum machine learning and quantum neural networks to continuously learn and adapt to new and evolving cyber threats, we may be able to develop more dynamic and responsive cybersecurity systems that can automatically detect, classify, and mitigate attacks in real-time, without requiring manual intervention or updates.

- Quantum-inspired classical algorithms: By studying and analyzing the principles and techniques behind quantum machine learning and quantum neural networks, we may be able to develop new and improved classical algorithms for cybersecurity that are inspired by quantum computing, but can run on classical hardware and provide similar benefits in terms of efficiency, robustness, and adaptability.

Of course, the realization of these and other potential applications of quantum machine learning and quantum neural networks in cybersecurity will require sustained research and development efforts, as well as careful consideration of the ethical, legal, and social implications of these technologies.

But if we can harness the power and potential of quantum machine learning and quantum neural networks in a responsible and beneficial way, we may be able to create a new paradigm for cybersecurity that is more intelligent, adaptive, and resilient than ever before.

So let us continue to explore and advance the frontiers of quantum machine learning and its applications in cybersecurity, and work towards a future where the intersection of these two transformative fields can help us to build a more secure, trustworthy, and prosperous digital world for all.

Section 8.5: Quantum Cybersecurity Challenges and Future Directions

As we have seen throughout this chapter, quantum computing and quantum technologies have the potential to revolutionize various aspects of cybersecurity, from cryptography and secure communication to machine learning and threat detection.

However, the development and deployment of quantum cybersecurity solutions also come with significant challenges and risks that need to be carefully considered and addressed.

One of the main challenges of quantum cybersecurity is the need for quantum-safe cryptography and security protocols that can resist attacks by quantum computers. While there is ongoing research and development of post-quantum cryptographic algorithms and quantum key distribution methods, there are still many open questions and uncertainties about their security, efficiency, and practicality.

Moreover, the transition from classical to quantum-safe cryptography will require significant efforts in terms of standardization, interoperability, and backward compatibility, as well as education and awareness-raising among developers, users, and policymakers. This transition will also need to be carefully managed to avoid creating new vulnerabilities or attack surfaces, and to ensure the continued availability and reliability of critical systems and services.

Another challenge of quantum cybersecurity is the potential for quantum computers to be used as a tool for cyber attacks and malicious activities. Just as quantum computers can be used to break classical cryptography, they can also be used to speed up and optimize various types of cyber attacks, such as password guessing, network scanning, and social engineering.

Moreover, the development of quantum technologies may also enable new types of cyber attacks that are not possible with classical computers, such as quantum hacking, quantum eavesdropping, and quantum denial-of-service attacks. These types of attacks could potentially exploit the unique properties of quantum systems, such as superposition, entanglement, and measurement, to bypass or compromise classical security controls and defenses.

To mitigate these risks, it will be important to develop and deploy quantum-safe security solutions that can detect, prevent, and respond to quantum-enabled cyber attacks, as well as to continue to advance the field of quantum cryptanalysis and quantum security testing.

A third challenge of quantum cybersecurity is the need for quantum-secure communication and networking infrastructures that can enable the secure and reliable transmission of quantum information and quantum keys. While there is ongoing research and development of quantum communication protocols and quantum networks, such as quantum key distribution and quantum repeaters, there are still many technical and logistical challenges to be overcome, such as the limited distance and rate of quantum communication, the need for specialized hardware and infrastructure, and the vulnerability of quantum channels to noise and interference.

Moreover, the deployment of quantum communication and networking solutions will require significant investments in terms of research, development, and infrastructure, as well as cooperation and coordination among various stakeholders, such as governments, industry, academia, and standards bodies.

Despite these challenges, there are also many exciting opportunities and future directions for quantum cybersecurity that could help to address these challenges and realize the full potential of quantum technologies for securing our digital world.

Some of these future directions include:

- Quantum-safe cryptography: Continuing to develop and standardize post-quantum cryptographic algorithms and protocols that can provide long-term security against quantum attacks, while also being efficient, interoperable, and backward-compatible with existing systems and applications.

- Quantum key distribution: Advancing the theory and practice of quantum key distribution methods that can enable the secure and confidential exchange of cryptographic keys over long distances and complex networks, using the principles of quantum physics and cryptography.

- Quantum networking: Building and deploying quantum communication and networking infrastructures that can support the secure and reliable transmission of quantum information and enable the development of new quantum applications and services, such as quantum sensing, quantum metrology, and quantum computing.

- Quantum machine learning: Leveraging the power of quantum computing and machine learning to develop new and enhanced methods for cybersecurity, such as quantum anomaly detection, quantum malware classification, and quantum network intrusion detection, that can provide more efficient, accurate, and adaptive security solutions.

- Quantum security testing: Developing and applying new methods and tools for testing and validating the security of quantum systems and protocols, such as quantum cryptanalysis, quantum fuzzing, and quantum penetration testing, to identify and mitigate potential vulnerabilities and attack vectors.

- Quantum risk management: Integrating quantum technologies and quantum security considerations into existing risk management frameworks and processes, such as threat modeling, risk assessment, and incident response, to ensure a comprehensive and holistic approach to cybersecurity in the quantum era.

- Quantum governance: Establishing and promoting policies, standards, and best practices for the responsible and ethical development and use of quantum technologies, such as quantum cryptography, quantum machine learning, and quantum networking, to ensure their alignment with social values and norms and to prevent their misuse or abuse.

Of course, realizing these future directions for quantum cybersecurity will require sustained investments, collaborations, and innovations across multiple domains and sectors, as well as a strong commitment to the principles of openness, transparency, and inclusivity.

Moreover, it will also require a proactive and adaptive approach to cybersecurity that can anticipate and respond to the rapidly evolving landscape of quantum technologies and their implications for security, privacy, and trust.

But if we can rise to these challenges and seize these opportunities, we have the potential to create a new paradigm for cybersecurity that is more secure, resilient, and adaptive than ever before – a paradigm that can leverage the power of quantum technologies to protect our digital assets, identities, and freedoms, while also promoting the responsible and beneficial use of these technologies for the betterment of society as a whole.

So let us continue to push the boundaries of what is possible with quantum cybersecurity, and work towards a future where the intersection of quantum computing and cybersecurity can help us to build a more secure, trustworthy, and prosperous digital world for all.

Chapter 8 Conclusion

In this chapter, we have explored the exciting and rapidly evolving field of quantum computing and its implications for cybersecurity and artificial intelligence. We have seen how the unique properties and capabilities of quantum systems, such as superposition, entanglement, and interference, can be harnessed to develop new and enhanced methods for cryptography, machine learning, and cybersecurity.

We have discussed the potential of quantum computers to break classical cryptographic algorithms and the need for post-quantum cryptography and quantum-safe security solutions that can resist attacks by both classical and quantum adversaries. We have also examined the concept of quantum machine learning and its applications in cybersecurity, such as anomaly detection, malware classification, and network intrusion detection.

Moreover, we have highlighted some of the key challenges and risks associated with the development and deployment of quantum technologies for cybersecurity, such as the need for standardization, interoperability, and backward compatibility, the potential for quantum computers to be used as a tool for cyber attacks, and the technical and logistical challenges of building and deploying quantum communication and networking infrastructures.

Despite these challenges, we have also identified many exciting opportunities and future directions for quantum cybersecurity, such as the continued development and standardization of post-quantum cryptography and quantum key distribution, the advancement of quantum networking and communication protocols, the leveraging of quantum machine learning for enhanced cybersecurity, the development of new methods and tools for quantum security testing and validation, the integration of quantum technologies into existing risk management frameworks and processes, and the establishment of policies, standards, and best practices for the responsible and ethical development and use of quantum technologies.

As we have seen throughout this chapter, the intersection of quantum computing and cybersecurity represents a new frontier in the ongoing battle to secure our digital world against an ever-evolving landscape of cyber threats and vulnerabilities. By harnessing the power and potential of quantum technologies, we have the opportunity to create a new paradigm for cybersecurity that is more secure, resilient, and adaptive than ever before – a paradigm that can leverage the unique properties and capabilities of quantum systems to protect our critical infrastructure, data, and identities from both classical and quantum attacks.

However, realizing this vision will require more than just technological innovation and progress. It will also require a deep understanding of the complex interplay between quantum computing, cybersecurity, and artificial intelligence, as well as a strong commitment to the principles of responsible and ethical innovation, multistakeholder collaboration and coordination, and proactive and adaptive risk management.

Moreover, it will require ongoing investments in research, education, and training to develop the next generation of quantum cybersecurity professionals and to foster a culture of continuous learning and improvement in the face of rapid technological change and uncertainty.

Ultimately, the success of quantum cybersecurity will depend on our ability to balance the benefits and risks of these powerful new technologies, and to ensure that they are developed and used in a way that promotes the greater good of society, while also respecting individual privacy, autonomy, and human rights.

As we look to the future of quantum computing and its implications for cybersecurity and artificial intelligence, we must remain vigilant, proactive, and adaptive in the face of new and emerging threats and challenges. We must continue to push the boundaries of what is possible with these technologies, while also being mindful of their limitations and potential unintended consequences.

At the same time, we must also work to build bridges and foster collaboration across disciplines, sectors, and borders, recognizing that the challenges and opportunities of quantum cybersecurity are not just technical or scientific in nature, but also social, economic, and political.

By working together to advance the state of the art in quantum cybersecurity, while also grappling with the complex ethical, legal, and societal implications of these technologies, we can help to shape a future that is not only more secure and technologically advanced, but also more just, equitable, and humane.

So let us embrace the challenges and opportunities of quantum cybersecurity with courage, creativity, and compassion, and let us work towards a future where the power of quantum computing can be harnessed for the greater good of all humanity, while also safeguarding the fundamental values and principles that define us as individuals and as a society.

The road ahead may be uncertain and the journey may be long, but the destination is clear and the stakes are high. With quantum computing as our guide and human ingenuity as our compass, we can navigate the uncharted waters of this new frontier with confidence, resilience, and hope, and emerge stronger, wiser, and more secure than ever before.

NINE

— • —

CHAPTER 9: AI FOR CYBERSECURITY POLICIES AND GOVERNANCE

Section 9.1: Introduction to AI Governance and Policy Considerations

The rapid advancements in artificial intelligence (AI) and its increasing integration into various aspects of our lives have brought about significant opportunities as well as challenges. As AI systems become more sophisticated and autonomous, it is crucial to consider the governance and policy implications of these technologies, particularly in the context of cybersecurity.

AI governance refers to the principles, policies, and practices that guide the development, deployment, and use of AI systems to ensure that they are safe, reliable, and aligned with human values and societal norms. It encompasses a wide range of considerations, including ethics, accountability, transparency, fairness, privacy, security, and safety.

In the realm of cybersecurity, AI governance is especially critical due to the high stakes involved. AI systems are being increasingly used for a variety of cybersecurity tasks, such as threat detection, incident response, network monitoring, and risk assessment. While these applications have the potential to significantly enhance our cybersecurity capabilities, they also raise important questions and concerns that need to be carefully addressed.

One key policy consideration for AI in cybersecurity is the issue of transparency and explainability. Many AI systems, particularly those based on deep learning, are often seen as "black boxes" that make decisions based on complex and opaque algorithms. This lack of transparency can make it difficult to understand how these systems arrive at their conclusions and to hold them accountable for their actions.

In the context of cybersecurity, this opacity can be particularly problematic. For example, if an AI system incorrectly identifies a legitimate network activity as malicious and takes action to block or disrupt it, it may be difficult to determine why the system made that decision and how to prevent similar mistakes in the future. This lack   of transparency can also erode trust in AI-based cybersecurity solutions and make it harder for organizations to comply with regulatory requirements around data protection and privacy.

Another important policy consideration is the issue of bias and fairness in AI systems. AI algorithms are only as unbiased as the data they are trained on, and if that data contains historical biases or underrepresents certain groups, the resulting AI models may perpetuate or even amplify those biases.

In the cybersecurity context, biased AI systems could lead to disproportionate targeting or profiling of certain individuals or groups, such as subjecting them to additional scrutiny or restricting their access to resources. This not only raises serious ethical concerns but could also open up organizations to legal and reputational risks.

Privacy is another key policy consideration for AI in cybersecurity. Many AI-based cybersecurity solutions rely on the collection and analysis of vast amounts of data, including potentially sensitive information about individuals and their online activities. If not properly protected, this data could be vulnerable to breaches, misuse, or unauthorized access, compromising individual privacy and security.

Organizations deploying AI for cybersecurity need to have robust data governance policies in place to ensure that data is collected, stored, and used in a responsible and compliant manner. This includes providing clear notice and obtaining consent from individuals, implementing strong security controls to protect data, and being transparent about how data is being used by AI systems.

Accountability is another critical aspect of AI governance in cybersecurity. When AI systems make decisions or take actions that have significant consequences, there needs to be clarity around who is responsible and liable for those outcomes.

In the case of a security breach or incident involving an AI system, for example, it may not always be clear whether the responsibility lies with the developers of the AI system, the organization deploying it, or the individuals interacting with it. Establishing clear lines of accountability and liability is essential for ensuring that AI is used responsibly and that any negative impacts can be properly addressed and remedied.

Safety and control are also important policy considerations for AI in cybersecurity. As AI systems become more autonomous and sophisticated, there is a risk that they could behave in unpredictable or harmful ways, particularly in complex and dynamic environments like cyberspace.

Ensuring that AI systems are safe and controllable requires careful design, testing, and oversight throughout their development and deployment. This includes techniques like adversarial testing to identify and mitigate potential vulnerabilities, as well as human-in-the-loop approaches to maintain meaningful human control and oversight over AI decision-making.

Finally, collaboration and coordination are essential for effective AI governance in cybersecurity. Given the global and interconnected nature of cyberspace, no single organization or nation can address these challenges alone. Developing consistent and interoperable approaches to AI governance requires multi-stakeholder engagement and international cooperation.

This includes not only collaboration among technical experts and policymakers, but also engagement with civil society, academia, and the private sector to ensure that AI governance frameworks are inclusive, equitable, and aligned with diverse societal values and priorities.

Effective AI governance in cybersecurity is not just a matter of developing the right policies and principles, but also of putting them into practice through concrete mechanisms and processes. This requires ongoing monitoring, assessment, and adjustment to ensure that governance frameworks remain relevant and effective as AI technologies and cybersecurity threats continue to evolve.

Some key mechanisms and processes for AI governance in cybersecurity include:

- Risk assessment and management: Regularly assessing the potential risks and impacts of AI systems in cybersecurity, and developing strategies to mitigate and manage those risks throughout the AI lifecycle.

- Ethical and human rights impact assessments: Systematically evaluating the potential ethical and human rights implications of AI systems in cybersecurity, and taking steps to prevent and address any negative impacts.

- Transparency and accountability mechanisms: Implementing mechanisms to ensure that the development and use of AI in cybersecurity is transparent, explainable, and accountable, such as through documentation, auditing, and reporting requirements.

- Stakeholder engagement and public participation: Engaging diverse stakeholders and the broader public in the development and governance of AI in cybersecurity, to ensure that these technologies are aligned with societal values and priorities.

- Regulatory and policy frameworks: Developing and implementing consistent and interoperable regulatory and policy frameworks for AI governance in cybersecurity, at both the national and international levels.

- Capacity building and education: Building the necessary skills, knowledge, and capacity among policymakers, practitioners, and the public to effectively govern and engage with AI in cybersecurity.

Ultimately, the goal of AI governance in cybersecurity is to ensure that these powerful technologies are developed and used in ways that promote security, privacy, fairness, and accountability, while also fostering innovation and realizing the full potential benefits of AI for society.

Achieving this goal will require ongoing collaboration, learning, and adaptation as the AI and cybersecurity landscapes continue to evolve. It will also require a willingness to grapple with difficult questions and trade-offs, and to make hard choices in the face of complex and often competing priorities.

But if we can rise to this challenge and put in place effective governance frameworks and practices for AI in cybersecurity, we can help to build a future in which these technologies are not only more secure and reliable, but also more trustworthy and beneficial for all.

In the following sections, we will explore some of the key policy and governance issues and approaches for AI in cybersecurity in more depth, looking at topics such as AI ethics and principles, AI security and robustness, and AI governance frameworks and standards. Through this exploration, we aim to provide a comprehensive and actionable roadmap for policymakers, practitioners, and other stakeholders looking to navigate the complex landscape of AI governance in cybersecurity.

Section 9.2: AI Ethics and Principles for Cybersecurity

The development and deployment of AI systems in cybersecurity raise significant ethical considerations that must be carefully addressed to ensure that these technologies are not only effective and secure but also fair, transparent, and accountable. AI ethics refers to the principles and values that should guide the design, development, and use of AI systems to ensure that they are aligned with human values and promote the well-being of individuals and society.

In the context of cybersecurity, AI ethics takes on particular importance due to the high stakes involved. Cybersecurity AI systems often have access to sensitive data and can make decisions or take actions that have significant consequences for individuals and organizations. As such, it is crucial that these systems are developed and used in ways that respect fundamental human rights, such as privacy, non-discrimination, and due process.

One of the key ethical principles for AI in cybersecurity is transparency. Given the opaque and complex nature of many AI algorithms, it can be difficult for individuals to understand how these systems make decisions and what factors they take into account. This lack of transparency can undermine trust in AI systems and make it difficult to hold them accountable for their actions.

To promote transparency, organizations developing and deploying cybersecurity AI should be clear and open about how these systems work, what data they use, and how they make decisions. This may involve providing clear and accessible explanations of AI algorithms and models, as well as enabling independent auditing and testing of these systems to verify their performance and identify potential biases or errors.

Fairness and non-discrimination are also critical ethical principles for AI in cybersecurity. AI systems can perpetuate or amplify existing societal biases if they are trained on biased data or if their algorithms are not designed to be fair and inclusive. In the cybersecurity context, this could lead to disproportionate targeting or profiling of certain individuals or groups, or to the denial of access to resources or services based on protected characteristics such as race, gender, or religion.

To promote fairness and non-discrimination, organizations should take steps to ensure that the data used to train cybersecurity AI systems is diverse and representative and that the algorithms used are tested for bias and fairness. They should also provide mechanisms for individuals to challenge or appeal decisions made by AI systems and to seek redress for any harmful or discriminatory impacts.

Accountability is another key ethical principle for AI in cybersecurity. Given the potential for AI systems to cause harm or make mistakes, it is essential that there are clear lines of responsibility and liability for their actions. This includes not only the developers and deployers of AI systems but also the individuals and organizations that use them or are affected by their decisions.

To promote accountability, organizations should establish clear governance frameworks and processes for the development and use of cybersecurity AI, including mechanisms for monitoring and auditing these systems, as well as processes for reporting and addressing any incidents or violations. They should also ensure that there are appropriate legal and regulatory frameworks in place to hold AI systems and their operators accountable for any harms or abuses.

Privacy is also a critical ethical consideration for AI in cybersecurity. Many cybersecurity AI systems rely on the collection and analysis of vast amounts of data, including sensitive personal information. If this data is not properly protected or if it is used in ways that violate individual privacy rights, it can lead to serious harms and undermine trust in these systems.

To promote privacy, organizations should ensure that cybersecurity AI systems are designed and used in ways that minimize the collection and retention of personal data and that provide individuals with appropriate notice and control over their data. They should also implement strong technical and organizational measures to protect data from unauthorized access, use, or disclosure.

Finally, human agency and oversight are essential ethical principles for AI in cybersecurity. While AI systems can provide valuable insights and automate certain tasks, it is important that they do not completely replace human judgment and decision-making. There should always be meaningful human control and oversight over the actions and decisions of cybersecurity AI systems, particularly in high-stakes situations where the consequences of errors or biases could be severe.

To promote human agency and oversight, organizations should ensure that cybersecurity AI systems are designed and used in ways that preserve human control and intervention, such as through human-in-the-loop approaches or the ability to override or modify AI decisions. They should also provide training and support to help individuals understand and effectively interact with these systems.

In addition to these core ethical principles, there are also a number of best practices and guidelines that organizations can follow to promote responsible and trustworthy AI in cybersecurity. These include:

- Developing and adhering to clear ethical principles and guidelines for the design, development, and use of cybersecurity AI systems, aligned with international human rights standards and best practices.

- Conducting regular risk assessments and impact assessments to identify and mitigate potential harms or unintended consequences of cybersecurity AI systems.

- Engaging in multi-stakeholder collaboration and dialogue to ensure that the development and governance of cybersecurity AI is informed by diverse perspectives and expertise.

- Investing in research and development to advance the state of the art in secure, transparent, and accountable AI systems for cybersecurity.

- Providing training and education to help individuals and organizations understand and effectively use cybersecurity AI systems in ways that are ethical and responsible.

Ultimately, the goal of AI ethics in cybersecurity is to ensure that these powerful technologies are developed and used in ways that promote the public good and respect fundamental human rights and values. By adhering to these principles and best practices, organizations can help to build trust in cybersecurity AI and ensure that these systems are a force for good in the world.

However, implementing AI ethics in cybersecurity is not without its challenges. There may be tensions or trade-offs between different ethical principles, such as between transparency and security or between fairness and efficiency. There may also be challenges in translating high-level ethical principles into concrete practices and processes, particularly in complex and rapidly evolving domains like cybersecurity.

To address these challenges, it is important to engage in ongoing dialogue and collaboration among diverse stakeholders, including policymakers, practitioners, researchers, civil society organizations, and affected communities. It is also important to continually monitor and assess the impacts of cybersecurity AI systems and to be willing to adapt and adjust governance frameworks and practices as needed.

Effective AI ethics in cybersecurity requires a combination of proactive foresight, ongoing vigilance, and a commitment to continuous learning and improvement. It also requires a willingness to make hard choices and to prioritize the well-being and rights of individuals and society over short-term gains or efficiencies.

But if we can rise to this challenge and put in place robust and adaptive ethical frameworks and practices for AI in cybersecurity, we can help to ensure that these technologies are developed and used in ways that are not only effective and secure but also fair, transparent, and accountable. And in doing so, we can help to build a future in which AI and cybersecurity are forces for good that promote the well-being and flourishing of all.

Section 9.3: AI Security and Robustness for Cybersecurity Systems

As AI systems become increasingly integrated into cybersecurity applications, ensuring their security and robustness is of paramount importance. AI security refers to the protection of AI systems against malicious attacks, unauthorized access, or unintended behavior that could compromise their integrity, confidentiality, or availability. AI robustness, on the other hand, refers to the ability of AI systems to maintain their performance and reliability in the face of changing or unforeseen circumstances, such as new or evolving cyber threats.

The security and robustness of cybersecurity AI systems are critical for several reasons. Firstly, these systems often have access to sensitive data and control critical infrastructure, making them attractive targets for malicious actors. A successful attack on a cybersecurity AI system could result in data breaches, system disruptions, or even physical harm.

Secondly, the complexity and opacity of many AI algorithms make them vulnerable to various types of attacks and manipulations. For example, adversarial attacks involve crafting input data that is specifically designed to deceive or mislead AI models, causing them to make incorrect or harmful decisions. Similarly, data poisoning attacks involve manipulating the training data used to build AI models to introduce biases or backdoors that can be exploited later.

Finally, the dynamic and unpredictable nature of cyber threats means that cybersecurity AI systems must be able to adapt and maintain their performance in the face of changing and unforeseen circumstances. If these systems are not robust and resilient, they may fail to detect or respond to new or evolving threats, leaving organizations vulnerable to attacks.

To address these challenges and ensure the security and robustness of cybersecurity AI systems, organizations should adopt a range of best practices and techniques, such as:

- Secure development practices: Ensuring that cybersecurity AI systems are designed and developed using secure coding practices, such as input validation, error handling, and cryptographic techniques.

- Adversarial testing: Conducting regular testing of cybersecurity AI systems using adversarial examples and other techniques to identify and mitigate potential vulnerabilities and weaknesses.

- Anomaly detection: Implementing anomaly detection techniques to identify unusual or suspicious behavior in cybersecurity AI systems that could indicate a security breach or malfunction.

- Redundancy and diversity: Building redundancy and diversity into cybersecurity AI systems, such as using multiple models or algorithms to provide backup and cross-check-ing capabilities.

- Continuous monitoring and updating: Continuously monitoring the performance and behavior of cybersecurity AI systems and regularly updating them to address new threats or vulnerabilities.

- Interpretability and explainability: Developing techniques to make cybersecurity AI systems more interpretable and explainable, so that their decision-making processes can be understood and audited.

- Secure hardware and infrastructure: Ensuring that the hardware and infrastructure used to run cybersecurity AI systems are secure and protected against physical and cyber attacks.

In addition to these technical measures, organizations should also establish clear policies and processes for the governance and oversight of cybersecurity AI systems. This includes developing and enforcing standards and guidelines for the development, testing, deployment, and monitoring of these systems, as well as establishing mechanisms for reporting and responding to security incidents or violations.

One important aspect of AI security and robustness in cybersecurity is the need for collaboration and information sharing among organizations and stakeholders. Given the global and interconnected nature of cyber threats, no single organization can address these challenges alone. Sharing threat intelligence, best practices, and lessons learned can help organizations to better understand and mitigate the risks associated with cybersecurity AI systems.

Another important consideration is the need for human oversight and control over cybersecurity AI systems. While these systems can provide valuable automation and decision support capabilities, it is important that they do not operate entirely autonomously without human intervention or supervision. There should always be mechanisms for human operators to monitor, override or shut down AI systems if necessary, particularly in high-stakes or safety-critical situations.

Finally, it is important to recognize that ensuring the security and robustness of cybersecurity AI systems is an ongoing and evolving challenge. As new threats and vulnerabilities emerge, organizations must continually adapt and update their approaches to AI security and robustness. This requires ongoing investment in research and development, as well as a commitment to continuous learning and improvement.

Some key areas for future research and innovation in AI security and robustness for cybersecurity include:

- Adversarial machine learning: Continuing to develop and refine techniques for detecting and mitigating adversarial attacks on AI systems, such as adversarial training, defensive distillation, and generative adversarial networks (GANs).

- Secure and privacy-preserving AI: Developing techniques for building AI systems that can operate securely and preserve privacy, such as federated learning, homomorphic encryption, and differential privacy.

- Explainable and interpretable AI: Advancing techniques for making AI systems more transparent and understandable, such as rule extraction, feature importance analysis, and counterfactual explanations.

- Autonomous security: Exploring the use of AI and other autonomous systems for cybersecurity applications, such as automated threat detection, incident response, and policy enforcement, while ensuring appropriate human oversight and control.

- Quantum-safe AI: Preparing for the potential impact of quantum computing on AI security and robustness, such as developing quantum-resistant cryptographic algorithms and protocols.

Ultimately, the goal of AI security and robustness in cybersecurity is to ensure that these powerful technologies are developed and used in ways that are secure, reliable, and trustworthy. By adopting best practices and investing in ongoing research and innovation, organizations can help to build a future in which AI and cybersecurity are mutually reinforcing and beneficial to society as a whole.

In the words of Andrew Wiles, the mathematician who proved Fermat's Last Theorem:

"The tools of modern technology are not just enabling us to do old things better, they're enabling us to do   things that were previously impossible. But with that power comes a great responsibility to ensure that we use these tools wisely and ethically."

As we continue to push the boundaries of what is possible with AI and cybersecurity, it is essential that we keep this responsibility at the forefront of our minds and actions. We must work to ensure that the benefits of these technologies are realized while mitigating their risks and potential harms.

By fostering a culture of security, ethics, and responsibility in the development and use of AI for cybersecurity, we can help to build a future that is not only more secure and resilient but also more just, equitable, and beneficial for all.

Section 9.4: AI Governance Frameworks and Standards for Cybersecurity

Effective governance of AI in cybersecurity requires not only adherence to ethical principles and best practices but also the development and implementation of clear frameworks and standards to guide the design, development, deployment, and use of these systems.

AI governance frameworks provide a structured approach to managing the risks and opportunities associated with AI in cybersecurity, while also promoting transparency, accountability, and trust in these systems. These frameworks typically include a set of principles, guidelines, and processes for the governance of AI, as well as mechanisms for monitoring, auditing, and enforcing compliance.

Some key elements of AI governance frameworks for cybersecurity include:

- Risk assessment and management: Regularly assessing the risks and potential impacts of AI systems in cybersecurity, including risks to security, privacy, fairness, and other ethical considerations, and developing strategies to mitigate and manage these risks.

- Policies and procedures: Establishing clear policies and procedures for the development, testing, deployment, and use of AI in cybersecurity, including guidelines for data collection and use, model training and validation, and human oversight and control.

- Roles and responsibilities: Defining clear roles and responsibilities for the various stakeholders involved in the governance of AI in cybersecurity, including developers, operators, users, and regulators, and ensuring that there are appropriate mechanisms for accountability and redress.

- Monitoring and auditing: Implementing mechanisms for monitoring and auditing the performance and behavior of AI systems in cybersecurity, including regular testing and evaluation, incident reporting and response, and compliance with relevant laws and regulations.

- Transparency and explainability: Ensuring that the decision-making processes and outputs of AI systems in cybersecurity are transparent and explainable to relevant stakeholders, including developers, operators, users, and regulators.

- Stakeholder engagement: Engaging with a wide range of stakeholders, including industry, academia, civil society, and government, to ensure that the governance of AI in cybersecurity is informed by diverse perspectives and expertise.

In addition to these general principles, there are also a number of specific standards and guidelines that have been developed to support the governance of AI in cybersecurity. These include:

- The NIST AI Risk Management Framework: Developed by the National Institute of Standards and Technology (NIST), this framework provides a structured approach to managing the risks associated with AI systems, including guidance on risk assessment, mitigation, and communication.

- The IEEE Ethical Aligned Design: Developed by the Institute of Electrical and Electronics Engineers (IEEE), this document provides a set of principles and guidelines for the ethical and responsible design of autonomous and intelligent systems, including AI systems used in cybersecurity.

- The OECD Principles on AI: Developed by the Organisation for Economic Co-operation and Development (OECD), these principles provide a framework for the responsible development and use of AI, including principles related to transparency, accountability, and privacy.

- The EU Ethics Guidelines for Trustworthy AI: Developed by the European Commission's High-Level Expert Group on AI, these guidelines provide a framework for the ethical and trustworthy development and use of AI, including principles related to human agency and oversight, privacy and data governance, and societal and environmental well-being.

While these frameworks and standards provide valuable guidance for the governance of AI in cybersecurity, it is important to recognize that they are not one-size-fits-all solutions. The specific governance approaches and practices adopted by organizations will depend on a range of factors, including the nature and complexity of the AI systems being used, the level of risk and potential impact associated with these systems, and the regulatory and legal environment in which they operate.

Moreover, effective AI governance in cybersecurity requires ongoing monitoring, evaluation, and adaptation to ensure that governance frameworks and practices remain relevant and effective as the technology and threat landscape continue to evolve. This requires a commitment to continuous learning and improvement, as well as a willingness to engage in ongoing dialogue and collaboration with diverse stakeholders.

One key challenge in implementing AI governance frameworks and standards for cybersecurity is the need to balance the benefits and risks of these technologies. While AI has the potential to significantly enhance cybersecurity capabilities and automate many routine tasks, it also introduces new risks and challenges, such as the potential for bias, errors, and unintended consequences.

To address these challenges, organizations must take a proactive and holistic approach to AI governance, one that considers not only the technical aspects of these systems but also their broader social, economic, and political implications. This may involve engaging in public dialogue and debate around the ethical and societal implications of AI in cybersecurity, as well as working to build trust and confidence in these systems among stakeholders and the general public.

Another important consideration is the need for international cooperation and coordination in the governance of AI in cybersecurity. Given the global and interconnected nature of cyberspace, effective governance of these technologies requires a shared understanding and approach across national borders and jurisdictions.

This may involve the development of international standards and best practices for AI governance in cybersecurity, as well as mechanisms for sharing information and collaborating on the development and deployment of these technologies. It may also require the establishment of global frameworks for accountability and redress in the event of harm or abuse arising from the use of AI in cybersecurity.

Ultimately, the goal of AI governance frameworks and standards for cybersecurity is to ensure that these technologies are developed and used in ways that are secure, reliable, and aligned with human values and societal priorities. By adopting a proactive, collaborative, and adaptive approach to AI governance, organizations can help to build a future in which the benefits of these technologies are realized while mitigating their risks and potential harms.

As Turing Award winner Geoffrey Hinton has said:

"The danger of AI is not that it will make us obsolete; the danger is that we will use it to make bad decisions. We need to think about how we can control these systems and use them for good."

By embracing the principles and practices of responsible AI governance in cybersecurity, we can work to ensure that these powerful technologies are used for good, and that they support the creation of a more secure, just, and equitable digital future for all.

Section 9.5: The Future of AI Governance in Cybersecurity

The rapid pace of technological change and the increasing integration of AI into all aspects of our lives and work have made the governance of AI in cybersecurity a critical priority for organizations, governments, and society as a whole. As we look to the future, it is clear that the challenges and opportunities associated with AI governance in cybersecurity will only continue to grow and evolve.

One of the key drivers of this evolution will be the continued advancement of AI technologies themselves. As AI systems become more sophisticated and autonomous, the risks and potential impacts associated with their use in cybersecurity will also increase. This will require ongoing research and innovation to develop new approaches to AI governance that can keep pace with these technological changes.

Some of the key areas where we can expect to see significant developments in AI governance for cybersecurity in the coming years include:

- Explainable AI: As AI systems become more complex and opaque, there will be a growing need for techniques and tools that can make these systems more transparent and explainable to human users and regulators. This will be particularly important in high-stakes domains like cybersecurity, where the decisions and actions of AI systems can have significant consequences.

- Adversarial AI: The use of AI to develop more sophisticated and targeted cyber attacks will require new approaches to AI security and robustness, including the development of adversarial AI techniques that can detect and defend against these attacks.

- Human-AI collaboration: As AI systems become more integrated into cybersecurity workflows and decision-making processes, there will be a need for new models of human-AI collaboration that can leverage the strengths of both humans and machines while also ensuring appropriate oversight and control.

- Responsible AI: The ethical and societal implications of AI in cybersecurity will continue to be a major focus of AI governance efforts, with a growing emphasis on developing and implementing principles and practices for responsible AI that prioritize fairness, transparency, accountability, and human rights.

- Global cooperation: Given the global and interconnected nature of cyberspace, effective AI governance in cybersecurity will require increased international cooperation and coordination, including the development of shared standards, best practices, and mechanisms for accountability and redress.

To meet these challenges and opportunities, organizations and policymakers will need to adopt a proactive and adaptive approach to AI governance in cybersecurity. This will require ongoing investment in research and development, as well as collaboration and dialogue among diverse stakeholders, including industry, academia, civil society, and government.

Some key strategies and recommendations for advancing AI governance in cybersecurity in the future include:

- Developing and implementing clear and consistent policies and procedures for the design, development, deployment, and use of AI in cybersecurity, based on established ethical principles and best practices.

- Investing in research and development to advance the state of the art in AI security, robustness, and interpretability, as well as in the social and ethical implications of these technologies.

- Building capacity and expertise in AI governance among cybersecurity professionals, policymakers, and other stakeholders through education, training, and skills development programs.

- Fostering multi-stakeholder collaboration and dialogue to ensure that the development and governance of AI in cybersecurity is informed by diverse perspectives and expertise, and that the benefits and risks of these technologies are widely understood and addressed.

- Promoting the development and adoption of international standards and best practices for AI governance in cybersecurity, as well as mechanisms for monitoring, auditing, and enforcing compliance with these standards.

Ultimately, the goal of AI governance in cybersecurity should be to ensure that these powerful technologies are developed and used in ways that promote security, privacy, fairness, accountability, and human values, while also fostering innovation and realizing the full potential of AI for cybersecurity and society as a whole.

To achieve this goal, we will need to embrace a culture of responsible innovation and governance in AI and cybersecurity, one that prioritizes the well-being and flourishing of individuals and communities, and that seeks to create a future in which the benefits of these technologies are widely shared and their risks and potential harms are effectively mitigated.

In the words of Max Tegmark, professor of physics at MIT and co-founder of the Future of Life Institute:

"The future is not something that just happens to us; it's something we create. We have the power to shape the future of AI, and with it, the future of cybersecurity and society as a whole. Let's use that power wisely, and work together to build a future that reflects our deepest values and aspirations."

As we look to the future of AI governance in cybersecurity, it is clear that we have both an opportunity and a responsibility to shape these technologies in ways that promote the greater good. By embracing the principles and practices of responsible AI governance, and by working together across disciplines and sectors to address the challenges and opportunities ahead, we can help to build a future in which AI and cybersecurity are forces for good, and in which the benefits of these technologies are realized for the betterment of all.

Chapter 9 Conclusion

In this chapter, we have explored the critical role of AI governance and policy in ensuring the responsible and effective development and use of AI technologies in cybersecurity. We have seen how the increasing integration of AI into cybersecurity systems and applications raises a range of ethical, social, and technical challenges that must be carefully addressed to ensure that these technologies are secure, reliable, and aligned with human values and societal priorities.

We started by examining the key policy considerations and ethical principles that should guide the governance of AI in cybersecurity, including transparency, fairness, accountability, privacy, and human agency. We discussed the importance of developing and implementing clear policies and procedures for the design, development, deployment, and use of AI in cybersecurity, as well as the need for ongoing monitoring, auditing, and enforcement of these policies.

We then delved into the specific challenges and best practices associated with ensuring the security and robustness of AI systems in cybersecurity, including techniques for adversarial testing, anomaly detection, interpretability, and secure development. We highlighted the importance of investing in ongoing research and development to advance the state of the art in AI security and robustness, as well as the need for collaboration and information sharing among organizations and stakeholders.

Next, we explored the role of AI governance frameworks and standards in providing a structured approach to managing the risks and opportunities associated with AI in cybersecurity. We discussed some of the key frameworks and standards that have been developed to date, including the NIST AI Risk Management Framework, the IEEE Ethical Aligned Design, and the EU Ethics Guidelines for Trustworthy AI, and highlighted the importance of adopting a proactive, collaborative, and adaptive approach to

AI governance.

Finally, we looked to the future of AI governance in cybersecurity, and discussed some of the key challenges and opportunities that lie ahead. We highlighted the need for ongoing investment in research and development, as well as collaboration and dialogue among diverse stakeholders, to ensure that AI governance keeps pace with the rapid advancement of these technologies. We also emphasized the importance of responsible innovation and the need to prioritize the well-being and flourishing of individuals and communities in the development and use of AI in cybersecurity.

Throughout this chapter, we have seen that effective AI governance in cybersecurity requires a multifaceted and ongoing effort that involves technical, social, and policy considerations. It requires a commitment to ethical principles and best practices, as well as a willingness to engage in ongoing learning, adaptation, and collaboration in the face of rapid technological change and evolving societal expectations.

Ultimately, the goal of AI governance in cybersecurity should be to ensure that these powerful technologies are developed and used in ways that promote the greater good, and that help to build a future that is more secure, just, and beneficial for all. To achieve this goal, we will need to work together across disciplines and sectors to address the challenges and opportunities ahead, and to shape the future of AI and cybersecurity in ways that reflect our deepest values and aspirations.

As we move forward, it will be essential to continue to invest in research, education, and capacity building to advance the state of the art in AI governance and to ensure that the benefits of these technologies are widely shared. This will require ongoing collaboration and dialogue among diverse stakeholders, including industry, academia, civil society, and government, as well as a commitment to responsible innovation and the ethical development and use of AI.

It will also be important to recognize that AI governance in cybersecurity is not a one-time effort, but rather an ongoing process that requires continuous monitoring, evaluation, and adaptation as the technology and threat landscape continue to evolve. By embracing a culture of continuous learning and improvement, and by working together to develop and implement effective governance frameworks and practices, we can help to ensure that AI and cybersecurity are forces for good in the world.

As we conclude this chapter, it is worth reflecting on the words of Stephen Hawking, who said:

"The rise of powerful AI will be either the best or the worst thing ever to happen to humanity. We do not yet know which."

The future of AI in cybersecurity, and indeed in all aspects of our lives, is not yet written. It will be shaped by the choices and actions we take today and in the years to come. By embracing the principles and practices of responsible AI governance, and by working together to address the challenges and opportunities ahead, we can help to ensure that the future of AI and cybersecurity is one that we can all be proud of.

So let us move forward with curiosity, courage, and compassion, and work to build a future in which the power of AI is harnessed for the greater good of all humanity, and in which the benefits of these transformative technologies are realized in ways that are secure, equitable, and aligned with our deepest values and aspirations.

TEN

— • —

CHAPTER 10: CYBERSECURITY LANDSCAPING AND AI

Section 10.1: Introduction to Cybersecurity Landscaping

In the ever-evolving world of cybersecurity, understanding the current landscape is crucial for organizations to effectively protect their digital assets and mitigate potential risks. Cybersecurity landscaping refers to the process of identifying, analyzing, and assessing the various elements that make up an organization's cybersecurity posture. This includes understanding the threats, vulnerabilities, and risks that an organization faces, as well as the tools, technologies, and strategies that are available to defend against them.

The importance of cybersecurity landscaping cannot be overstated. Cyber threats are becoming increasingly sophisticated and frequent, with attackers constantly finding new ways to exploit vulnerabilities and bypass security controls. At the same time, the cybersecurity landscape is becoming more complex and dynamic, with new technologies, regulations, and best practices emerging all the time.

In this context, cybersecurity landscaping serves several key purposes:

1. Risk assessment: By understanding the current threat landscape and the specific risks that an organization faces, security teams can prioritize their efforts and allocate resources more effectively.

2. Compliance: Many industries are subject to specific cybersecurity regulations and standards, such as HIPAA in healthcare or PCI-DSS in retail. Cybersecurity landscaping helps organizations ensure that they are meeting these requirements and avoiding potential penalties.

3. Benchmarking: By comparing their own cybersecurity posture to industry standards and best practices, organizations can identify areas for improvement and track their

progress over time.

4. Strategic planning: Cybersecurity landscaping provides a foundation for developing long-term cybersecurity strategies and roadmaps, helping organizations stay ahead of emerging threats and technologies.

The process of cybersecurity landscaping typically involves several key steps:

1. Asset inventory: The first step is to identify and catalog all of the digital assets that an organization owns or controls, including hardware, software, data, and network components.

2. Threat modeling: Next, security teams need to understand the specific threats that could potentially target those assets, based on factors such as the organization's industry, size, and geographic location.   3. Vulnerability assessment: Once the threats have been identified, the next step is to assess the organization's current vulnerabilities and weaknesses that could be exploited by those threats. This may involve a range of techniques, such as penetration testing, code review, and security audits.

4. Risk analysis: Based on the results of the vulnerability assessment, security teams can then analyze the potential impact and likelihood of different risks, and prioritize them based on their severity and urgency.

5. Control mapping: Finally, the results of the risk analysis can be used to map out the specific security controls and countermeasures that are needed to mitigate each risk, based on industry standards and best practices.

While cybersecurity landscaping has traditionally been a manual and time-consuming process, the increasing complexity and scale of modern IT environments has made it increasingly difficult for human analysts to keep up. This is where artificial intelligence (AI) and machine learning (ML) are starting to play a key role.

AI and ML technologies can help automate and streamline many aspects of cybersecurity landscaping, from asset discovery and threat modeling to vulnerability scanning and risk analysis. By analyzing vast amounts of data from multiple sources, AI algorithms can identify patterns and anomalies that might indicate potential security risks, and provide actionable insights to help security teams respond more quickly and effectively.

Some key areas where AI is being applied in cybersecurity landscaping include:

1. Network monitoring: AI-powered tools can continuously monitor network traffic and behavior, looking for signs of unusual or suspicious activity that might indicate a potential security breach.

2. Threat intelligence: AI can help gather and analyze threat intelligence from multiple

sources, such as social media, dark web forums, and security blogs, to provide real-time insights into emerging threats and attack vectors.

3. Vulnerability management: AI can automate the process of scanning systems and applications for known vulnerabilities, and prioritize patching and remediation efforts based on the risk level of each vulnerability.

4. Predictive analytics: By analyzing historical data on past security incidents and attacks, AI can help predict future threats and vulnerabilities, allowing organizations to proactively address potential risks before they become actual breaches.

Despite these benefits, however, the use of AI in cybersecurity landscaping also presents some challenges and risks that need to be carefully considered. For example, AI systems can be vulnerable to bias and errors if they are trained on incomplete or inaccurate data sets, leading to false positives or missed threats. There are also concerns around the transparency and explainability of AI algorithms, particularly in high-stakes scenarios where the consequences of a wrong decision could be severe.

To address these challenges, it is important for organizations to take a strategic and holistic approach to AI in cybersecurity landscaping. This may involve developing clear policies and guidelines around the use of AI, ensuring that AI systems are regularly tested and validated, and investing in ongoing training and education for security teams to help them understand and effectively leverage these technologies.

Ultimately, the goal of cybersecurity landscaping is to provide organizations with a clear and comprehensive understanding of their cybersecurity posture, and to enable them to make informed decisions about how to allocate resources and prioritize efforts to reduce risk and improve security. By leveraging the power of AI and other advanced technologies, organizations can gain a more accurate and timely picture of the ever-changing cybersecurity landscape, and stay one step ahead of the threats that they face.

In the following sections, we will explore some of the key technologies and techniques that are being used in AI-powered cybersecurity landscaping, and discuss some of the emerging trends and best practices in this rapidly evolving field.

Section 10.2: Cybersecurity Threat Landscaping with AI

One of the most critical aspects of cybersecurity landscaping is understanding the constantly evolving threat landscape. Cybersecurity threat landscaping refers to the process of identifying, analyzing, and prioritizing the various threats that an organization faces, based on factors such as the likelihood and potential impact of each threat.

Traditionally, threat landscaping has been a largely manual process, relying on human analysts to gather and interpret threat intelligence from a variety of sources, such as security blogs, news articles, and industry reports. However, the sheer volume and complexity of threat data has made it increasingly difficult for human analysts to keep up, leading to gaps in coverage and delays in response times.

This is where artificial intelligence (AI) and machine learning (ML) are starting to play a key role. AI-powered threat landscaping tools can automatically collect and analyze vast amounts of threat data from multiple sources, identifying patterns and correlations that might indicate emerging threats or attack vectors.

Some key benefits of using AI for threat landscaping include:

1. Speed and scale: AI algorithms can process and analyze threat data much faster than human analysts, allowing organizations to identify and respond to threats in near real-time.

2. Accuracy and consistency: By leveraging machine learning techniques, AI systems can learn to identify and classify threats with a high degree of accuracy and consistency, reducing the risk of false positives or missed threats.

3. Predictive capabilities: By analyzing historical data on past threats and attacks, AI can help predict future threats and vulnerabilities, allowing organizations to proactively address potential risks before they become actual breaches.

4. Automation and efficiency: AI can automate many of the manual and time-consuming tasks involved in threat landscaping, such as data collection, normalization, and correlation, freeing up human analysts to focus on higher-level analysis and decision-making.

There are several key techniques and approaches that are being used in AI-powered threat landscaping, including:

1. Natural Language Processing (NLP): NLP techniques can be used to automatically extract relevant threat information from unstructured text data, such as security blogs, news articles, and social media posts. By analyzing the language and context of these sources, NLP algorithms can identify key entities, relationships, and events related to specific threats or attack vectors.

2. Graph Analytics: Graph analytics techniques can be used to model and analyze the complex relationships between different entities in the threat landscape, such as attackers, victims, and infrastructure. By mapping out these relationships, graph analytics

can help identify hidden connections and patterns that might indicate coordinated or sophisticated attacks.

3. Deep Learning: Deep learning techniques, such as convolutional neural networks (CNNs) and recurrent neural networks (RNNs), can be used to automatically learn and detect complex patterns in threat data, such as malware signatures or network anomalies. By training on large datasets of labeled examples, deep learning models can achieve high levels of accuracy and generalization in identifying new and unknown threats.

4. Reinforcement Learning: Reinforcement learning techniques can be used to develop adaptive and autonomous threat hunting systems that can learn and evolve over time based on feedback and rewards. By exploring and experimenting with different strategies and actions, reinforcement learning agents can continuously improve their ability to detect and respond to emerging threats.

While AI-powered threat landscaping offers many benefits, it also presents some challenges and risks that need to be carefully considered. For example, the quality and reliability of threat data can vary widely depending on the sources and methods used to collect it, which can impact the accuracy and effectiveness of AI models. There are also concerns around the potential for adversarial attacks, where attackers deliberately manipulate or poison the training data used by AI models to evade detection or cause false positives.

To address these challenges, it is important for organizations to adopt a multi-layered and holistic approach to threat landscaping that combines AI with human expertise and other security best practices. This may involve developing clear guidelines and standards for data collection and labeling, regularly testing and validating AI models against known threats and attack scenarios, and investing in ongoing training and education for security teams to help them effectively leverage and interpret AI-generated insights.

Some key best practices for effective threat landscaping with AI include:

1. Diversify data sources: To ensure comprehensive coverage and reduce the risk of bias or blind spots, organizations should collect threat data from a wide range of internal and external sources, including network logs, security tools, threat intelligence feeds, and open-source intelligence (OSINT).

2. Prioritize context and relevance: Not all threat data is created equal, and it is important to prioritize and filter data based on its relevance and potential impact to the organization. This may involve developing custom threat models and risk profiles based on the organization's specific assets, vulnerabilities, and business objectives.

3. Integrate with existing security tools and processes: To maximize the value and im-

pact of AI-powered threat landscaping, it is important to integrate it with existing security tools and processes, such as SIEM, SOAR, and incident response platforms. This can help ensure a seamless and coordinated response to identified threats and vulnerabilities.

4. Foster collaboration and information sharing: Threat landscaping is not a solo activity, and it is important to foster collaboration and information sharing across different teams, departments, and organizations. This may involve participating in industry-specific threat intelligence sharing communities, such as Information Sharing and Analysis Centers (ISACs), or leveraging open-source threat intelligence platforms, such as MISP or OpenCTI.

5. Continuously monitor and adapt: The threat landscape is constantly evolving, and it is important to continuously monitor and adapt threat landscaping efforts to keep pace with new and emerging threats. This may involve regularly updating and retraining AI models, as well as conducting periodic assessments and simulations to test the effectiveness of current defenses and identify areas for improvement.

Ultimately, the goal of threat landscaping with AI is to provide organizations with a more comprehensive, accurate, and timely understanding of the threats they face, and to enable them to make more informed and proactive decisions about how to mitigate those threats. By leveraging the power of AI and other advanced technologies, organizations can gain a significant advantage in the ongoing battle against cyber threats, and better protect their critical assets and operations.

In the following sections, we will explore some of the specific applications and use cases of AI in threat landscaping, and discuss some of the emerging trends and innovations in this rapidly evolving field.

Section 10.3: Cybersecurity Risk Landscaping with AI

In addition to understanding the threat landscape, another critical aspect of cybersecurity landscaping is assessing and prioritizing the various risks that an organization faces. Cybersecurity risk landscaping refers to the process of identifying, analyzing, and evaluating the potential impact and likelihood of different cybersecurity risks, based on factors such as the value of the assets at risk, the effectiveness of existing controls, and the potential consequences of a breach or attack.

Traditionally, risk landscaping has been a largely qualitative and subjective process, relying on the expertise and judgment of human analysts to assess and prioritize risks based on their knowledge of the organization's specific context and requirements. However, the increasing complexity and dynamism of modern IT environments has made it increasingly difficult for human analysts to accurately and consistently assess risks across the entire organization.

This is where artificial intelligence (AI) and machine learning (ML) are starting to play a key role. AI-powered risk landscaping tools can automatically collect and analyze vast amounts of data from multiple sources, such as asset inventories, vulnerability scans, and threat intelligence feeds, to provide a more objective and data-driven assessment of cybersecurity risks.

Some key benefits of using AI for risk landscaping include:

1. Consistency and objectivity: By leveraging machine learning algorithms and standardized risk assessment frameworks, AI systems can provide a more consistent and objective assessment of risks across the entire organization, reducing the potential for bias or subjectivity.

2. Scalability and efficiency: AI can automate many of the manual and time-consuming tasks involved in risk assessment, such as data collection, normalization, and correlation, allowing organizations to assess and prioritize risks more quickly and efficiently.

3. Continuous monitoring and adaptation: AI systems can continuously monitor and analyze risk data in real-time, adapting to changes in the environment and providing up-to-date and actionable insights to help organizations stay ahead of emerging risks.

4. Predictive and prescriptive analytics: By analyzing historical data on past incidents and losses, AI can help predict the likelihood and potential impact of future risks, as well as recommend specific actions and controls to mitigate those risks.

There are several key techniques and approaches that are being used in AI-powered risk landscaping, including:

1. Anomaly detection: Anomaly detection techniques can be used to identify unusual or unexpected patterns in risk data, such as spikes in vulnerability scan results or deviations from baseline risk scores. By flagging these anomalies for further investigation, AI systems can help organizations quickly identify and respond to potential risks before they become actual incidents.

2. Clustering and segmentation: Clustering and segmentation techniques can be used to group similar assets or risks based on common characteristics or attributes, such as asset type, business criticality, or risk level. By organizing risks into meaningful categories and segments, AI systems can help organizations prioritize and allocate resources more

effectively.

3. Predictive modeling: Predictive modeling techniques, such as regression analysis and decision trees, can be used to estimate the likelihood and potential impact of different risks based on historical data and relevant risk factors. By developing and training predictive models on past incidents and losses, AI systems can provide more accurate and reliable risk assessments and forecasts.

4. Multi-criteria decision analysis: Multi-criteria decision analysis techniques, such as Analytic Hierarchy Process (AHP) and TOPSIS, can be used to evaluate and prioritize risks based on multiple criteria or objectives, such as cost, impact, and feasibility. By providing a structured and transparent approach to risk prioritization, AI systems can help organizations make more informed and defensible risk management decisions.

While AI-powered risk landscaping offers many benefits, it also presents some challenges and risks that need to be carefully considered. For example, the quality and completeness of risk data can vary widely depending on the sources and methods used to collect it, which can impact the accuracy and reliability of AI models. There are also concerns around the interpretability and explainability of AI-generated risk assessments, particularly in high-stakes scenarios where the consequences of a wrong decision could be severe.

To address these challenges, it is important for organizations to adopt a transparent and collaborative approach to risk landscaping that combines AI with human expertise and oversight. This may involve developing clear guidelines and standards for data collection and validation, regularly testing and benchmarking AI models against known risks and scenarios, and investing in ongoing training and education for risk management teams to help them effectively leverage and interpret AI-generated insights.

Some key best practices for effective risk landscaping with AI include:

1. Align with business objectives and risk appetite: To ensure that risk assessments are relevant and actionable, it is important to align them with the organization's specific business objectives and risk appetite. This may involve developing custom risk assessment criteria and thresholds based on the organization's industry, size, and risk tolerance.

2. Integrate with existing risk management frameworks and processes: To maximize the value and impact of AI-powered risk landscaping, it is important to integrate it with existing risk management frameworks and processes, such as NIST, ISO, or COSO. This can help ensure a consistent and comprehensive approach to risk management across the entire organization.

3. Foster cross-functional collaboration and communication: Risk landscaping is not a siloed activity, and it is important to foster collaboration and communication across different teams and departments, such as IT, security, compliance, and business units. This can help ensure that risk assessments are comprehensive, accurate, and aligned with the organization's overall risk management strategy.

4. Continuously monitor and adapt: The risk landscape is constantly evolving, and it is important to continuously monitor and adapt risk landscaping efforts to keep pace with new and emerging risks. This may involve regularly updating and retraining AI models, as well as conducting periodic risk assessments and simulations to test the effectiveness of current controls and identify areas for improvement.

5. Emphasize transparency and explainability: To build trust and confidence in AI-powered risk assessments, it is important to emphasize transparency and explainability in the development and use of AI models. This may involve providing clear documentation and visualization of risk assessment criteria and results, as well as enabling human analysts to review and validate AI-generated insights.

Ultimately, the goal of risk landscaping with AI is to provide organizations with a more comprehensive, objective, and actionable understanding of the cybersecurity risks they face, and to enable them to make more informed and effective decisions about how to manage and mitigate those risks. By leveraging the power of AI and other advanced technologies, organizations can gain a significant advantage in the ongoing battle against cyber risks, and better protect their critical assets and operations.

In the following sections, we will explore some of the specific applications and use cases of AI in risk landscaping, and discuss some of the emerging trends and innovations in this rapidly evolving field.

Section 10.4: AI for Cybersecurity Compliance Landscaping

Compliance is a critical aspect of cybersecurity, requiring organizations to adhere to various legal, regulatory, and industry standards related to data protection, privacy, and security. Cybersecurity compliance landscaping refers to the process of identifying, analyzing, and assessing an organization's compliance posture with respect to these standards, and determining the actions and controls needed to maintain compliance over time.

Traditionally, compliance landscaping has been a largely manual and resource-intensive process, requiring compliance teams to review and interpret complex legal and regulatory requirements, assess the organization's current controls and processes against those requirements, and develop and implement remediation plans to address any gaps or deficiencies.

However, the increasing complexity and dynamism of modern compliance environments, coupled with the rapid pace of technological change and the growing volume and variety of data being generated and processed by organizations, has made it increasingly difficult for compliance teams to keep up using traditional approaches.

This is where artificial intelligence (AI) and machine learning (ML) are starting to play a key role. AI-powered compliance landscaping tools can automatically collect and analyze vast amounts of data from multiple sources, such as legal and regulatory databases, industry standards and frameworks, and internal policies and procedures, to provide a more comprehensive and up-to-date assessment of an organization's compliance posture.

Some key benefits of using AI for compliance landscaping include:

1. Automated compliance monitoring and reporting: AI can automate many of the manual and time-consuming tasks involved in compliance monitoring and reporting, such as data collection, normalization, and analysis, allowing compliance teams to focus on higher-value activities such as risk assessment and remediation planning.

2. Improved accuracy and consistency: By leveraging natural language processing (NLP) and machine learning techniques, AI systems can accurately and consistently interpret complex legal and regulatory requirements, reducing the potential for human error or misinterpretation.

3. Real-time insights and alerts: AI systems can continuously monitor compliance data in real- time, providing instant alerts and notifications when potential compliance issues or gaps are identified, allowing organizations to quickly respond and mitigate risks before they escalate.

4. Predictive and prescriptive analytics: By analyzing historical compliance data and trends, AI can help predict potential future compliance risks and recommend specific actions and controls to proactively address those risks.

There are several key techniques and approaches that are being used in AI-powered compliance landscaping, including:

1. Natural Language Processing (NLP): NLP techniques can be used to automatically extract relevant compliance requirements and obligations from unstructured text data, such as legal and regulatory documents, industry standards, and internal policies. By analyzing the language and context of these sources, NLP algorithms can identify key entities,

relationships, and obligations related to specific compliance domains or requirements.

2. Machine Learning (ML): Machine learning techniques, such as supervised learning and reinforcement learning, can be used to automatically classify and prioritize compliance risks based on historical data and feedback. By training on labeled examples of past compliance incidents and remediation actions, ML models can learn to identify patterns and indicators of potential compliance issues, and recommend appropriate actions to mitigate those issues.

3. Knowledge Graphs: Knowledge graphs can be used to model and visualize the complex relationships and dependencies between different compliance requirements, controls, and assets. By mapping out these relationships, knowledge graphs can help identify potential gaps or inconsistencies in an organization's compliance posture, and provide a more holistic and contextual view of compliance risks and remediation options.

4. Robotic Process Automation (RPA): RPA techniques can be used to automate repetitive and rule-based compliance tasks, such as data entry, report generation, and workflow management. By leveraging AI-powered bots to handle these tasks, compliance teams can free up time and resources to focus on more strategic and value-added activities.

While AI-powered compliance landscaping offers many benefits, it also presents some challenges and risks that need to be carefully considered. For example, the quality and accuracy of compliance data can vary widely depending on the sources and methods used to collect it, which can impact the reliability and effectiveness of AI models. There are also concerns around the interpretability and explainability of AI-generated compliance assessments, particularly in highly regulated industries where the consequences of non-compliance can be severe.

To address these challenges, it is important for organizations to adopt a responsible and ethical approach to AI in compliance landscaping, one that combines the power of AI with human expertise and oversight. This may involve developing clear guidelines and standards for data governance and model development, regularly testing and validating AI models against known compliance scenarios, and investing in ongoing training and education for compliance teams to help them effectively leverage and interpret AI-generated insights.

Some key best practices for effective compliance landscaping with AI include:

1. Align with business objectives and risk appetite: To ensure that compliance assessments are relevant and actionable, it is important to align them with the organization's specific business objectives and risk appetite. This may involve developing custom com-

pliance assessment criteria and thresholds based on the organization's industry, size, and risk tolerance.

2. Integrate with existing compliance frameworks and processes: To maximize the value and impact of AI-powered compliance landscaping, it is important to integrate it with existing compliance frameworks and processes, such as ISO, NIST, or COBIT. This can help ensure a consistent and comprehensive approach to compliance management across the entire organization.

3. Foster cross-functional collaboration and communication: Compliance landscaping is not a siloed activity, and it is important to foster collaboration and communication across different teams and departments, such as legal, risk, IT, and business units. This can help ensure that compliance assessments are comprehensive, accurate, and aligned with the organization's overall compliance strategy.

4. Continuously monitor and adapt: The compliance landscape is constantly evolving, and it is important to continuously monitor and adapt compliance landscaping efforts to keep pace with new and emerging requirements and risks. This may involve regularly updating and retraining AI models, as well as conducting periodic compliance assessments and audits to test the effectiveness of current controls and identify areas for improvement.

5. Emphasize transparency and accountability: To build trust and confidence in AI-powered compliance assessments, it is important to emphasize transparency and accountability in the development and use of AI models. This may involve providing clear documentation and explanation of compliance assessment methodologies and results, as well as enabling human analysts to review and validate AI-generated insights.

Ultimately, the goal of compliance landscaping with AI is to provide organizations with a more comprehensive, efficient, and effective way to identify, assess, and manage compliance risks, and to enable them to maintain a strong and resilient compliance posture in the face of rapidly evolving legal, regulatory, and industry requirements. By leveraging the power of AI and other advanced technologies, organizations can gain a significant advantage in the ongoing battle to stay compliant and secure in today's complex and dynamic cybersecurity landscape.

In the following sections, we will explore some of the specific applications and use cases of AI in compliance landscaping, and discuss some of the emerging trends and innovations in this rapidly evolving field.

Section 10.5: The Future of AI in Cybersecurity Landscaping

As we have seen throughout this chapter, artificial intelligence (AI) and machine learning (ML) are playing an increasingly important role in cybersecurity landscaping, helping organizations to more effectively identify, assess, and manage the complex and evolving risks and threats they face in today's digital world.

From automating threat intelligence gathering and analysis, to enabling more objective and data-driven risk assessments, to streamlining compliance monitoring and reporting, AI is transforming the way organizations approach cybersecurity landscaping, and providing powerful new tools and capabilities to help them stay ahead of the curve.

However, the use of AI in cybersecurity landscaping is still in its early stages, and there is much more to be done to fully realize the potential of these technologies. In this section, we will explore some of the key trends and developments that are shaping the future of AI in cybersecurity landscaping, and discuss some of the opportunities and challenges that lie ahead.

One of the most significant trends in AI for cybersecurity landscaping is the growing adoption of deep learning and other advanced ML techniques. Deep learning, which involves training neural networks with multiple layers to learn complex patterns and representations from large datasets, has shown tremendous promise in areas such as malware detection, network anomaly detection, and user behavior analytics.

By leveraging the power of deep learning, organizations can develop more accurate and adaptive models for identifying and responding to cyber threats, and can uncover hidden patterns and insights that may not be visible to traditional rule-based or signature-based approaches.

Another key trend is the increasing use of unsupervised and semi-supervised learning techniques, which can help organizations to identify previously unknown or emerging threats without the need for labeled training data. These techniques, which include clustering, anomaly detection, and one-class classification, can be particularly useful in scenarios where labeled data is scarce or expensive to obtain, or where the nature of the threat is constantly evolving.

In addition to these technical advancements, there is also a growing recognition of the importance of human-AI collaboration in cybersecurity landscaping. While AI can provide powerful automation and analytics capabilities, it is not a replacement for human expertise and judgment, particularly in complex and high-stakes scenarios.

As such, many organizations are exploring ways to develop more collaborative and interactive AI systems that can augment and support human decision-making, rather than simply replacing it. This may involve developing explainable AI techniques that can provide clear and transparent explanations of the reasoning behind AI-generated insights and recommendations, as well as user interfaces and workflows that enable analysts to easily review, validate, and act on those insights.

Another important trend is the increasing focus on privacy and security in the development and deployment of AI systems for cybersecurity landscaping. As these systems become more sophisticated and influential, there is a growing concern about the potential for bias, errors, and unintended consequences, particularly in sensitive domains such as law enforcement, healthcare, and financial services.

To address these concerns, there is a growing emphasis on developing AI systems that are transparent, accountable, and aligned with human values and ethics. This may involve incorporating privacy-preserving techniques such as differential privacy and homomorphic encryption into AI models, as well as developing governance frameworks and standards for the responsible development and use of AI in cybersecurity.

Finally, there is a growing recognition of the need for more interdisciplinary and collaborative approaches to AI in cybersecurity landscaping. As the complexity and scale of cyber threats continue to grow, it is becoming increasingly clear that no single organization or domain has all the answers, and that effective cybersecurity landscaping requires input and expertise from a wide range of fields, including computer science, data science, social science, law, and policy.

To foster this kind of interdisciplinary collaboration, there is a growing emphasis on developing shared data, tools, and platforms for AI in cybersecurity, as well as on building bridges between academia, industry, government, and civil society to share knowledge and best practices.

Some key opportunities and challenges for the future of AI in cybersecurity landscaping include:

1. Developing more adaptive and resilient AI models that can keep pace with the rapidly evolving threat landscape, and that can continue to learn and improve over time.

2. Integrating AI with other advanced technologies such as blockchain, quantum computing, and 5G to create more secure and efficient cybersecurity solutions.

3. Addressing the ethical and societal implications of AI in cybersecurity, including

issues of bias, privacy, transparency, and accountability.

4. Building a skilled and diverse workforce of AI and cybersecurity professionals who can effectively develop, deploy, and manage these complex systems.

5. Fostering greater international cooperation and collaboration on AI and cybersecurity issues, to ensure a more secure and stable digital ecosystem for all.

Ultimately, the future of AI in cybersecurity landscaping is both exciting and challenging, with tremendous potential to transform the way we identify, assess, and manage cyber risks and threats, but also with significant hurdles and uncertainties to overcome.

To fully realize this potential, it will require ongoing investment, innovation, and collaboration across multiple sectors and disciplines, as well as a deep commitment to the responsible and ethical development and use of these powerful technologies.

But if we can rise to this challenge, and harness the power of AI in a way that is both effective and aligned with our values and aspirations, we have the opportunity to create a more secure, resilient, and trustworthy digital future for all.

As we look ahead to this future, it is clear that AI will play an increasingly central role in cybersecurity landscaping, and that the organizations that are able to effectively leverage these technologies will be best positioned to navigate the complex and dynamic cybersecurity landscape of tomorrow.

But it is also clear that the success of AI in cybersecurity will depend not just on technical prowess, but also on our ability to grapple with the broader social, ethical, and policy implications of these technologies, and to ensure that they are developed and used in ways that benefit society as a whole.

As such, it is incumbent upon all of us - researchers, practitioners, policymakers, and citizens alike - to actively engage in shaping the future of AI in cybersecurity, and to work together to build a digital world that is both secure and equitable, both innovative and responsible.

With the right approach, the right mindset, and the right collaboration, we have the opportunity to unlock the full potential of AI in cybersecurity landscaping, and to create a future in which the power of these technologies is harnessed for the greater good of all.

So let us embrace this opportunity with both enthusiasm and care, and let us work together to shape a future in which AI and cybersecurity are powerful allies in the quest for a more secure, resilient, and equitable digital world.

Chapter 10 Conclusion

In this chapter, we have explored the critical role of AI in cybersecurity landscaping, and the many ways in which these technologies are transforming the way organizations identify, assess, and manage the complex and evolving risks and threats they face in today's digital world.

We began by discussing the importance of cybersecurity landscaping in general, and the challenges and limitations of traditional approaches to this critical task. We then explored how AI and machine learning are being used to automate and enhance various aspects of cybersecurity landscaping, from threat intelligence gathering and analysis, to risk assessment and prioritization, to compliance monitoring and reporting.

Throughout the chapter, we have seen how AI is providing organizations with powerful new tools and capabilities to help them stay ahead of the curve in the face of an ever-changing cybersecurity landscape. From deep learning models that can identify previously unknown threats and vulnerabilities, to knowledge graphs that can provide a more holistic and contextual view of the cybersecurity ecosystem, to natural language processing techniques that can extract key insights and requirements from unstructured data sources, AI is revolutionizing the way we approach cybersecurity landscaping.

At the same time, we have also explored some of the challenges and risks associated with the use of AI in cybersecurity landscaping, including issues of data quality and bias, model interpretability and explainability, and the need for human oversight and collaboration in complex and high-stakes scenarios.

We have discussed some of the key best practices and strategies for effective AI-powered cybersecurity landscaping, including aligning with business objectives and risk appetite, integrating with existing frameworks and processes, fostering cross-functional collaboration and communication, continuously monitoring and adapting to new threats and requirements, and emphasizing transparency and accountability in the development and use of AI models.

Finally, we have looked to the future of AI in cybersecurity landscaping, exploring some of the key trends and developments that are shaping this rapidly evolving field, from the growing adoption of deep learning and unsupervised learning techniques, to the increasing focus on human-AI collaboration and the responsible development and use of AI systems, to the need for more interdisciplinary and collaborative approaches to cybersecurity research and practice.

As we have seen throughout this chapter, the use of AI in cybersecurity landscaping is not without its challenges and risks, and there is still much work to be done to fully realize the potential of these technologies. However, the benefits and opportunities of AI-powered cybersecurity landscaping are also clear and compelling, and the organizations that are able to effectively leverage these technologies will be well-positioned to navigate the complex and dynamic cybersecurity landscape of the future.

Ultimately, the success of AI in cybersecurity landscaping will depend not just on technological advances, but also on our ability to grapple with the broader social, ethical, and policy implications of these technologies, and to ensure that they are developed and used in ways that benefit society as a whole.

This will require ongoing investment, innovation, and collaboration across multiple sectors and disciplines, as well as a deep commitment to the responsible and ethical development and use of AI in cybersecurity. It will also require a willingness to engage in open and honest dialogue about the challenges and opportunities of these technologies, and to work together to find solutions that balance the needs of security, privacy, fairness, and accountability.

But if we can rise to this challenge, and harness the power of AI in a way that is both effective and aligned with our values and aspirations, we have the opportunity to create a more secure, resilient, and trustworthy digital future for all.

As we conclude this chapter, we invite readers to continue exploring the exciting and rapidly evolving field of AI in cybersecurity landscaping, and to join us in shaping a future in which the power of these technologies is leveraged for the greater good of all.

Whether you are a researcher, practitioner, policymaker, or simply someone who is passionate about the potential of AI to transform our world for the better, there is a role for you to play in this important and ongoing effort.

So let us move forward with both enthusiasm and care, and let us work together to build a future in which AI and cybersecurity are powerful allies in the quest for a more secure, resilient, and equitable digital world.

Eleven

— • —

Chapter 11: AI and Cybersecurity Awareness and Education

Section 11.1: The Importance of Cybersecurity Awareness and Education in the Age of AI

As artificial intelligence (AI) continues to reshape the cybersecurity landscape, it is becoming increasingly clear that technology alone is not enough to protect organizations and individuals from the growing array of cyber threats they face. While AI-powered tools and techniques can provide powerful new capabilities for detecting, preventing, and responding to cyber attacks, they are only effective if they are deployed and used in the right way, by people who understand their strengths, limitations, and potential risks.

This is where cybersecurity awareness and education come in. In today's digital age, where cyber threats are becoming more sophisticated, frequent, and costly than ever before, it is essential that everyone - from top executives and IT professionals to front-line employees and everyday consumers - has a basic understanding of the risks and best practices associated with cybersecurity.

Cybersecurity awareness refers to the knowledge, attitudes, and behaviors that individuals and organizations need to protect themselves and their assets from cyber threats. This includes understanding the types of threats that exist, the potential impacts of those threats, and the steps that can be taken to prevent or mitigate them.

Cybersecurity education, on the other hand, refers to the formal and informal learning opportunities that are available to help individuals and organizations develop the skills and knowledge they need to effectively manage cybersecurity risks. This can include everything from online training courses and certification programs to in-person workshops and hands-on labs.

The importance of cybersecurity awareness and education in the age of AI cannot be overstated. As AI-powered tools and techniques become more widespread and influential in the cybersecurity domain, it is essential that the people who are responsible for developing, deploying, and using these technologies have a deep understanding of their capabilities, limitations, and potential risks.

For example, while AI can be incredibly effective at detecting and blocking certain types of cyber attacks, such as malware and phishing attempts, it is not a silver bullet. AI models can be biased, brittle, and opaque, and they can be vulnerable to adversarial attacks that are specifically designed to exploit their weaknesses.

As such, it is critical that cybersecurity professionals and decision-makers have a strong foundation in the principles and best practices of AI security, including topics such as data governance, model validation, and ethical considerations. They need to be able to ask the right questions, interpret the results of AI-powered tools and techniques, and make informed decisions about when and how to use them.

At the same time, it is also important that everyday employees and consumers have a basic understanding of the role that AI plays in cybersecurity, and the steps they can take to protect themselves and their organizations from cyber threats. This includes being aware of common attack vectors, such as   phishing emails and social engineering tactics, as well as best practices for safe online behavior, such as using strong passwords, enabling two-factor authentication, and keeping software and devices up to date.

Effective cybersecurity awareness and education programs can help to foster a culture of cybersecurity within organizations, where everyone understands the importance of protecting sensitive data and systems, and feels empowered to play a role in doing so. This can be particularly important in the context of AI, where the risks and challenges are often complex and rapidly evolving.

Some key benefits of investing in cybersecurity awareness and education in the age of AI include:

1. Reducing the risk of human error: Many cyber attacks succeed because of human error, such as clicking on a malicious link or falling for a social engineering scam. By educating employees about these risks and best practices, organizations can reduce the likelihood of these types of mistakes.

2. Enhancing the effectiveness of AI-powered tools: AI-powered cybersecurity tools

are only as effective as the people who use them. By providing training and education on how to properly deploy, configure, and interpret these tools, organizations can maximize their value and minimize the risk of false positives or negatives.

3. Fostering innovation and collaboration: Cybersecurity is a complex and multidisciplinary field, requiring input and expertise from a wide range of stakeholders, including IT professionals, data scientists, legal experts, and business leaders. By providing opportunities for cross-functional learning and collaboration, organizations can break down silos and foster a more holistic and effective approach to cybersecurity.

4. Attracting and retaining top talent: Cybersecurity is a highly competitive field, with a growing demand for skilled professionals who can navigate the challenges of the AI-powered threat landscape. By investing in cybersecurity awareness and education programs, organizations can demonstrate their commitment to employee development and attract top talent to their teams.

5. Maintaining compliance and mitigating risk: Many industries are subject to strict cybersecurity regulations and standards, such as HIPAA in healthcare or PCI-DSS in retail. By providing regular cybersecurity awareness and education training, organizations can ensure that their employees are up to date on the latest requirements and best practices, reducing the risk of costly fines or reputational damage.

Despite these benefits, however, many organizations still struggle to prioritize cybersecurity awareness and education, particularly in the face of competing priorities and limited resources. This is a dangerous oversight, as the cost of a single cyber attack can far outweigh the investment required to provide effective training and education programs.

To address this challenge, it is important for organizations to take a strategic and proactive approach to cybersecurity awareness and education, one that is aligned with their overall business objectives and risk appetite. This may involve developing custom training programs that are tailored to the specific needs and roles of different employee groups, as well as leveraging emerging technologies such as gamification and virtual reality to make the learning experience more engaging and effective.

It is also important for organizations to partner with external experts and organizations, such as academic institutions, industry associations, and cybersecurity vendors, to stay up to date on the latest trends and best practices in the field. By collaborating and sharing knowledge and resources, organizations can more effectively navigate the complex and rapidly evolving landscape of AI and cybersecurity.

Ultimately, the importance of cybersecurity awareness and education in the age of

AI cannot be overstated. As the threat landscape continues to evolve and expand, it is essential that individuals and organizations have the knowledge, skills, and tools they need to protect themselves and their assets from cyber attacks. By investing in effective training and education programs, and fostering a culture of cybersecurity throughout the organization, we can build a more secure and resilient digital future for all.

In the following sections, we will explore some of the key strategies and best practices for developing and implementing effective cybersecurity awareness and education programs in the age of AI, as well as some of the emerging trends and technologies that are shaping the future of this critical field.

Section 11.2: Strategies for Developing Effective Cybersecurity Awareness and Education Programs

Developing effective cybersecurity awareness and education programs is a complex and multifaceted challenge, requiring a strategic and holistic approach that takes into account the unique needs, risks, and culture of each organization. While there is no one-size-fits-all solution, there are several key strategies and best practices that can help organizations to design and implement programs that are engaging, effective, and sustainable over time.

One of the most important strategies for developing effective cybersecurity awareness and education programs is to start with a clear understanding of the organization's specific cybersecurity risks and priorities. This may involve conducting a comprehensive risk assessment to identify the most critical assets, vulnerabilities, and threats facing the organization, as well as the potential impacts of a cyber attack on the business, customers, and stakeholders.

Based on this risk assessment, organizations can then develop a set of clear and measurable learning objectives for their cybersecurity awareness and education programs. These objectives should be aligned with the organization's overall cybersecurity strategy and goals, and should be tailored to the specific needs and roles of different employee groups, such as executives, IT professionals, and front-line staff.

Another key strategy is to design programs that are engaging and interactive, using a variety of learning formats and modalities to keep participants interested and motivated. This may include a mix of online and in-person training sessions, hands-on labs and simulations, gamification and rewards programs, and other creative approaches that make the learning experience fun and memorable.

For example, some organizations have had success with using escape room-style challenges to teach cybersecurity concepts and best practices, where participants must work together to solve a series of puzzles and challenges related to topics such as password security, phishing prevention, and incident response. Others have used virtual reality and augmented reality technologies to create immersive and realistic training scenarios that allow participants to practice their skills in a safe and controlled environment.

In addition to being engaging, effective cybersecurity awareness and education programs should also be comprehensive and continuous, covering a wide range of topics and skills that are relevant to the organization's specific needs and risks. This may include topics such as:

- Basic cybersecurity concepts and terminology
- Common types of cyber threats and attack vectors
- Best practices for safe online behavior and password management
- Recognizing and reporting suspicious activity or incidents
- Compliance with relevant laws, regulations, and standards
- Incident response and business continuity planning
- Emerging trends and technologies in AI and cybersecurity

To ensure that the learning is retained and applied over time, it is important to provide ongoing reinforcement and support, such as regular refresher training sessions, newsletters and other communications, and opportunities for hands-on practice and feedback.

Another important strategy is to leverage the power of storytelling and real-world examples to make the learning more relevant and impactful. By sharing stories and case studies of actual cyber attacks and their consequences, organizations can help participants to understand the real-world risks and impacts of cybersecurity threats, and to see the value and importance of the skills and best practices they are learning.

For example, a healthcare organization might share the story of a ransomware attack that shut down critical systems and put patient lives at risk, highlighting the importance of regular software updates and backup procedures. A financial services firm might share the story of a social engineering scam that led to the theft of millions of dollars, emphasizing the need for strong authentication and verification processes.

In addition to these strategies, there are several other best practices that can help organizations to develop effective cybersecurity awareness and education programs, including:

- Securing executive buy-in and support for the program, and aligning it with the organization's overall business strategy and goals

- Involving a diverse range of stakeholders in the design and delivery of the program, including IT, HR, legal, and communications professionals

- Providing clear and consistent messaging and branding for the program, and communicating its value and importance to all employees

- Measuring and evaluating the effectiveness of the program over time, using metrics such as participation rates, knowledge retention, and behavior change

- Continuously updating and adapting the program to keep pace with the evolving threat landscape and the organization's changing needs and priorities

Ultimately, the key to developing effective cybersecurity awareness and education programs is to take a strategic, comprehensive, and user-centric approach that is tailored to the unique needs and culture of each organization. By investing in high-quality, engaging, and continuous learning opportunities, organizations can build a strong foundation of cybersecurity knowledge and skills that can help to protect their assets, reputation, and bottom line in the face of evolving cyber threats.

Of course, developing and implementing effective cybersecurity awareness and education programs is not without its challenges and pitfalls. Some common obstacles that organizations may face include:

- Limited budgets and resources for training and education initiatives

- Competing priorities and demands on employees' time and attention

- Resistance or lack of engagement from certain employee groups or departments

- Difficulty in measuring and demonstrating the ROI of awareness and education efforts

- Rapidly evolving technologies and threat landscapes that require constant updates and adaptations to training content and delivery methods

To overcome these challenges, organizations may need to get creative and strategic in their approach to cybersecurity awareness and education. This may involve partnering with external training providers or industry associations to access high-quality content and expertise, leveraging internal subject matter experts and champions to help deliver and promote the program, and using data and metrics to demonstrate the value and impact of the initiative to key stakeholders and decision-makers.

Another important consideration is the need to tailor cybersecurity awareness and education programs to the specific needs and learning styles of different employee groups and demographics. For example, younger employees may prefer more interactive and gamified learning experiences, while older employees may prefer more traditional classroom-style training. Employees in technical roles may require more in-depth and hands-on training on specific tools and techniques, while non-technical employees may need more focus on basic cybersecurity concepts and best practices.

To address these diverse needs and preferences, organizations may need to develop a range of training modalities and formats, such as self-paced e-learning courses, instructor-led workshops, webinars, podcasts, and mobile apps. They may also need to use a variety of teaching methods and techniques, such as case studies, role-playing exercises, simulations, and hands-on labs, to engage learners and reinforce key concepts and skills.

Ultimately, the goal of any cybersecurity awareness and education program should be to create a culture of cybersecurity within the organization, where all employees understand the importance of protecting sensitive data and systems, and feel empowered and motivated to play their part in doing so. This requires not only effective training and education, but also strong leadership, clear communication, and ongoing reinforcement and support from all levels of the organization.

By taking a strategic, comprehensive, and user-centric approach to cybersecurity awareness and education, and by continuously adapting and improving their programs over time, organizations can build a strong and resilient cybersecurity posture that can withstand the ever-evolving threats of the digital age. With the right mindset, tools, and resources, we can all become more informed, empowered, and secure digital citizens, and help to create a safer and more trustworthy online world for all.

Section 11.3: The Role of AI in Enhancing Cybersecurity Awareness and Education

As artificial intelligence (AI) continues to transform the landscape of cybersecurity, it is also playing an increasingly important role in enhancing the effectiveness and impact of cybersecurity awareness and education programs. From personalized learning experiences to intelligent threat simulations, AI-powered tools and techniques are helping organizations to deliver more engaging, interactive, and adaptive training that can keep pace with the rapidly evolving threat landscape.

One of the key ways that AI is being used to enhance cybersecurity awareness and education is through the development of personalized learning experiences. By leveraging machine learning algorithms and data analytics, AI-powered training platforms can analyze individual learners' behavior, performance, and preferences, and tailor the content and delivery of training to their specific needs and learning styles.

For example, an AI-powered training platform might use natural language processing (NLP) techniques to analyze a learner's responses to open-ended questions or simulations, and provide customized feedback and recommendations based on their strengths and weaknesses. It might also use predictive analytics to identify learners who are at risk of falling behind or disengaging from the training, and proactively intervene with targeted support and resources.

Another way that AI is being used to enhance cybersecurity awareness and education is through the creation of intelligent threat simulations and exercises. By leveraging AI-powered tools and techniques, organizations can create realistic and dynamic training scenarios that can adapt to learners' actions and decisions in real-time, providing a more immersive and challenging learning experience.

For example, an AI-powered phishing simulation tool might use machine learning algorithms to analyze a learner's email behavior and craft personalized phishing emails that are tailored to their specific interests and vulnerabilities. The tool might then use NLP techniques to analyze the learner's responses and provide immediate feedback and guidance on how to identify and avoid phishing scams in the future.

AI-powered threat simulations can also be used to test and evaluate the effectiveness of an organization's cybersecurity defenses and incident response plans. By simulating realistic attack scenarios and monitoring how employees and systems respond, organizations can identify weaknesses and gaps in their security posture, and use the insights to improve their training and awareness programs.

In addition to these applications, AI is also being used to automate and streamline many of the manual and time-consuming tasks associated with cybersecurity training and education. For example, AI-powered tools can be used to automatically generate and update training content based on the latest threat intelligence and best practices, reducing the burden on human instructors and ensuring that learners always have access to the most current and relevant information.

AI can also be used to monitor and analyze learner engagement and performance data, providing real-time insights and recommendations to instructors and program managers on how to optimize the training experience and improve learning outcomes. This can include identifying trends and patterns in learner behavior, predicting future performance, and recommending targeted interventions or resources for struggling learners.

Despite these benefits, however, the use of AI in cybersecurity awareness and education also raises some important ethical and practical considerations. For example, there are concerns about the potential for AI-powered training tools to perpetuate biases or create unintended consequences, such as reinforcing stereotypes or encouraging risky behavior.

There are also questions about the transparency and accountability of AI-powered training systems, particularly when they are making decisions or recommendations that can have significant impacts on learners' careers or personal lives. Organizations must ensure that their AI-powered training tools are designed and deployed in a responsible and ethical manner, with clear oversight and governance mechanisms in place.

Another challenge is the need for organizations to have the right skills and expertise to effectively leverage AI in their cybersecurity awareness and education programs. This requires not only technical knowledge of AI and machine learning, but also a deep understanding of adult learning principles, instructional design, and cybersecurity best practices.

To address these challenges, organizations may need to invest in specialized training and education for their own workforce, as well as partner with external experts and vendors who can provide the necessary tools and support. They may also need to engage in ongoing research and experimentation to identify best practices and lessons learned, and to continuously improve and adapt their AI-powered training programs over time.

Ultimately, the role of AI in enhancing cybersecurity awareness and education is still evolving, and there is much work to be done to fully realize its potential. However, by taking a thoughtful and strategic approach, and by leveraging the power of AI in a responsible and ethical manner, organizations can create more effective, engaging, and impactful training programs that can help to build a culture of cybersecurity and protect against the ever-evolving threats of the digital age.

In the words of cybersecurity expert Bruce Schneier, "AI will be the next battleground in cybersecurity, and the side that masters it first will have a significant advantage." By investing in AI-powered cybersecurity awareness and education, organizations can help to ensure that they are on the winning side of this battle, and that their employees and systems are better prepared to face the challenges and opportunities of the AI-driven future.

Section 11.4: Measuring the Effectiveness of Cybersecurity Awareness and Education Programs

Measuring the effectiveness of cybersecurity awareness and education programs is a critical but often overlooked aspect of building a strong and resilient cybersecurity posture. Without clear and meaningful metrics and evaluation methods, organizations may struggle to demonstrate the value and impact of their training initiatives, and may miss opportunities to identify areas for improvement and optimization.

However, measuring the effectiveness of cybersecurity awareness and education programs can be a complex and multifaceted challenge, requiring a holistic and strategic approach that takes into account a range of factors and considerations. Some key strategies and best practices for measuring the effectiveness of these programs include:

1. Defining clear and measurable learning objectives: Before launching any cybersecurity awareness and education program, it is essential to define clear and specific learning objectives that are aligned with the organization's overall cybersecurity goals and priorities. These objectives should be measurable and achievable, and should focus on the knowledge, skills, and behaviors that learners need to acquire to be effective in their roles.

2. Collecting and analyzing learner data: To measure the effectiveness of cybersecurity awareness and education programs, organizations need to collect and analyze data on learner engagement, performance, and outcomes. This may include data on course completion rates, assessment scores, simulation results, and other metrics that can provide insights into how well learners are absorbing and applying the content.

3. Conducting pre- and post-training assessments: One effective way to measure the impact of cybersecurity awareness and education programs is to conduct assessments before and after the training, to gauge learners' knowledge and skills levels and to track their progress over time. These assessments can take many forms, such as quizzes, surveys, or practical exercises, and can be administered online or in-person.

4. Monitoring behavior change: While assessments can provide valuable insights into learners' knowledge and skills, they do not necessarily reflect how well learners are applying those skills in their day-to-day work. To measure the impact of cybersecurity awareness and education programs on actual behavior change, organizations may need to use other methods, such as phishing simulation tests, security audits, or employee surveys.

5. Tracking security metrics: Another way to measure the effectiveness of cybersecurity

awareness and education programs is to track key security metrics over time, such as the number of security incidents, the time to detect and respond to threats, and the overall cost of security breaches. By monitoring these metrics and analyzing trends and patterns, organizations can gain insights into how well their training programs are contributing to a stronger and more resilient cybersecurity posture.

6. Gathering feedback and insights: In addition to quantitative data, organizations should also gather qualitative feedback and insights from learners, instructors, and other stakeholders involved in the cybersecurity awareness and education program. This may include surveys, focus groups, interviews, or other methods that can provide valuable context and nuance to the data, and can help to identify areas for improvement or optimization.

7. Using AI and machine learning: As discussed in the previous section, AI and machine learning technologies can play a powerful role in enhancing the effectiveness and impact of cybersecurity awareness and education programs. By leveraging these technologies to analyze learner data, personalize content and delivery, and provide intelligent recommendations and feedback, organizations can gain deeper insights into the effectiveness of their training programs and identify opportunities for improvement.

8. Continuously monitoring and adapting: Finally, measuring the effectiveness of cybersecurity awareness and education programs is not a one-time event, but rather an ongoing process that requires continuous monitoring, evaluation, and adaptation. Organizations should regularly review and analyze their training metrics and feedback, and use the insights to make data-driven decisions about how to optimize and improve their programs over time.

Of course, implementing these strategies and best practices is not without its challenges and considerations. For example, collecting and analyzing learner data can raise important privacy and security concerns, particularly when dealing with sensitive or confidential information. Organizations must ensure that they have robust data governance and protection policies in place, and that they are transparent with learners about how their data is being used and secured.

Another challenge is the need to balance the desire for comprehensive and detailed metrics with the practical realities of limited time, resources, and attention spans. Organizations must be strategic and selective in choosing the metrics and methods that are most relevant and meaningful for their specific needs and goals, and must avoid overwhelming learners or instructors with excessive or irrelevant data collection and analysis.

There is also the risk of focusing too narrowly on short-term or superficial metrics, such as course completion rates or quiz scores, at the expense of more meaningful and long-term outcomes, such as behavior change or security incident reduction. Organizations must take a holistic and strategic approach to measuring the effectiveness of their cybersecurity awareness and education programs, and must be willing to invest in the time, resources, and expertise needed to gather and analyze the right data and insights.

Despite these challenges, however, the benefits of measuring the effectiveness of cybersecurity awareness and education programs are clear and compelling. By taking a data-driven and evidence-based approach to training and education, organizations can demonstrate the value and impact of their initiatives, identify areas for improvement and optimization, and ultimately build a stronger and more resilient cybersecurity posture that can withstand the ever-evolving threats of the digital age.

As the famous management consultant Peter Drucker once said, "If you can't measure it, you can't improve it." By embracing the power of metrics and measurement in their cybersecurity awareness and education programs, organizations can create a virtuous cycle of continuous learning, adaptation, and improvement that can help to protect their most valuable assets and stakeholders from harm.

Section 11.5: Emerging Trends and Best Practices in Cybersecurity Awareness and Education

As the landscape of cybersecurity continues to evolve and expand, so too do the strategies and approaches for building effective cybersecurity awareness and education programs. From the rise of gamification and microlearning to the growing emphasis on diversity and inclusion, there are many exciting trends and best practices emerging in this field that are worth exploring and adopting.

One of the most significant trends in cybersecurity awareness and education is the shift towards more personalized and adaptive learning experiences. Rather than taking a one-size-fits-all approach to training, organizations are increasingly using data analytics and machine learning to tailor content and delivery to the specific needs, preferences, and learning styles of individual learners.

For example, some organizations are using AI-powered chatbots and virtual assistants to provide learners with on-demand support and guidance, while others are using adaptive learning platforms that can dynamically adjust the difficulty and pace of training based on learners' performance and engagement levels. By creating more targeted and responsive learning experiences, organizations can help to increase learner motivation, retention, and application of cybersecurity knowledge and skills.

Another trend that is gaining traction in cybersecurity awareness and education is the use of gamification and game-based learning. By incorporating elements of play, competition, and rewards into training programs, organizations can create more engaging and memorable learning experiences that can help to drive behavior change and skill development.

For example, some organizations are using cybersecurity-themed escape rooms, capture-the-flag exercises, and other immersive challenges to teach learners about topics such as social engineering, incident response, and secure coding practices. Others are using gamified learning platforms that allow learners to earn points, badges, and other rewards for completing training modules and demonstrating their knowledge and skills.

In addition to these trends, there is also a growing recognition of the importance of diversity and inclusion in cybersecurity awareness and education. As the threat landscape becomes more complex and global in nature, organizations need to ensure that their training programs are accessible, relevant, and inclusive to learners from all backgrounds and perspectives.

This may involve creating training content and materials in multiple languages and formats, using diverse and representative examples and case studies, and actively seeking out and amplifying the voices and experiences of underrepresented groups in the cybersecurity field. By promoting diversity and inclusion in their training programs, organizations can not only create a more welcoming and supportive learning environment, but also tap into a wider range of skills, perspectives, and innovations that can help to strengthen their overall cybersecurity posture.

Another best practice that is gaining traction in cybersecurity awareness and education is the use of microlearning and just-in-time training. Rather than relying on long, comprehensive training sessions that can be overwhelming and difficult to retain, organizations are increasingly breaking down their training content into smaller, more focused modules that can be easily consumed and applied in real-time.

For example, some organizations are using short, interactive videos or infographics to teach learners about specific cybersecurity topics or best practices, while others are using mobile apps or chatbots to provide learners with quick reference guides or decision-support tools that they can access on-demand. By providing learners with targeted, actionable training at the point of need, organizations can help to increase knowledge retention and application, and create a more agile and responsive cybersecurity culture.

Finally, there is a growing emphasis on the importance of continuous learning and improvement in cybersecurity awareness and education. Given the rapidly evolving nature of the threat landscape, organizations cannot afford to treat training as a one-time event or a compliance checkbox. Instead, they need to create a culture of ongoing learning and development, where cybersecurity knowledge and skills are regularly updated, reinforced, and applied.

This may involve creating learning pathways and certification programs that allow learners to continuously build and demonstrate their expertise, as well as establishing feedback loops and metrics that can help to identify areas for improvement and optimization in training programs. By fostering a culture of continuous learning and improvement, organizations can create a more resilient and adaptable cybersecurity workforce that can keep pace with the ever-changing demands of the digital age.

Of course, implementing these trends and best practices is not without its challenges and considerations. For example, creating personalized and adaptive learning experiences requires significant investments in data collection, analysis, and infrastructure, as well as careful attention to issues of privacy, security, and ethical use of learner data.

Similarly, incorporating gamification and game-based learning into cybersecurity training programs requires careful design and testing to ensure that the games are both engaging and effective, and do not create unintended consequences or reinforce negative behaviors or stereotypes.

There is also the challenge of balancing the need for continuous learning and improvement with the practical realities of limited time, resources, and attention spans. Organizations must be strategic and selective in choosing the training topics, formats, and frequencies that are most relevant and impactful for their specific needs and goals, and must avoid overwhelming or disengaging learners with excessive or irrelevant training demands.

Despite these challenges, however, the benefits of adopting these emerging trends and best practices in cybersecurity awareness and education are clear and compelling. By creating more personalized, engaging, inclusive, and continuous learning experiences, organizations can help to build a stronger, more diverse, and more resilient cybersecurity workforce that can adapt and thrive in the face of ever-evolving cyber threats.

Moreover, by investing in effective cybersecurity awareness and education programs, organizations can not only reduce their risk of cyber attacks and data breaches, but also create a more positive and empowering culture of cybersecurity that can benefit all stakeholders, from employees and customers to partners and society at large.

As the famous futurist Alvin Toffler once said, "The illiterate of the 21st century will not be those who cannot read and write, but those who cannot learn, unlearn, and relearn." By embracing the power of continuous learning and improvement in their cybersecurity awareness and education programs, organizations can help to create a more literate, agile, and secure digital future for all.

Chapter 11 Conclusion

In this chapter, we have explored the critical importance of cybersecurity awareness and education in the age of artificial intelligence, and the key strategies, best practices, and emerging trends that organizations can adopt to build more effective and impactful training programs.

We began by discussing the vital role that cybersecurity awareness and education play in protecting organizations and individuals from the growing array of cyber threats they face in today's digital world. We highlighted the need for everyone, from executives and IT professionals to front-line employees and everyday consumers, to have a basic understanding of the risks and best practices associated with cybersecurity, particularly in the context of AI-powered tools and techniques.

We then delved into some of the key strategies and best practices for developing effective cybersecurity awareness and education programs, including starting with a clear understanding of the organization's specific risks and priorities, designing programs that are engaging and interactive, using a variety of learning formats and modalities, leveraging the power of storytelling and real-world examples, providing ongoing reinforcement and support, and continuously updating and adapting the program to keep pace with the evolving threat landscape.

Next, we explored the role of AI in enhancing the effectiveness and impact of cybersecurity awareness and education programs, from personalized learning experiences to intelligent threat simulations. We discussed the benefits and challenges of using AI-powered tools and techniques in cybersecurity training, and highlighted the need for organizations to take a responsible and ethical approach to leveraging these technologies.

We then turned our attention to the importance of measuring the effectiveness of cybersecurity awareness and education programs, and the key strategies and best practices for collecting and analyzing data on learner engagement, performance, and outcomes. We emphasized the need for organizations to take a holistic and strategic approach to measuring the effectiveness of their training programs, and to use the insights and feedback gathered to continuously improve and optimize their initiatives.

Finally, we explored some of the emerging trends and best practices in cybersecurity awareness and education, including the shift towards more personalized and adaptive learning experiences, the use of gamification and game-based learning, the growing emphasis on diversity and inclusion, the adoption of microlearning and just-in-time training, and the importance of fostering a culture of continuous learning and improvement.

Throughout this chapter, we have seen that building effective cybersecurity awareness and education programs is a complex and multifaceted challenge, requiring a strategic and holistic approach that takes into account the unique needs, risks, and culture of each organization. It requires ongoing investment, experimentation, and adaptation, as well as a deep commitment to the responsible and ethical use of technology in the service of human learning and development.

At the same time, we have also seen the immense potential and benefits of investing in cybersecurity awareness and education, particularly in the age of AI. By creating more engaging, personalized, and impactful learning experiences, organizations can help to build a stronger, more diverse, and more resilient cybersecurity workforce that can adapt and thrive in the face of ever-evolving cyber threats.

Moreover, by fostering a culture of continuous learning and improvement in cybersecurity, organizations can not only reduce their risk of cyber attacks and data breaches, but also create a more positive and empowering digital future for all stakeholders, from employees and customers to partners and society at large.

As we look ahead to the future of cybersecurity awareness and education, it is clear that there is still much work to be done to fully realize the potential of these programs, particularly in the context of AI and other emerging technologies. However, by embracing the strategies, best practices, and trends discussed in this chapter, and by taking a proactive and collaborative approach to building and measuring the effectiveness of these programs, we can create a more secure, literate, and empowered digital world for all.

In the words of the renowned futurist and author John Naisbitt, "We are drowning in information but starved for knowledge." By investing in effective cybersecurity awareness and education programs, we can help to bridge this gap, and create a more knowledgeable, skilled, and resilient cybersecurity workforce that can navigate the challenges and opportunities of the AI-driven future with confidence and purpose.

TWELVE

— • —

CHAPTER 12: AI AND CYBERSECURITY ETHICS AND SOCIAL RESPONSIBILITY

Section 12.1: The Importance of Ethical AI and Cybersecurity Practices

As artificial intelligence (AI) continues to transform the landscape of cybersecurity, it is becoming increasingly clear that the development and deployment of these technologies must be guided by a strong ethical framework and a deep sense of social responsibility. Without a clear understanding of the moral implications and potential consequences of AI-powered cybersecurity tools and techniques, organizations risk not only undermining the trust and confidence of their stakeholders, but also contributing to a range of unintended harms and negative outcomes for individuals and society as a whole.

At its core, the concept of ethical AI and cybersecurity practices is about ensuring that the design, development, and use of these technologies is aligned with fundamental human values and principles, such as fairness, transparency, accountability, and respect for individual privacy and autonomy. It is about recognizing that AI and cybersecurity are not neutral or value-free endeavors, but rather inherently political and socially constructed activities that have real-world impacts on people's lives and well-being.

The importance of ethical AI and cybersecurity practices is particularly salient in the context of the growing power and reach of these technologies, and the increasing reliance of organizations and individuals on AI-powered tools and systems. As AI becomes more sophisticated and ubiquitous, it is no longer sufficient to simply focus on the technical aspects of cybersecurity, such as detecting and preventing attacks or protecting data and assets. Rather, organizations must also grapple with the broader social, political, and ethical implications of their cybersecurity practices, and take proactive steps to ensure that their use of AI is aligned with the values and interests of all stakeholders.

Some of the key ethical and social responsibility issues that organizations must consider when developing and deploying AI-powered cybersecurity tools and systems include:

1. Bias and discrimination: One of the most significant ethical challenges associated with AI and cybersecurity is the potential for these technologies to perpetuate or amplify existing social biases and discriminatory practices. For example, if an AI-powered cybersecurity system is trained on data that is biased or unrepresentative of certain groups or populations, it may produce results that are unfair or discriminatory towards those groups, even if unintentionally. Similarly, if an AI system is designed or deployed in a way that disproportionately targets or harms certain individuals or communities, it may reinforce existing power imbalances and social inequities.

2. Privacy and data protection: Another key ethical concern related to AI and cybersecurity is the potential for these technologies to infringe on individual privacy rights and undermine data protection principles. As AI systems become more sophisticated and able to process and analyze vast amounts of personal and sensitive data, there is a risk that this information could be used in ways that violate individuals' reasonable expectations of privacy, or that expose them to new forms of surveillance, profiling, or manipulation. Organizations must ensure that their use of AI and cybersecurity tools is consistent with applicable data protection laws and regulations, and that they have robust safeguards in place to protect the privacy and security of individuals' data.

3. Transparency and accountability: Given the complexity and opacity of many AI algorithms and systems, there is a risk that the decision-making processes and outcomes of these technologies may be difficult or impossible to understand, explain, or challenge. This lack of transparency can undermine public trust and confidence in AI and cybersecurity practices, and make it difficult to hold organizations accountable for any harms or negative consequences that may result from their use of these technologies. To address these concerns, organizations must strive to make their AI and cybersecurity practices as transparent and explainable as possible, and to establish clear mechanisms for accountability and redress in the event of errors, failures, or abuses.

4. Human agency and oversight: As AI systems become more autonomous and capable of making decisions and taking actions without human intervention, there is a risk that they may undermine human agency and control over important aspects of our lives and

society. In the context of cybersecurity, this could include AI systems that make decisions about who is a security threat or how to respond to cyber attacks without adequate human oversight or input. To mitigate these risks, organizations must ensure that their use of AI and cybersecurity tools is subject to appropriate human control and oversight, and that there are clear policies and procedures in place for monitoring and intervening in the operation of these systems as needed.

5. Social and economic impacts: Finally, the development and deployment of AI and cybersecurity technologies can have significant social and economic impacts that go beyond the immediate concerns of individual organizations or stakeholders. For example, the increasing automation of cybersecurity tasks and the growing reliance on AI-powered tools and systems may lead to job losses or skill obsolescence for human cybersecurity professionals, or may exacerbate existing digital divides and inequalities in access to cyber-security resources and expertise. Organizations must be mindful of these broader social and economic implications of their AI and cybersecurity practices, and work to ensure that the benefits and risks of these technologies are distributed fairly and equitably across society.

To address these and other ethical and social responsibility challenges associated with AI and cybersecurity, organizations must adopt a proactive and holistic approach that prioritizes the values of fairness, transparency, accountability, and respect for   human rights and dignity. This may involve developing and implementing clear ethical guidelines and principles for the design, development, and use of AI and cybersecurity technologies, as well as establishing robust governance and oversight mechanisms to ensure that these guidelines are followed in practice.

It may also involve investing in ongoing training and education for employees and stakeholders on the ethical and social implications of AI and cybersecurity, and fostering a culture of ethical awareness and responsibility throughout the organization. Additional-ly, organizations may need to engage in ongoing dialogue and collaboration with external stakeholders, such as policymakers, civil society organizations, and affected communities, to ensure that their AI and cybersecurity practices are aligned with broader societal values and interests.

Ultimately, the goal of ethical AI and cybersecurity practices is to ensure that these powerful technologies are developed and used in ways that promote the greater good and minimize harm to individuals and society. By prioritizing these values and taking a proactive and responsible approach to the ethical and social implications of their AI and cybersecurity practices, organizations can help to build a more secure, equitable, and trustworthy digital future for all.

Section 12.2: Designing and Implementing Ethical AI and Cybersecurity Frameworks

Designing and implementing ethical AI and cybersecurity frameworks is a critical step in ensuring that organizations are able to realize the full potential of these technologies while minimizing the risks and negative consequences associated with their use. These frameworks provide a structured and systematic approach to identifying, assessing, and addressing the ethical and social implications of AI and cybersecurity practices, and help to ensure that these technologies are developed and deployed in ways that are consistent with fundamental human values and principles.

At a high level, an ethical AI and cybersecurity framework should include several key components, such as:

1. Ethical principles and values: The framework should clearly articulate the core ethical principles and values that should guide the design, development, and use of AI and cybersecurity technologies. These may include principles such as fairness, transparency, accountability, privacy, security, and respect for human rights and dignity. The framework should also provide guidance on how to prioritize and balance these principles in cases where they may come into conflict with one another.

2. Risk assessment and management: The framework should include a process for identifying and assessing the potential ethical and social risks associated with AI and cybersecurity technologies, as well as strategies for mitigating and managing these risks. This may involve conducting impact assessments to evaluate the potential harms and benefits of these technologies, as well as developing contingency plans and response strategies for addressing any negative consequences that may arise.

3. Governance and oversight: The framework should establish clear roles, responsibilities, and accountability mechanisms for ensuring that AI and cybersecurity practices are aligned with ethical principles and values. This may involve creating a dedicated ethics board or committee to oversee the development and deployment of these technologies, as well as establishing policies and procedures for monitoring and auditing their use.

4. Transparency and explainability: The framework should emphasize the importance of transparency and explainability in AI and cybersecurity practices, and provide guid-

ance on how to make these technologies more understandable and accountable to stakeholders. This may involve developing clear and accessible documentation on the design, functionality, and limitations of AI and cybersecurity systems, as well as establishing mechanisms for stakeholders to challenge or appeal decisions made by these systems.

5. Stakeholder engagement and collaboration: The framework should recognize the importance of engaging and collaborating with a wide range of stakeholders in the development and deployment of AI and cybersecurity technologies, including employees, customers, partners, policymakers, and civil society organizations. This may involve establishing forums for ongoing dialogue and feedback on the ethical and social implications of these technologies, as well as working with external experts and organizations to ensure that best practices and standards are being followed.

To implement an ethical AI and cybersecurity framework effectively, organizations may need to take several key steps, such as:

1. Conducting a comprehensive assessment of their current AI and cybersecurity practices to identify any potential ethical or social risks or gaps.

2. Developing a clear and actionable plan for addressing these risks and gaps, including specific goals, timelines, and resources needed.

3. Providing training and education to employees and stakeholders on the ethical and social implications of AI and cybersecurity, and how to apply the framework in practice.

4. Establishing clear metrics and key performance indicators (KPIs) for measuring the effectiveness and impact of the framework, and using this data to continuously improve and refine the framework over time.

5. Engaging in ongoing dialogue and collaboration with external stakeholders to ensure that the framework remains relevant and responsive to evolving ethical and social concerns and best practices.

Designing and implementing an effective ethical AI and cybersecurity framework is not a one-time event, but rather an ongoing process that requires sustained commitment, resources, and leadership from all levels of the organization. It also requires a willingness to engage in difficult conversations and make tough decisions about the trade-offs and priorities involved in developing and deploying these technologies in an ethical and responsible manner.

However, the benefits of investing in an ethical AI and cybersecurity framework are clear and compelling. By proactively addressing the ethical and social implications of these technologies, organizations can help to build trust and confidence among stakeholders, mitigate potential legal and reputational risks, and position themselves as leaders in the responsible development and use of AI and cybersecurity.

Moreover, by prioritizing ethical and socially responsible practices in their AI and cybersecurity efforts, organizations can help to create a more secure, equitable, and sustainable digital future for all. They can help to ensure that the benefits of these technologies are distributed fairly and widely, and that the risks and negative consequences are minimized and mitigated to the greatest extent possible.

Ultimately, the goal of designing and implementing an ethical AI and cybersecurity framework is not to stifle innovation or limit the potential of these technologies, but rather to ensure that they are developed and used in ways that are consistent with our deepest values and aspirations as a society. By taking a proactive and principled approach to these issues, organizations can help to unlock the full potential of AI and cybersecurity to drive positive social and economic outcomes, while also fulfilling their ethical and moral obligations to their stakeholders and the broader public.

Section 12.3: Promoting Transparency, Accountability, and Fairness in AI and Cybersecurity

Promoting transparency, accountability, and fairness in AI and cybersecurity is a critical aspect of ensuring that these technologies are developed and used in an ethical and socially responsible manner. These principles are essential for building trust and confidence in AI and cybersecurity systems, and for ensuring that they are aligned with fundamental human values and principles.

Transparency refers to the idea that the design, development, and use of AI and cybersecurity technologies should be open and understandable to all stakeholders, including users, policymakers, and the general public. This means that organizations should be clear and transparent about the purposes and functionalities of these technologies, as well as their limitations and potential risks. It also means that the decision-making processes and outcomes of these technologies should be explainable and interpretable, so that stakeholders can understand how and why particular decisions or actions were taken.

Accountability, on the other hand, refers to the idea that organizations should be held responsible for the consequences and impacts of their AI and cybersecurity practices, and should have clear mechanisms in place for addressing any harms or negative outcomes that may arise. This means that organizations should have robust governance and oversight structures in place to ensure that these technologies are being used in accordance with ethical principles and values, and that there are clear processes for identifying and mitigating potential risks and harms.

Fairness, meanwhile, refers to the idea that AI and cybersecurity technologies should be developed and used in ways that are equitable and non-discriminatory, and that do not perpetuate or amplify existing social biases or inequities. This means that organizations should take proactive steps to ensure that the data and algorithms used to train and operate these technologies are representative and unbiased, and that the outcomes and decisions produced by these technologies are fair and equitable for all stakeholders.

To promote transparency, accountability, and fairness in AI and cybersecurity, organizations can take several key steps, such as:

1. Developing clear and accessible documentation on the design, functionality, and limitations of AI and cybersecurity systems, and making this documentation available to all stakeholders.

2. Establishing clear governance and oversight structures for AI and cybersecurity practices, including dedicated ethics boards or committees, as well as policies and procedures for monitoring and auditing the use of these technologies.

3. Conducting regular impact assessments and risk analyses to identify potential biases, harms, or unintended consequences of AI and cybersecurity technologies, and developing strategies for mitigating these risks.

4. Providing training and education to employees and stakeholders on the importance of transparency, accountability, and fairness in AI and cybersecurity, and how to apply these principles in practice.

5. Engaging in ongoing dialogue and collaboration with external stakeholders, including policymakers, civil society organizations, and affected communities, to ensure that AI and cybersecurity practices are aligned with broader societal values and interests.

6. Establishing clear mechanisms for stakeholders to challenge or appeal decisions made by AI and cybersecurity systems, and for providing redress and compensation in cases where harms or negative outcomes have occurred.

By taking these and other steps to promote transparency, accountability, and fairness in AI and cybersecurity, organizations can help to build trust and confidence in these technologies, and ensure that they are developed and used in ways that are ethical, responsible, and socially beneficial.

However, promoting these principles is not always easy or straightforward, and may involve difficult trade-offs and challenges. For example, efforts to increase transparency and explainability in AI and cybersecurity systems may sometimes come at the cost of performance or efficiency, or may raise concerns about the protection of intellectual property or sensitive information.

Similarly, efforts to ensure fairness and non-discrimination in these technologies may require significant investments in data collection, cleaning, and preprocessing, as well as ongoing monitoring and testing to identify and mitigate potential biases or disparities.

Despite these challenges, however, the importance of promoting transparency, accountability, and fairness in AI and cybersecurity cannot be overstated. These principles are essential for ensuring that these technologies are developed and used in ways that are consistent with our deepest values and aspirations as a society, and for building a more secure, equitable, and trustworthy digital future for all.

Ultimately, the goal of promoting these principles is not to stifle innovation or limit the potential of AI and cybersecurity, but rather to ensure that these technologies are developed and used in ways that benefit everyone, and that minimize the risks and negative consequences for individuals and society as a whole.

By embracing transparency, accountability, and fairness as core values in their AI and cybersecurity practices, organizations can help to create a more ethical, responsible, and socially beneficial digital ecosystem, one that leverages the power of these technologies to drive positive change and progress, while also respecting and protecting the rights and interests of all stakeholders.

Section 12.4: Addressing Bias and Discrimination in AI and Cybersecurity Systems

Addressing bias and discrimination in AI and cybersecurity systems is a critical aspect of ensuring that these technologies are developed and used in an ethical and socially responsible manner. Bias and discrimination can occur at various stages of the AI and cybersecurity lifecycle, from the data collection and preprocessing phase to the design and deployment of algorithms and models.

Bias in AI and cybersecurity systems can take many forms, including:

1. Data bias: This occurs when the data used to train and develop AI and cybersecurity systems is not representative of the population or domain being modeled, or when it contains historical or societal biases that are reflected in the data.

2. Algorithmic bias: This occurs when the algorithms and models used in AI and cybersecurity systems are designed or implemented in ways that discriminate against certain groups or individuals, either intentionally or unintentionally.

3. Evaluation bias: This occurs when the metrics and methods used to evaluate the performance and effectiveness of AI and cybersecurity systems are biased or discriminatory, leading to unfair or inaccurate assessments of these technologies.

4. Deployment bias: This occurs when AI and cybersecurity systems are deployed or used in ways that disproportionately impact or harm certain groups or individuals, such as through targeted surveillance or profiling.

The consequences of bias and discrimination in AI and cybersecurity systems can be severe and far-reaching. They can perpetuate and amplify existing social inequities and power imbalances, leading to unfair treatment, denial of opportunities, and other forms of harm for marginalized or vulnerable groups. They can also undermine public trust and confidence in these technologies, and hinder their ability to drive positive social and economic outcomes.

To address bias and discrimination in AI and cybersecurity systems, organizations can take several key steps, such as:

1. Conducting regular audits and assessments of AI and cybersecurity systems to identify potential sources of bias and discrimination, and developing strategies for mitigating these risks.

2. Ensuring that the data used to train and develop AI and cybersecurity systems is diverse, representative, and free from historical or societal biases, and that it is collected and processed in an ethical and responsible manner.

3. Designing and implementing algorithms and models that are transparent, explainable, and accountable, and that incorporate fairness and non-discrimination as core principles and objectives.

4. Providing training and education to employees and stakeholders on the importance of addressing bias and discrimination in AI and cybersecurity, and how to identify and mitigate these risks in practice.

5. Engaging in ongoing dialogue and collaboration with external stakeholders, including policymakers, civil society organizations, and affected communities, to ensure that AI and cybersecurity practices are aligned with broader societal values and interests around fairness and non-discrimination.

6. Establishing clear mechanisms for individuals and groups to challenge or appeal

decisions made by AI and cybersecurity systems that they believe to be biased or discriminatory, and for providing redress and compensation in cases where harms or negative outcomes have occurred.

By taking these and other steps to address bias and discrimination in AI and cybersecurity, organizations can help to ensure that these technologies are developed and used in ways that are fair, equitable, and socially responsible.

However, addressing bias and discrimination in AI and cybersecurity is not always easy or straightforward, and may require significant investments of time, resources, and expertise. It may also involve difficult trade-offs and challenges, such as balancing the need for fairness and non-discrimination with other important objectives, such as performance, efficiency, and innovation.

Despite these challenges, however, the importance of addressing bias and discrimination in AI and cybersecurity cannot be overstated. These issues are not just technical or operational concerns, but fundamental moral and ethical imperatives that go to the heart of our values and aspirations as a society.

By prioritizing fairness, non-discrimination, and social responsibility in their AI and cybersecurity practices, organizations can help to build a more just, equitable, and inclusive digital future for all. They can help to ensure that the benefits and opportunities of these technologies are distributed fairly and widely, and that the risks and harms are minimized and mitigated to the greatest extent possible.

Ultimately, the goal of addressing bias and discrimination in AI and cybersecurity is not to achieve some abstract or unattainable ideal of perfect fairness or neutrality, but rather to ensure that these technologies are developed and used in ways that respect and promote the dignity, autonomy, and well-being of all individuals and communities.

By embracing this goal as a core value and principle in their AI and cybersecurity practices, organizations can help to create a more ethical, responsible, and socially beneficial digital ecosystem, one that leverages the power of these technologies to drive positive change and progress, while also upholding the fundamental rights and freedoms of all people.

Section 12.5: Promoting Diversity, Equity, and Inclusion in AI and Cybersecurity

Promoting diversity, equity, and inclusion (DEI) in AI and cybersecurity is a critical aspect of ensuring that these technologies are developed and used in an ethical and socially responsible manner. DEI is about creating a culture and environment where all individuals, regardless of their race, gender, ethnicity, sexual orientation, age, ability, or other characteristics, feel valued, respected, and included, and have equal opportunities to participate and succeed in these fields.

The importance of DEI in AI and cybersecurity cannot be overstated. These technologies are increasingly shaping and influencing every aspect of our lives, from healthcare and education to finance and criminal justice. However, the people who design, develop, and deploy these technologies are often not representative of the diverse populations and communities that they serve and impact.

This lack of diversity and inclusivity in AI and cybersecurity can have serious consequences, including:

1. Perpetuating and amplifying existing biases and inequities in society, such as racial and gender discrimination, through the design and deployment of biased algorithms and models.

2. Limiting the perspectives, experiences, and insights that are brought to bear on the development and use of these technologies, leading to narrow and incomplete solutions that fail to address the needs and concerns of diverse stakeholders.

3. Reducing the trust and confidence that individuals and communities have in these technologies, and hindering their ability to drive positive social and economic outcomes for all.

4. Reinforcing and exacerbating existing power imbalances and social inequities, by concentrating the benefits and opportunities of these technologies in the hands of a privileged few, while excluding or marginalizing others.

To address these and other challenges, organizations can take several key steps to promote DEI in AI and cybersecurity, such as:

1. Developing and implementing clear and actionable DEI strategies and plans that are aligned with the organization's mission, values, and goals, and that are supported by leadership at all levels.

2. Conducting regular audits and assessments of the organization's DEI practices and outcomes, and using this data to identify areas for improvement and to track progress over time.

3. Providing training and education to employees and stakeholders on the importance of DEI in AI and cybersecurity, and how to identify and address bias, discrimination, and

other barriers to inclusion in these fields.

4. Establishing employee resource groups (ERGs) and other forums for underrepresented groups to connect, support, and advocate for one another, and to provide input and feedback on the organization's DEI efforts.

5. Partnering with external organizations and communities, such as universities, nonprofits, and professional   associations, to promote diversity and inclusion in AI and cybersecurity, and to build a more diverse and representative talent pipeline for these fields.

6. Establishing clear and transparent criteria and processes for hiring, promotion, and compensation decisions, and ensuring that these processes are free from bias and discrimination.

7. Celebrating and showcasing the contributions and achievements of diverse individuals and teams in AI and cybersecurity, and using these examples to inspire and encourage others to pursue careers in these fields.

By taking these and other steps to promote DEI in AI and cybersecurity, organizations can help to create a more diverse, equitable, and inclusive digital ecosystem, one that leverages the full potential and creativity of all individuals and communities.

Moreover, by prioritizing DEI as a core value and principle in their AI and cybersecurity practices, organizations can help to build a more just, fair, and socially responsible digital future for all. They can help to ensure that the benefits and opportunities of these technologies are distributed equitably and widely, and that the risks and harms are minimized and mitigated to the greatest extent possible.

However, promoting DEI in AI and cybersecurity is not always easy or straightforward, and may require significant investments of time, resources, and commitment from all levels of the organization. It may also involve difficult conversations and challenges, such as confronting and dismantling deeply entrenched biases, power structures, and cultural norms that have historically excluded or marginalized certain groups.

Despite these challenges, however, the importance of DEI in AI and cybersecurity cannot be overstated. These issues are not just matters of social justice or moral imperative, but are also critical to the long-term success, resilience, and impact of these technologies.

By embracing diversity, equity, and inclusion as core values and principles in their AI and cybersecurity practices, organizations can tap into a wider range of perspectives, experiences, and insights, leading to more innovative, effective, and socially beneficial solutions. They can also build stronger, more resilient, and more trusted relationships with the diverse communities and stakeholders that they serve and impact.

Ultimately, the goal of promoting DEI in AI and cybersecurity is to create a more just, equitable, and inclusive digital world, one that empowers and uplifts all individuals and communities, regardless of their background or identity. By working towards this goal, we can help to ensure that the transformative potential of these technologies is realized in a way that benefits everyone, and that leaves no one behind.

Chapter 12 Conclusion

In this chapter, we have explored the critical importance of ethics and social responsibility in the development and use of AI and cybersecurity technologies. We have seen how these technologies, while holding immense potential for driving positive change and progress, also raise significant moral and ethical challenges that must be proactively addressed to ensure that their benefits are realized in a fair, equitable, and socially responsible manner.

We began by discussing the importance of ethical AI and cybersecurity practices, and how these practices are essential for building trust and confidence in these technologies, and for ensuring that they are aligned with fundamental human values and principles. We highlighted several key ethical and social responsibility issues that organizations must consider when developing and deploying AI and cybersecurity systems, including bias and discrimination, privacy and data protection, transparency and accountability, human agency and oversight, and social and economic impacts.

We then explored the process of designing and implementing ethical AI and cybersecurity frameworks, and how these frameworks can provide a structured and systematic approach to identifying, assessing, and addressing the ethical and social implications of these technologies. We discussed several key components of an effective ethical AI and cybersecurity framework, including ethical principles and values, risk assessment and management, governance and oversight, transparency and explainability, and stakeholder engagement and collaboration.

Next, we delved into the importance of promoting transparency, accountability, and fairness in AI and cybersecurity systems, and how these principles are critical for ensuring that these technologies are developed and used in an ethical and socially responsible manner. We discussed several key steps that organizations can take to promote these principles, such as developing clear and accessible documentation, establishing robust governance and oversight structures, conducting regular impact assessments and risk analyses, providing training and education to employees and stakeholders, engaging in ongoing dialogue and collaboration with external stakeholders, and establishing clear mechanisms for stakeholder challenge and redress.

We then turned our attention to the critical issue of addressing bias and discrimination in AI and cybersecurity systems, and how these issues can perpetuate and amplify existing social inequities and power imbalances, leading to unfair treatment, denial of opportunities, and other forms of harm for marginalized or vulnerable groups. We discussed several key steps that organizations can take to address bias and discrimination in these technologies, such as conducting regular audits and assessments, ensuring diverse and representative data, designing transparent and accountable algorithms and models, providing training and education on bias and discrimination, engaging in ongoing dialogue and collaboration with affected communities, and establishing clear mechanisms for challenge and redress.

Finally, we explored the importance of promoting diversity, equity, and inclusion in AI and cybersecurity, and how these values are critical for creating a more just, equitable, and socially responsible digital ecosystem. We discussed several key steps that organizations can take to promote DEI in these fields, such as developing and implementing clear DEI strategies and plans, conducting regular audits and assessments, providing training and education on DEI, establishing employee resource groups and other forums for underrepresented groups, partnering with external organizations and communities to build diverse talent pipelines, establishing clear and transparent criteria and processes for hiring and promotion, and celebrating and showcasing the contributions and achievements of diverse individuals and teams.

Throughout this chapter, we have seen that ethics and social responsibility are not just abstract or aspirational ideals, but are critical and urgent imperatives that must be actively and continuously pursued in the development and use of AI and cybersecurity technologies. We have seen how these technologies, while holding immense potential for driving positive change and progress, also raise significant moral and ethical challenges that must be proactively addressed to ensure that their benefits are realized in a fair, equitable, and socially responsible manner.

Moreover, we have seen that promoting ethics and social responsibility in AI and cybersecurity is not just a matter of compliance or risk management, but is also a critical driver of innovation, resilience, and long-term success. By embracing these values and principles as core to their mission and operations, organizations can tap into a wider range of perspectives, insights, and opportunities, leading to more effective, impactful, and socially beneficial solutions.

Ultimately, the goal of ethics and social responsibility in AI and cybersecurity is to create a more just, equitable, and inclusive digital world, one that empowers and uplifts all individuals and communities, regardless of their background or identity. By working towards this goal, we can help to ensure that the transformative potential of these technologies is realized in a way that benefits everyone, and that leaves no one behind.

As we conclude this chapter, it is important to recognize that the work of promoting ethics and social responsibility in AI and cybersecurity is ongoing and never-ending. It requires sustained commitment, collaboration, and vigilance from all stakeholders, including developers, users, policymakers, and civil society.

But if we can rise to this challenge, and embrace ethics and social responsibility as core values and principles in our AI and cybersecurity practices, we can help to build a more just, equitable, and socially beneficial digital future for all. We can help to ensure that these technologies are developed and used in ways that respect and promote the dignity, autonomy, and well-being of all individuals and communities, and that contribute to the greater good of society as a whole.

So let us move forward with a sense of urgency and purpose, and work together to create a world where AI and cybersecurity are powerful forces for positive change and progress, guided by the uncompromising principles of ethics, fairness, transparency, and social responsibility. Let us strive to be the best versions of ourselves, both as individuals and as a society, and use these technologies to build a brighter, more just, and more equitable future for all.

THIRTEEN

— · —

CHAPTER 13: THE FUTURE OF AI IN CYBERSECURITY

Section 13.1: Emerging Trends and Technologies in AI and Cybersecurity

As we have seen throughout this book, the intersection of artificial intelligence (AI) and cybersecurity is a rapidly evolving and highly dynamic field, with new trends, technologies, and innovations emerging all the time. In this section, we will explore some of the most exciting and promising developments in this space, and discuss their potential implications for the future of cybersecurity.

One of the most significant trends in AI and cybersecurity is the growing use of deep learning and neural networks for threat detection and response. Deep learning is a subset of machine learning that involves training artificial neural networks on large datasets to automatically learn and extract complex patterns and features. In the context of cybersecurity, deep learning can be used to analyze vast amounts of network traffic, system logs, and other data sources to identify anomalies, detect malicious activities, and predict potential threats.

For example, deep learning-based intrusion detection systems (IDS) can learn to recognize the unique patterns and behaviors of different types of cyber attacks, such as malware infections, phishing attempts, and denial-of-service (DoS) attacks, and can automatically flag suspicious activities for further investigation. Similarly, deep learning-based malware detection systems can analyze the code and behavior of software programs to identify known and unknown malware variants, even if they have been obfuscated or encrypted to evade traditional signature-based detection methods.

Another emerging trend in AI and cybersecurity is the use of generative adversarial networks (GANs) for threat modeling and simulation. GANs are a type of deep learning architecture that involves training two neural networks in competition with each other: a generator network that learns to create realistic fake data, and a discriminator network that learns to distinguish between real and fake data. In the context of cybersecurity, GANs can be used to generate realistic simulations of different types of cyber attacks, such as phishing emails, malicious URLs, and network intrusions, which can then be used to train and test AI-based defense systems.

For example, a GAN-based phishing simulator could learn to generate highly convincing fake phishing emails that mimic the language, style, and structure of real phishing attempts, complete with personalized details and persuasive social engineering tactics. These simulated phishing emails could then be used to train and evaluate the effectiveness of AI-based email filtering and anti-phishing systems, helping to improve their accuracy and robustness against evolving threats.

Another promising application of GANs in cybersecurity is in the area of adversarial machine learning, which involves using GANs to generate adversarial examples that can fool and mislead AI-based defense systems. By training a GAN to create malicious inputs that are specifically designed to evade detection or cause misclassification, researchers can identify and fix potential vulnerabilities in AI models before they can be exploited by real-world attackers.

Beyond deep learning and GANs, there are many other emerging technologies and approaches in AI and cybersecurity that are worth noting. For example, reinforcement learning is a type of machine learning that involves training AI agents to make sequential decisions in complex environments, such as network security games or cyber-physical systems. By using reinforcement learning to optimize the actions and strategies of AI-based defense systems, researchers can create more adaptive, resilient, and effective cybersecurity solutions that can learn and evolve over time.

Another promising area of research is the use of explainable AI (XAI) for cybersecurity, which involves developing AI systems that can provide clear, interpretable explanations for their decisions and actions. By making AI-based cybersecurity systems more transparent and accountable, XAI can help to build trust and confidence in these technologies, and can enable human analysts to better understand and validate the results of AI-based threat detection and response.

Finally, there is growing interest in the use of quantum computing for cybersecurity, which involves harnessing the unique properties of quantum mechanics to perform complex computations and cryptographic operations. While still in the early stages of development, quantum computing has the potential to revolutionize many aspects of cybersecurity, from secure communication and data protection to advanced threat detection and cryptanalysis.

As quantum computers become more powerful and accessible, researchers are exploring new ways to leverage these technologies for AI-based cybersecurity, such as developing quantum machine learning algorithms that can analyze and classify vast amounts of data with unprecedented speed and accuracy.

Of course, these are just a few examples of the many exciting trends and technologies that are shaping the future of AI in cybersecurity. As the field continues to evolve and mature, we can expect to see many more innovative and transformative developments in the years ahead, from cognitive security and autonomous response systems to AI-powered deception technologies and beyond.

However, it is important to recognize that the future of AI in cybersecurity is not just about technological advancement, but also about the ethical, social, and human dimensions of these technologies. As we have discussed throughout this book, the development and deployment of AI-based cybersecurity solutions raise important questions and challenges around issues such as privacy, fairness, transparency, accountability, and social responsibility.

To ensure that the benefits of AI in cybersecurity are realized in a way that is equitable, inclusive, and socially responsible, it is essential that we continue to engage in ongoing dialogue and collaboration among all stakeholders, including researchers, developers, policymakers, and civil society. We must work together to develop and implement robust ethical frameworks and governance structures for AI in cybersecurity, and to ensure that these technologies are developed and used in ways that respect and promote the rights, dignity, and well-being of all individuals and communities.

Ultimately, the future of AI in cybersecurity is not just about the technology itself, but about the values, principles, and vision that guide its development and use. By embracing a holistic and human-centered approach to AI and cybersecurity, we can help to build a more secure, resilient, and equitable digital future for all.

Section 13.2: Preparing for the AI-Driven Cybersecurity Landscape: Strategies and Best Practices

As artificial intelligence (AI) continues to transform the landscape of cybersecurity, organizations of all sizes and sectors must adapt and evolve their strategies and practices to stay ahead of the curve. In this section, we will explore some of the key steps and best practices that organizations can take to prepare for the AI-driven future of cybersecurity.

The first and most critical step in preparing for the AI-driven cybersecurity landscape is to develop a clear and comprehensive understanding of the current and emerging threats and challenges that organizations face. This requires ongoing investment in threat intelligence and research, as well as active engagement with industry groups, government agencies, and other stakeholders to share information and best practices.

Organizations should also conduct regular risk assessments and vulnerability scans to identify potential weaknesses and gaps in their cybersecurity posture, and should prioritize the implementation of AI-based solutions that can help to mitigate these risks. This may include deploying AI-powered intrusion detection and prevention systems, malware analysis tools, and threat hunting platforms that can automatically detect and respond to emerging threats in real-time.

Another key strategy for preparing for the AI-driven cybersecurity landscape is to invest in the development and training of a skilled and diverse cybersecurity workforce. As the demand for AI and machine learning expertise in cybersecurity continues to grow, organizations must prioritize the recruitment, retention, and development of talent with the skills and knowledge needed to design, implement, and manage AI-based security solutions.

This may involve partnering with universities and other educational institutions to develop and deliver specialized training programs in AI and cybersecurity, as well as providing ongoing professional development opportunities for existing staff to stay up-to-date with the latest trends and technologies. It may also involve actively promoting diversity and inclusion in the cybersecurity workforce, to ensure that a wide range of perspectives and experiences are represented in the development and deployment of AI-based solutions.

In addition to investing in people and technology, organizations must also prioritize the development of robust governance and risk management frameworks for AI in cybersecurity. This includes establishing clear policies and procedures for the ethical and responsible development and use of AI-based security solutions, as well as implementing strong data privacy and protection measures to safeguard sensitive information and assets.

Organizations should also establish clear lines of accountability and oversight for AI-based security decisions and actions, and should regularly review and update their governance frameworks to ensure that they remain effective and relevant in the face of evolving threats and technologies.

Another critical best practice for preparing for the AI-driven cybersecurity landscape is to foster a culture of continuous learning and improvement within the organization. As the pace of technological change accelerates, organizations must be able to rapidly adapt and evolve their cybersecurity strategies and practices to stay ahead of emerging threats and challenges.

This requires a willingness to experiment with new technologies and approaches, as well as a commitment to ongoing testing, evaluation, and refinement of AI-based security solutions. It also requires a culture of openness and transparency, where successes and failures are shared and used as opportunities for learning and growth.

Finally, organizations must recognize that the AI-driven future of cybersecurity is not just about technology, but also about people and processes. To truly prepare for this future, organizations must prioritize the development of a holistic and integrated approach to cybersecurity that encompasses not just technical solutions, but also human factors such as awareness, training, and behavior.

This may involve investing in employee education and awareness programs to help staff understand and adopt secure behaviors and practices, as well as implementing strong access controls and authentication measures to prevent unauthorized access to sensitive data and systems. It may also involve developing and testing incident response and business continuity plans to ensure that the organization can quickly and effectively respond to and recover from cyber incidents.

Ultimately, preparing for the AI-driven cybersecurity landscape requires a proactive, adaptive, and collaborative approach that engages all stakeholders and leverages the full range of available resources and expertise. By embracing these strategies and best practices, organizations can position themselves to thrive in the face of evolving cyber threats and challenges, and can help to build a more secure and resilient digital future for all.

Section 13.3: Overcoming Challenges and Barriers to AI Adoption in Cybersecurity

Despite the many potential benefits and opportunities of AI in cybersecurity, there are also significant challenges and barriers that organizations must overcome to successfully adopt and implement these technologies. In this section, we will explore some of the key obstacles and hurdles that organizations may face when seeking to leverage AI for cybersecurity, and discuss strategies and approaches for addressing and overcoming these challenges.

One of the most significant challenges to AI adoption in cybersecurity is the lack of trust and transparency in these technologies. As AI-based security solutions become more complex and autonomous, there is growing concern among stakeholders about the potential for bias, errors, and unintended consequences in their decision-making and actions.

This lack of trust can be exacerbated by the "black box" nature of many AI algorithms, which can make it difficult for users to understand and interpret the reasoning behind their outputs and recommendations. To overcome this challenge, organizations must prioritize the development of explainable and interpretable AI models that provide clear and transparent insights into their inner workings and decision-making processes.

Another key barrier to AI adoption in cybersecurity is the shortage of skilled talent and expertise in this field. As the demand for AI and machine learning capabilities in cybersecurity continues to grow, many organizations are struggling to find and retain the talent they need to design, implement, and manage these technologies effectively.

This skills gap can be particularly acute in smaller organizations and those in non-technical industries, who may not have the resources or expertise to compete with larger tech companies and research institutions for top talent. To address this challenge, organizations must invest in the development and training of their existing workforce, as well as explore new models for collaboration and partnership with external experts and service providers.

A third major challenge to AI adoption in cybersecurity is the need for high-quality, diverse, and representative data to train and validate AI models. As we have discussed throughout this book, the effectiveness and fairness of AI-based security solutions depends heavily on the quality and diversity of the data used to develop them. However, many organizations struggle to access and curate the large volumes of relevant, labeled, and unbiased data needed to build robust and reliable AI models for cybersecurity.

To overcome this challenge, organizations must prioritize the development of strong data governance and management practices, as well as explore new approaches to data sharing and collaboration across industry and academia. This may involve investing in data annotation and labeling services, as well as participating in data consortia and open-source initiatives to pool and share cybersecurity data for AI research and development.

Another significant barrier to AI adoption in cybersecurity is the complexity and fragmentation of the cybersecurity technology landscape. With a wide range of vendors, products, and platforms competing for market share, organizations can struggle to navigate the noise and identify the AI-based solutions that are best suited to their specific needs and requirements. This complexity can also make it difficult to integrate AI technologies with existing security tools and workflows, leading to silos and inefficiencies in the overall security operations.

To address this challenge, organizations must take a strategic and holistic approach to AI adoption in cybersecurity, focusing on solutions that are interoperable, scalable, and aligned with their overall security architecture and goals. This may involve working with trusted partners and advisors to assess and select the right AI technologies for their needs, as well as investing in the development of standardized APIs and integration frameworks to enable seamless data sharing and collaboration across different security tools and platforms.

Finally, a major challenge to AI adoption in cybersecurity is the need for ongoing monitoring, testing, and validation of AI-based security solutions to ensure their effectiveness and resilience against evolving threats and attacks. As cyber criminals and nation-state actors become more sophisticated in their use of AI and machine learning techniques, there is a risk that AI-based defenses may become vulnerable to new forms of evasion, manipulation, and exploitation.

To mitigate this risk, organizations must prioritize the development of robust testing and evaluation frameworks for AI in cybersecurity, as well as invest in ongoing research and innovation to stay ahead of emerging threats and vulnerabilities. This may involve collaborating with academic and industry partners to develop new approaches to adversarial testing and red teaming, as well as exploring new technologies such as homomorphic encryption and secure multi-party computation to enable privacy-preserving AI for cybersecurity.

Ultimately, overcoming the challenges and barriers to AI adoption in cybersecurity will require a concerted and collaborative effort from all stakeholders, including technology vendors, researchers, policymakers, and end-user organizations. By working together to address these obstacles and develop new solutions and best practices, we can help to accelerate the adoption and impact of AI in cybersecurity, and build a more secure and resilient digital future for all.

Section 13.4: The Role of Policy and Regulation in Shaping the Future of AI and Cybersecurity

As artificial intelligence (AI) and cybersecurity technologies continue to advance and evolve, the role of policy and regulation in shaping their development and deployment is becoming increasingly critical. Governments and regulatory bodies around the world are grappling with the complex and multifaceted challenges of balancing the benefits and risks of these technologies, while also promoting innovation, competition, and social responsibility in the digital economy.

In this section, we will explore some of the key policy and regulatory issues and initiatives that are likely to shape the future of AI and cybersecurity, and discuss the potential implications and opportunities for organizations and society as a whole.

One of the most significant policy challenges in the realm of AI and cybersecurity is the need for clear and consistent ethical and governance frameworks to guide the development and use of these technologies. As we have discussed throughout this book, AI-based security solutions raise important questions and concerns around issues such as privacy, fairness, transparency, accountability, and social responsibility.

To address these challenges, policymakers and regulators are increasingly focusing on the development of ethical guidelines and principles for AI, such as the OECD Principles on Artificial Intelligence and the IEEE Ethically Aligned Design framework. These initiatives aim to provide a common set of values and best practices for the responsible development and deployment of AI technologies, while also promoting trust and confidence among stakeholders.

Another key policy issue in the realm of AI and cybersecurity is the need for strong and effective data protection and privacy regulations. As AI-based security solutions become more data-driven and autonomous, there is growing concern about the potential for

200   FORTRESS AI

misuse or abuse of personal and sensitive information, as well as the risks of data breaches and cyber attacks.

To address these risks, policymakers and regulators are developing and enforcing new data protection and privacy laws and regulations, such as the European Union's General Data Protection Regulation (GDPR) and the California Consumer Privacy Act (CCPA). These regulations aim to give individuals greater control over their personal data, while also imposing strict requirements on organizations that collect, process, and store this data.

In addition to data protection and privacy, another critical policy issue in the realm of AI and cybersecurity is the need for strong and effective cybersecurity standards and best practices. As the threat landscape continues to evolve and expand, organizations of all sizes and sectors are facing growing risks and challenges in securing their digital assets and operations.

To help organizations navigate these challenges, policymakers and industry groups are developing and promoting new cybersecurity standards and frameworks, such as the NIST Cybersecurity Framework and the ISO 27000 series of information security standards. These standards provide a common language and set of best practices for organizations to assess and manage their cybersecurity risks, while also enabling greater collaboration and information sharing across industry and government.

Another important policy issue in the realm of AI and cybersecurity is the need for greater investment in research and development (R&D) to drive innovation and progress in these fields. As the pace of technological change accelerates, there is a growing need for sustained and targeted investment in AI and cybersecurity R&D, to ensure that the benefits of these technologies are realized and the risks are effectively mitigated.

To support this goal, governments and funding agencies around the world are increasing their investments in AI and cybersecurity research, through initiatives such as the US National Science Foundation's Secure and Trustworthy Cyberspace program and the European Commission's Horizon 2020 research and innovation program. These investments aim to foster collaboration and knowledge sharing among researchers, industry, and government, while also promoting the development of new tools, techniques, and best practices for AI and cybersecurity.

Finally, a critical policy issue in the realm   Here is the continuation of the manuscript: of AI and cybersecurity is the need for international cooperation and coordination to address global challenges and promote a secure and resilient digital ecosystem. As cyber threats and attacks become increasingly sophisticated and transnational in nature, there is a growing recognition that no single country or organization can effectively address these challenges alone.

To promote greater international cooperation and coordination on AI and cybersecurity issues, policymakers and stakeholders are engaging in a range of initiatives and forums, such as the United Nations Group of Governmental Experts on Developments in the Field of Information and Telecommunications in the Context of International Security, and the Global Forum on Cyber Expertise. These efforts aim to build trust and confidence among nations, while also promoting the development of common norms, principles, and best practices for responsible behavior in cyberspace.

In addition to these global initiatives, there is also a growing trend towards regional and bilateral cooperation on AI and cybersecurity issues, particularly among like-minded countries and allies. For example, the United States and the European Union have established a range of dialogues and working groups on issues such as AI ethics and governance, data protection and privacy, and cybersecurity resilience and response.

These regional and bilateral efforts can help to promote greater alignment and interoperability among national policies and regulations, while also fostering innovation and economic growth through increased trade and investment in digital technologies and services.

Of course, the role of policy and regulation in shaping the future of AI and cybersecurity is not without its challenges and limitations. Policymakers and regulators must grapple with complex and rapidly evolving technologies and threat landscapes, while also balancing competing priorities and interests among diverse stakeholders.

There is also a risk that overly prescriptive or burdensome regulations could stifle innovation and competition in the AI and cybersecurity markets, while also creating barriers to entry for smaller and emerging players. Policymakers must therefore strive to develop flexible and adaptive frameworks that can keep pace with technological change, while also promoting open and inclusive markets and ecosystems.

Another key challenge is the need for greater public awareness and engagement on AI and cybersecurity issues, to ensure that policies and regulations are developed and implemented in a transparent, accountable, and socially responsible manner. This requires ongoing efforts to educate and empower citizens and communities to understand and participate in the governance of these technologies, while also promoting greater diversity and inclusion in the policymaking process.

Ultimately, the role of policy and regulation in shaping the future of AI and cybersecurity will require a collaborative and multi-stakeholder approach that engages governments, industry, academia, civil society, and the broader public. By working together to develop and implement effective and responsible policies and frameworks, we can help to ensure that the benefits of these technologies are realized in a way that promotes security, privacy, fairness, and social responsibility, while also fostering innovation and economic growth in the digital age.

Section 13.5: Building a Secure and Resilient AI-Driven Future: A Call to Action for Cybersecurity Leaders and Professionals

As we have seen throughout this book, the rapid advances in artificial intelligence (AI) and cybersecurity are transforming the digital landscape in profound and unprecedented ways. From enabling new forms of threat detection and response, to enhancing the efficiency and effectiveness of security operations, to driving innovation and growth across industries and sectors, the potential of these technologies to shape the future is truly remarkable.

At the same time, the rise of AI and cybersecurity also presents significant challenges and risks that must be carefully navigated and addressed. From the potential for bias and discrimination in AI-based security systems, to the growing sophistication and scale of cyber threats and attacks, to the complex ethical and social implications of these technologies, the stakes have never been higher for organizations and individuals alike.

In this final section of the book, we issue a call to action for cybersecurity leaders and professionals to step up and lead the way in building a secure and resilient AI-driven future. As the guardians and stewards of our digital assets and operations, cybersecurity professionals have a unique and critical role to play in shaping the development and deployment of AI technologies in a way that promotes security, privacy, fairness, and social responsibility.

To do this effectively, cybersecurity leaders and professionals must first and foremost prioritize the development of their own skills and expertise in AI and machine learning. This requires ongoing investment in training and education, as well as active engagement with the broader AI and cybersecurity communities to stay up-to-date on the latest trends, technologies, and best practices.

At the same time, cybersecurity leaders must also work to build strong and diverse teams that bring together a range of perspectives and experiences to tackle the complex challenges of AI and cybersecurity. This includes not only technical experts in areas such as data science, software engineering, and threat intelligence, but also experts in fields such as ethics, law, policy, and social science, who can help to ensure that AI-based security solutions are developed and used in a responsible and inclusive manner.

Another key imperative for cybersecurity leaders is to foster a culture of collaboration and information sharing within and across organizations. As the threat landscape continues to evolve and expand, it is essential that cybersecurity professionals work together to share intelligence, best practices, and lessons learned, in order to stay ahead of emerging threats and vulnerabilities.

This may involve participating in industry forums and working groups, as well as engaging in joint research and development initiatives with academic and government partners. It may also involve exploring new models for public-private partnerships and ecosystem collaboration, such as bug bounty programs, threat intelligence sharing platforms, and open-source software communities.

In addition to collaboration and information sharing, cybersecurity leaders must also prioritize the development and implementation of strong governance and risk management frameworks for AI and cybersecurity. This includes establishing clear policies and procedures for the responsible development and use of AI-based security solutions, as well as implementing robust testing and evaluation processes to ensure the safety, reliability, and effectiveness of these technologies.

Cybersecurity leaders must also work closely with executive management and boards of directors to ensure that AI and cybersecurity risks are properly understood and managed at the highest levels of the organization. This may involve regular briefings and reporting on the state of the organization's AI and cybersecurity posture, as well as developing and implementing incident response and business continuity plans to ensure resilience in the face of cyber attacks and disruptions.

Finally, and perhaps most importantly, cybersecurity leaders and professionals must embrace a proactive and adaptive mindset in the face of the rapidly evolving AI and cybersecurity landscape. Rather than simply reacting to new threats and vulnerabilities as they emerge, cybersecurity professionals must work to anticipate and prevent these challenges before they occur, through ongoing threat modeling, risk assessment, and scenario planning.

This requires a willingness to experiment with new technologies and approaches, as well as a commitment to continuous learning and improvement. It also requires a recognition that building a secure and resilient AI-driven future is not a one-time event, but rather an ongoing process that requires sustained effort, investment, and leadership over time.

Ultimately, the call to action for cybersecurity leaders and professionals is clear: to step up and lead the way in shaping the future of AI and cybersecurity in a way that promotes security, privacy, fairness, and social responsibility. This is not an easy task, and it will require significant challenges and obstacles to be overcome along the way.

But it is also a task that is essential to the long-term success and sustainability of our digital economy and society. By embracing the opportunities and challenges of AI and cybersecurity with courage, creativity, and collaboration, we can help to build a future that is more secure, resilient, and equitable for all.

So let us rise to this challenge, and work together to create a world in which the transformative power of AI and cybersecurity is harnessed for the greater good, and in which the benefits of these technologies are realized in a way that promotes trust, transparency, and social responsibility. Let us lead by example, and inspire others to join us in this critical mission, so that together, we can build a brighter and more secure future for generations to come.

Chapter 13 Conclusion

In this final chapter of the book, we have explored the exciting and rapidly evolving future of artificial intelligence (AI) in cybersecurity. We have seen how the convergence of these two powerful technologies is transforming the digital landscape in profound and unprecedented ways, creating both tremendous opportunities and significant challenges for organizations and individuals alike.

We began by examining some of the key emerging trends and technologies in AI and cybersecurity, such as deep learning, generative adversarial networks, and quantum computing, and discussed their potential implications for the future of threat detection, response, and prevention. We also highlighted the importance of explainable AI and human-machine collaboration in building trust and confidence in these technologies, and ensuring their responsible and ethical development and use.

We then turned our attention to the strategies and best practices that organizations can adopt to prepare for the AI-driven cybersecurity landscape, including investing in talent and skills development, establishing governance and risk management frameworks, fostering a culture of continuous learning and improvement, and prioritizing explainable and transparent AI solutions.

Next, we explored some of the key challenges and barriers to AI adoption in cybersecurity, such as the lack of trust and transparency, the shortage of skilled talent, the need for high-quality and diverse data, and the complexity and fragmentation of the technology landscape. We discussed potential approaches and solutions for overcoming these obstacles, including collaboration and partnerships, standardization and interoperability, and ongoing testing and validation of AI systems.

We also examined the critical role of policy and regulation in shaping the future of AI and cybersecurity, and highlighted some of the key initiatives and frameworks that are emerging to guide the responsible development and deployment of these technologies, such as the OECD Principles on AI and the IEEE Ethically Aligned Design framework. We discussed the need for international cooperation and coordination to address global challenges and promote a secure and resilient digital ecosystem, as well as the importance of public awareness and engagement in the governance of these technologies.

Finally, we issued a call to action for cybersecurity leaders and professionals to step up and lead the way in building a secure and resilient AI-driven future. We emphasized the need for ongoing skills development, team diversity, collaboration and information sharing, strong governance and risk management, and a proactive and adaptive mindset in the face of the rapidly evolving threat landscape.

Throughout this chapter and indeed the entire book, we have seen that the future of AI in cybersecurity is both exciting and challenging, full of tremendous potential and significant risks. As we move forward into this new era, it is clear that the success and sustainability of our digital economy and society will depend on our ability to navigate these opportunities and challenges with wisdom, courage, and collaboration.

This will require a concerted and coordinated effort from all stakeholders - from technology vendors and researchers to policymakers and civil society organizations - to ensure that the development and deployment of AI in cybersecurity is guided by clear ethical principles and values, and that the benefits of these technologies are realized in a way that promotes security, privacy, fairness, and social responsibility.

It will also require ongoing investment in research and innovation, as well as in the education and training of the next generation of cybersecurity leaders and professionals. By equipping these individuals with the skills and knowledge they need to navigate the complexities of the AI-driven cybersecurity landscape, we can help to build a workforce that is both technically proficient and ethically grounded, and that is well-positioned to drive positive change and progress in this critical field.

Ultimately, the future of AI in cybersecurity is not set in stone, but rather will be shaped by the actions and decisions that we take today, and in the years ahead. By embracing the opportunities and challenges of this new era with boldness, creativity, and a commitment to the greater good, we can help to build a future that is more secure, resilient, and equitable for all.

So let us rise to this challenge, and work together to create a world in which the transformative power of AI and cybersecurity is harnessed for the benefit and protection of all. Let us lead by example, and inspire others to join us in this critical mission, so that together, we can build a brighter and more secure future for generations to come.

FOURTEEN

— · —

CHAPTER 14: FINAL THOUGHTS

We come to the end of this comprehensive exploration into the transformative world of artificial intelligence and its profound impact on the field of cybersecurity. Throughout this book, we have delved into the myriad applications, challenges, and future potential of AI in bolstering our digital defenses against the ever-evolving landscape of cyber threats.

From the foundational concepts of AI and its key subdomains, to the practical implementation strategies across network security, endpoint protection, application security, and beyond, this book has provided a thorough roadmap for cybersecurity professionals looking to harness the power of AI in their work.

We have examined the critical importance of AI governance, the need for robust ethical frameworks, and the role of transparency, accountability, and fairness in building trust in AI-driven cybersecurity solutions. We have also highlighted the immense potential of emerging technologies like deep learning, adversarial machine learning, and quantum computing in shaping the future of cybersecurity.

But perhaps most importantly, this book has underscored the vital role that cybersecurity leaders and professionals must play in realizing the full potential of AI in a responsible and inclusive manner. It is through your tireless efforts, your commitment to continuous learning and collaboration, and your unwavering focus on the greater good that we can hope to build a more secure and resilient digital future for all.

As we close the pages of this book, let us remember that the journey of AI in cybersecurity is far from over. With each passing day, new challenges and opportunities will emerge, and it will be up to us to rise to the occasion with courage, creativity, and a steadfast commitment to the values of security, privacy, and social responsibility.

So let us go forth with renewed purpose and resolve, armed with the knowledge and insights contained within these pages. Let us continue to push the boundaries of what is possible with AI and cybersecurity, always striving to create a world that is safer, fairer, and more secure for all.

The future of cybersecurity lies in our hands. Together, let us seize this extraordinary opportunity, and build a legacy of innovation, collaboration, and progress that will endure for generations to come.

ABOUT THE AUTHOR

Ken Watson is a distinguished figure in cybersecurity, known for his groundbreaking work in integrating artificial intelligence with security measures to protect against sophisticated threats. With over two decades of experience, Ken has been instrumental in transforming cybersecurity practices, protecting both governmental and corporate sectors with innovative, forward-thinking solutions.

Ken's notable career is highlighted by his leadership in transitioning large-scale IT infrastructures to secure cloud platforms, conducting in-depth security audits within complex environments, and designing comprehensive cybersecurity frameworks. His strategies have fortified the digital defenses of Fortune 500 companies, showcasing his ability to navigate and neutralize a myriad of cyber threats.

Holding a Master's degree from New York University and a Bachelor's degree in Electrical Engineering from Columbia University, Ken's educational background is as extensive as his field expertise. His certifications—CISSP, CISA, CRISC, and CEH—reflect his deep commitment to cybersecurity excellence.

In his bestselling book, "Fortress AI," Ken explores the dynamic intersection of AI and cybersecurity. His work not only enhances the security landscape but also predicts and shapes future trends. Ken Watson is not just a pioneer in cybersecurity; he is a visionary who is defining the future of digital security.